CITIZENSHIP AND ORDER:

STUDIES IN FRENCH POLITICAL THOUGHT

The citizen, a figure capable of self-government in both the political and the personal sense, is a central and enduring theme of political thought. The role of the citizen in the modern state was a question raised persistently by French political theorists from Rousseau on, as they sought new principles of legitimacy to replace those of the *ancien régime*. Richard Vernon's studies in this volume examine a series of moments in French political thought when the possibility and meaning of citizenship were called into question.

Vernon considers the view held by Rousseau and later Durkheim that citizenship was sustained immediately by moral principles, a view that was criticized by others who refused any such identification of political and moral order. Vernon shows how this refusal governs, in different ways, the political thinking of theorists as diverse as Maistre, Proudhon, Tocqueville, Comte, Sorel, and Bergson. He explains why the idea of citizenship in its political sense was exposed to so many objections, objections that may in turn suggest a new approach to the topic of political legitimacy.

Citizenship may once have been legitimated by ideas of moral, religious, or cosmic order, but in a modern context it is the civic process itself that must exercise a legitimating function. Once, citizenship rested upon order; now, suggests Vernon, we may have to realize that order depends upon citizenship.

RICHARD VERNON is a professor in the Department of Political Science, University of Western Ontario.

RICHARD VERNON

Citizenship and Order: Studies in French Political Thought

UNIVERSITY OF TORONTO PRESS
Toronto Buffalo London

© University of Toronto Press 1986
Toronto Buffalo London
Printed in Canada
ISBN 0-8020-2588-9

Printed on acid-free paper

Canadian Cataloguing in Publication Data

Vernon, Richard, 1945–
    Citizenship and order
    Bibliography: p.
    Includes index.
    ISBN 0-8020-2588-9
    1. Political science – France – History. 2. Citizen-
ship – France – Philosophy. I. Title.
    JA84.F7V47 1986   320.5'0944   C86-093197-8

An earlier version of chapter 3 appeared in the *Canadian Journal of Political Science* 14 (1981). Chapter 6 is an expanded version of a paper that appeared in the *American Political Science Review* 75 (1981). Much of chapter 5 is reprinted from the *Journal of the History of Ideas* (copyright 1984) with the permission of the editors.

This book has been published with the help of a grant from the Social Science Federation of Canada, using funds provided by the Social Sciences and Humanities Research Council of Canada, and from the Publications Fund of the University of Toronto Press.

A la fin de l'Ancien Régime, tout le monde semblait être d'accord sur le principe de la transformation qui allait s'opérer: après avoir été le *fidèle* de l'Eglise et le *sujet* du roi, l'homme se sentait assez fort pour devenir *citoyen*; mais que fallait-il entendre par ce terme?

Georges Sorel

Contents

Introduction

In a phase of political theorizing that now seems quite distant, the French polity was the standard example of abnormality and failure. Among the older and larger nations of the West it was France that had most glaringly failed to achieve that paradigm of stable democracy that, it was believed, virtually defined the Western political condition. Its boundary maintenance, in the language of that time, was poor. It had not succeeded in disentangling political objectives, essentially negotiable, from the absolute objectives of religious commitments, or of ideologies either. It lacked a party system capable of shielding central power from the raw, unprocessed demands of particular interests. Its state had never found a satisfactory accommodation with its society. Its political culture remained fractured by its revolutionary past, its traditional and modern segments immobilizing one another mutually. It had not, in a word, developed, development being defined as the happy equilibrium into which, it then appeared to some, the Anglo-Saxon world had settled.[1]

Today such a mood of anglophone self-congratulation scarcely seems imaginable, quite different and much gloomier idioms having come to govern much recent political diagnosis: all our states are held to have 'failed'; all our societies confront 'ungovernability'; and all our legitimacies are said to be in (or to approach) 'crisis.' For this reason if for no other the modern history of political thought in France invites attention, as a record of preoccupations that may have come to seem almost familiar. If in different circumstances France figured as a counter-example, perhaps it could now figure as an example, and what French theorists have had to say about their endemic theme of legitimation crisis may have exemplary interest. What follows in these studies is a highly selective exploration. It does not amount to a history – it is too discontinuous for that – but offers a series of suggestions, developed in what is intended to be an orderly way, about how some major French political and social theorists might be read. These theorists are evidently very diverse, but I have tried to identify an issue of a general kind to which, from very different perspectives, they may be seen to have responded.

The topic of citizenship is related to but distinct from the topic of political obligation. To ask why one should obey a state is to ask for a rule or other prescription that will govern what one does. To ask why one should be a citizen is to ask, in part, what it is that one should be, for citizenship carries with it more than the notion of obedience to rules. For one thing, citizens are supposed to do more than obey: they are supposed to identify as their own the ends for which obedience is sought – obedience is given, not merely demanded. For another, citizenship refers more to the person than to the prescriptions, and the term carries with it the notion of an attitude or, even, a character. This character is defined by a long and pervasive tradition of republican or civic thinking that makes itself felt not only in Rousseau but also in other French thinkers in whom, perhaps, it is more of a surprise to find it. We find not only in Tocqueville's classic treatment but in Proudhon's later writings an effort to restore citizenship as a political value; in Durkheim we find an ideology of *civisme* in which any Rousseauan pessimism has been smoothed away, the values of the individual substituting functionally for those of the ancient Roman. Even writers critical of the republican tradition – or of the political tradition generally – often applaud the citizen-like virtues while assigning them to new and apolitical bearers. The civic tradition is, then, one that will demand attention in several of the works discussed below, although in those works – as in the case of Rousseau, as I shall claim – the impact of that tradition was highly modified by other traditions or languages. It is under constant stress in French thought and faces continual competition from other modes of thinking in which civic obligation is far less well normatively anchored.

What sustains citizenship? The belief that one is participating in an order of relations that is intelligible, significant, and proper. Citizens must believe that they occupy a shared situation to which meaning can be attributed and that represents more than the triumph of one will over another: a citizen cannot be 'a creature who obeys a creature who wills,' in Montesquieu's phrase, but must rather be a person who obeys because he sees in the polity something more than simple dominance. He sees the pattern of institutions and the distribution of power as making sense and as doing so objectively – not, that is, merely by way of reflecting his own or someone else's preference. Such making sense is what, in the first instance, may be termed *order*. And if order is taken to mean intelligibility of the relations that define and express a situation common to a polity's members, it is correlative with citizenship, which may be defined as the capacity of a polity's members to grasp and adapt their actions to such an order. One term refers to the ends or principles, held to be objectively valid, that political institutions express; the other refers to the process of making these ends or principles subjectively one's own.

But order has, of course, a narrower sense. It is sometimes taken to refer not merely to objective validity but to cosmological sanctions and to express an assumed relation between political order and the order of nature itself.[2] Taken in this sense, 'order' was among the most treasured words of Jean Bodin and others, and licensed a style of argumentation that later empiricism was to render obsolete. The meaning of order is not thus restricted here; but the use of order as a cosmological concept has a particular importance for the studies below in marking a limit to their scope. They concern theorists for whom a cosmological argument was not available and who were thus driven along alternative avenues of justification. What Bodin had called order had provided a powerful normative context for his valuing of citizenship, the claims as well as the duties of citizens receiving natural and, ultimately, divine endorsement. But such endorsement is undermined as order ceases to be imagined in such a way.

How does the idea of order change? In *Creative Evolution* Bergson was to make a famous distinction between order as willed and order as caused. In the first sense order is 'the mind finding itself again in things,' the recognition in the world of a structure corresponding to design – 'reality is ordered exactly to the degree to which it satisfies our thought.' But in the second sense, even a room that apparently is 'in disorder' is ordered: 'The position of each object is explained by the automatic movements of the person who sleeps in the room, or by the efficient causes, whatever they may be, that have caused each piece of furniture, clothing, etc., to be where it is.'[3] Beyond a doubt, it is order in the second sense that comes to play an increasingly central role in modern social science; indeed, it is precisely the exclusion of *willed* order and the substitution of causal for intentional explanation that is sometimes held to constitute social science – such, for example, is the view of Durkheim, among many others. But before Bergson and Durkheim, the concerns accompanying this theme were political rather than methodological. In describing *anarchie* Proudhon celebrated the *freeing* of society from the yoke of design and the substitution of economic for political order: outcomes would reflect the spontaneous interaction of manifold free contributions, not the forced imposition of a single, centrally devised program – a 'general tendency' would replace the 'general will.'[4] Likewise, Tocqueville contrasted the vanished 'aristocratic' assumption that all events can be traced to some will or intention with the new 'democratic' assumption that no events can: 'Historians who live in democratic ages ... attribute hardly any influence over the destinies of mankind to individuals, or over the fate of a people to the citizens. But they make great general causes responsible for the smallest particular events.'[5] Tocqueville was, however, less sanguine than Proudhon about the beneficial or liberating consequences of this transition: if relations and events are the unwitting products, not the conscious ends, of our actions, where is there a space for public responsibility, and what indeed would be its point? Quietism would seem to be the natural conclusion. But while his normative assessment is different from Proudhon's, the two are in significant agreement that order thus understood is not easily compatible with the preconditions for politics. Politics implies the existence of a point of leverage through which members of a society can amend or confirm their relations to one another; and if their relations are generated only mediately and indirectly, it is hard to see what political life can accomplish.

The causes that led to such new conceptions are complex, and no monocausal explanation stands much chance of carrying conviction. The upshot, however, according to one well-known recent commentary, is that as the idea of order in its original sense recedes, legitimacy altogether loses its connection with objective rightness; it becomes a wholly subjective thing.[6] A state is legitimate, it comes to be thought, if it is supposed to be or if its commands meet with frequent compliance. Older definitions place legitimacy 'upon foundations external to and independent of the mere assertion or opinion of the claimant' or upon 'some source of authority beyond or above himself'; whereas 'the new definitions all dissolve legitimacy into belief or opinion.' Social science, it would appear, is doubly regrettable. On the one hand, by insisting on

finding order in the unintended products of human action, it super-
sedes older ways of thinking in which the natural and social environ-
ment had figured as something immediately intelligible and as charged
with normative meaning. On the other, by virtue of the same
empirical and statistical bias it insists on transforming the question of
legitimacy into a question of how many people think what.[7]

That there was once an age of consensus, when God or nature
provided an agreed source of authority, and that the passing of such an
age had dire consequences for political legitimation are propositions to
which most of the thinkers considered here would have assented. Once,
Tocqueville noted, there was 'an ancient order of things whose
legitimacy was not contested,' but 'there comes a time in the life of
nations when old customs are changed, mores destroyed, beliefs
shaken, and the prestige of memories has vanished, but when none the
less enlightenment has remained incomplete and political rights are ill
assured or restricted. Then men see their country only by a weak and
doubtful light.'[8] Comte, too, distinguished between the 'normal' state
of consensus and the pathological state of 'criticism' into which the
Enlightenment had plunged Europe, as traditional beliefs lost their
force before positive ones were in a position to take their place. For
Proudhon, by contrast, there was to be no such process of replacement:
society had become definitively critical and the very concept of authority
had had its day, for deference would be replaced by autonomy. These
three contemporaries, whose attitudes to their own society so remarkably prefigure later trends of opinion, were thus in agreement on one
point at least: that Enlightenment had generated a crisis of legitimacy.

Yet there is an evident reluctance to accept any total or final
separation between these two kinds of legitimacy, the legitimacy
conferred by consent or compliance on the one hand and by correspondence to objectively validated norms on the other. That is, there is a
reluctance – with which perhaps we may still sympathize today – to
declare any regime legitimate simply on the grounds that it is obeyed,
or to declare a regime legitimate simply on the grounds that it is proper,
even if nobody obeys it at all. The concept of legitimacy appears to
occupy the contested middle ground between competing criteria. Thus
even so radical a theorist of personal consent as Proudhon, who denied
(on occasion) that any absolute whatever could survive the sovereignty
of will, insisted nevertheless that organization must reflect the
structure of rational order. Reverting to a traditional and emphatically
pre-revolutionary idiom of 'correspondences,' he rests his federalist

proposals upon the 'admirable accord among zoology, political economy, and politics':[9] the federal principle of division and co-operation is underwritten by nature itself. Conversely, even so stern an opponent of democracy as Comte, for whom (no less than for Bodin) principles of organization were a matter of cognition and not will, insisted nevertheless upon the necessity of consent: the recognition that government requires willing acceptance, he claimed, was the one political truth contributed by the malign age of revolution. Though freedom of thought was a principle of disorder, the order that denied it was to be founded upon its free renunciation.[10]

It requires little ingenuity to suggest an underlying reason for Proudhon's and Comte's concessions. Here, surely, we may see the impact of French political circumstances as they are often viewed, circumstances in which state and society lacked effective intermediation, political structures failing to connect with patterns of social interest and participation. Fundamental social and ideational divisions impeded the establishment of a political order recognizable to all major interests as their own: *incivisme* was the much lamented response. For all their differences, French social and political theorists of the post-revolutionary period sought above all a point of contact between organization and consciousness, a point at which interest and sentiment would promote instead of block the pursuit of general ends: for what was organized was not generally willed, while what was willed did not lend itself to general organization. It is just in this respect that the concepts of citizenship and order assume a central place: it was recognized that participation would be sustained only by the presence of compellingly intelligible ends *and* that the political weight of even the most impressively validated ends would depend upon the degree to which they won assent.

In few theorists has this tension been so systematically acute as in Rousseau, who struggles in *Social Contract* to resolve or evade it but perhaps succeeds only in reproducing it in a peculiarly baffling form.[11] Rousseau of course provides an elaborate account of the conditions under which assent is to be given by citizens. Every vote must be counted; the 'right question' must be posed by the voters themselves; there must be no 'intriguing groups' and no communication prior to public discussion. It might seem that it is the observance of such procedures that lends authority to the outcome: does a law have authority if consent is (properly) given, if it is 'self-prescribed'? If authority in an older sense has been displaced, are we offered a new conception of *procedural* authority? To state the position in that way would seem to involve at least one omission. For Rousseau offers something closer to the view that consent, rather than being actually *constitutive* of rightness, is as it were *declaratory* of it; that the point of the procedures is to make it more probable that consent will be given to an outcome that in some way is antecedently right and merely awaits constitutional expression. Consent given when all the ideal conditions are in force is termed the 'general will': and we may note that the most immediate source for that term is in Diderot's *Encyclopaedia* article on 'Natural Right,' where it stands, in effect, for the law of nature – 'A pure act of understanding that reasons in the silence of the passions about what man can demand of his fellow man and about what his fellow man can rightfully demand of him.'

For all his use of the natural-jurisprudence tradition, Rousseau has an undeniable sociological realism. He is aware of the relativity of law and custom and even of human personality, which he sees as being shaped and transformed by institutions. But he is not thereby led to a merely sociological definition of legitimacy, as frequency of compliance; he insists on retaining an objective dimension, which he finds in what he calls the 'art of generalizing,' or in the moral principle of generalization. He denies, against Diderot, that the art of generalizing is innate or natural; he denies, against Diderot and the philosophes generally, that one can be truly universal in adopting a point of reference for the art or principle: we can apply it only within the context of familiarity and mutuality provided by an organized community. But these important qualifications aside, the acts of the general will have a *moral* rightness in expressing a generalizing as opposed to a particularizing intention; only what can be generally willed – as opposed to a claim for privilege – can be proper. Here Rousseau's position is not wholly dissimilar to much later theories – German rather than French – of legitimation crisis. A state, Rousseau demands, must have features that reflect no partial and privileged will: it must display a will that is that of 'no one' and is in that sense general or unassignable. A state that is effectively identical to a partial will – as it is in either the Machiavellian or the Marxian accounts[12] – is not really a state at all but an 'aggregation' constituting simply an item of personal or class property. Likewise, one currently influential theorist identifies in modern states a problem of 'generalizability.'[13] A political order, if it is to be sustained rationally, can make good its claim to obedience only by relating its demands to a genuinely shared situation. If its demands systematically confer privileges upon some interests and involve the suppression of others, then it has abandoned reason for coercion, for reason inherently implies a commitment to consistency of meaning. If an interest is to be sustained by reason, it must necessarily be one that is generalizable – that is, not arbitrarily ascribed; and the 'ideal-speech situation,' in which what is truly general is to be discovered, shares something with Rousseau's 'assembly,' as well as posing, perhaps, some interestingly similar problems.[14]

Rousseau's proposed solution creates a context within which, or at least a background against which, all the issues discussed in these studies may be placed. For it is immediately obvious that Rousseau's legitimation of politics as a moral order cannot accomplish what earlier notions of order had done. Compare, for example, the legitimating resources available to Bodin and those available to Rousseau in *Social Contract*. Bodin's citizen is housed in an ordained structure of things, and the role of mediation that he plays could be described as an ontologically necessary one; but no such claims can be made for Rousseau's. When Rousseau says 'it is of *man* that I have to speak,'[15] it is clear that he intends 'man' to be understood as an effectively contextless being for whom order must be produced. Man cannot be shown a normatively charged pattern of things in which his place and role are evident: if he is to have norms, they must be generated out of human circumstances themselves. In this respect Rousseau inherited and elaborated upon the claims of earlier theorists of *droit humain*, who had taken on the task of showing that there were norms that were compelling to human reason even without the further support of revelation. And in this respect Rousseau in turn was followed by theorists who believed that human society drew its principles from 'its own nature and condition' (Comte),[16] or that it had to recognize itself as 'a human institution' (Proudhon),[17] or that for it 'there is no power but within itself' (Tocqueville).[18]

One question thus posed is Maistre's: Can the political theory of contextless man do what a political theology had done? Maistre thought not, for 'Men never respect what they have made.' This question is no irrelevance: some version or echo of it is still to be found in Durkheim and Bergson in the early years of this century, as well as in still more recent accounts of the meaning of *secularization*. But in Maistre's case as in much later cases, as I shall argue, the theme tends strongly towards a shallow pragmatism. What is really lamented, it often seems, is not the loss of knowledge but merely the loss of consensus; for considered functionally, as a basis for generating respect (or authority, or community), beliefs evidently require to be shared but not necessarily to be true. This point alone, apart from other more elaborate considerations, should cast doubt upon any literal-minded parallel between membership in a political association and participation in a cognitive enterprise.

It is a less familiar but more centrally political question that demands attention. It is not that of the source or normative strength of moral principles or obligations, or of the possibility of a secular morality. It is that of the specifically political bearing of morality. What is it in moral principles that requires us to identify ourselves as citizens and not as something else? For Rousseau had discovered generality of will in all associations; it was, indeed, in its possession of a general will that something qualified as an association as opposed to an aggregation. But he had *also* sought to privilege political association over other forms of association, and in doing both things confronted political associations with problems of legitimation that may be insoluble. Why should it be the state that serves as the essential focus of moral commitment? Why should not levels of organization below the state do this (as Proudhon and Comte both believed, for very different reasons)? Or levels beyond the state (a possibility mentioned by Rousseau himself but taken up less sceptically by Bergson)? Or is there any *essential* focus at all (a question raised by Proudhon's federalism)? Or if there is, what reason is there to suppose it to be territorial? The 'art of generalizing' that Rousseau had attached to citizenship is practised by Comte's savant in rising above pedantic disciplinary specialism, or by Sorel's industrial worker in advancing from the idea of a local to that of a general strike: and the rise to prominence of both the savant and the syndicalist is meant to displace the state altogether. We find, then – as we do not find to the same degree in, say, British thought of the period – a willingness to question not only the organizational scale of the state but the very principle of territoriality that is fundamental to state organization. Citizenship is thus confronted with challenges of a very basic kind: nothing less than the identity of its primary locus is at issue, so that even if the *values* of citizenship can somehow be rescued, they will not necessarily sustain civic *purposes*.

The theme outlined above has governed the selection of the theorists considered below, as well as the approach taken to their writings. The diversity of these theorists and of their texts demands respect, and to exaggerate what they have in common would be to sacrifice truth to unity. In general, while drawing parallels and contrasts, I have tried to write each study in such a way that it would make sense if read independently of the others. I have tried to allow the theorists considered to say what they wanted to say even as I suggest ways in which we might understand them. The studies are grouped in four pairs, each corresponding to one of four aspects or moments of the general issue sketched above; there is, of course, much overlapping, but we may nevertheless distinguish among four aspects into which the issue can be divided.

First, I try to show how and why, against the background of earlier thinking, Rousseau evolved a theory of citizenship that was inherently problematic. Why did the notion of citizenship have to take on such a severe burden of legitimation, and why did it fail to carry it? And how were its failures exploited by Rousseau's critics of both the left (Proudhon) and the right (Maistre)? Second, I examine two notable post-revolutionary theories of citizenship, those of the later, federalist, Proudhon and of Tocqueville: what views of politics did their arguments offer or imply, and how were those views different from Rousseau's? Third, an alternative trend of thinking is considered, that of Comte and Sorel, who, despite many differences, both sought to empty the political realm of citizenship and to transpose its qualities – in a greatly modified form – elsewhere. Fourth, essays on the political thought of Durkheim and Bergson discuss two contrasting accounts of the relationship between civic obligation and religious belief.

My principal concern has been to show that a common set of problems is engaged by some writings of fairly disparate kinds. Another question, however, is that of the solution. The essays in Part II may seem to suggest one, and in the Conclusion to these studies some hints found in the later Proudhon and (more especially) in Tocqueville are briefly taken up. It is citizenship, not order, that legitimates. It is a mistake to suppose that legitimation rests on the discovery (or invention) of new forms of order functionally equivalent to, say, Bodin's: if a secular political theory cannot do what a political theology can do, that is not because it fails but because it does something different. It cannot posit ultimate ends that then confer legitimacy upon institutions *de haut en bas*. It must, on the contrary, describe institutions whose operation confers legitimacy upon the ends adopted. To value citizenship is, evidently, to favour some modes of operation and to reject others as incapable of conferring legitimacy.

In a commentary already quoted above John H. Schaar writes: 'Theory, ... by making power legitimate, turns it into authority.'[19] This seems to me to be fundamentally mistaken. It is not a theory that creates legitimacy, nor even (as a relativist would claim) the acceptance of a theory; it is rather the manner in which a conclusion is reached that makes it legitimate. The importance of the idea of citizenship lies precisely in the fact that it draws our attention to the manner in which things are done; its further importance is that it suggests that questions of political legitimacy are not settled by deduction from non-political premises, such as a moral or cosmological theory, but require reflection on political circumstances themselves. But this view may carry more weight after some of the alternatives to it have been assessed.

PART I: LEGITIMIZING CITIZENSHIP

1

From Bodin to Rousseau

The idea of the citizen is not of course an essentially democratic one, although in revolutionary and post-revolutionary writings it often comes to be systematically entangled with the ideals of political (and sometimes also social) democracy. The idea was already solidly entrenched in the political thinking of the *ancien régime*, nowhere more clearly so than in Jean Bodin's *Six Books of the Commonwealth*; and already the idea of citizenship was intimately connected there with a notion of order, another theme to which Bodin's thinking gives an altogether crucial place. Bodin's great work has been well described as the *Summa* of sixteenth-century political thought;[1] much less serene and accomplished, no doubt, than Aquinas's, it has somewhat comparably synthetic intentions and likewise is encyclopaedic in its scope, locating citizenship (as Aquinas too had done) in a framework that lent to it an incontestable dignity. But to start with Bodin is not to suggest that here we have a beginning; on the contrary, it is to suggest that we must look elsewhere for a beginning, for Bodin's conception of politics, however great its influence, does not admit the sort of problems that later political theory was to raise. Housed in order, Bodin's citizen is inherently protected from the questions that Rousseau had to answer and that were to engage still later theorists whether they were satisfied with Rousseau's answers or not.

Bodin brings at least three themes together in (an intended) synthetic harmony. One of these is a conception of citizenship that, despite Bodin's reservations about Aristotle, is Aristotelian through and through; another is a conception of the pluralist character of political association, a conception for which Bodin, together with Althusius, is sometimes cited as an essential ancestor; a third is the notion of sovereignty, the authorship of which Bodin is often thought to have shared with Hobbes. In certain later contexts these three themes have often stood in triangular relations of opposition: notions of citizenship as an ideal have been set against pluralistic models of political process, while pluralism has taken as its prime enemy the doctrine of sovereignty; and in turn theories of sovereignty have sometimes been regarded as essentially hostile to the rights that the ideal of citizenship proclaims. But these later oppositions may spring, Bodin's book reminds us, from contingent and particular historical articulations of the themes in question; what he offers is a vision in which the three stand to each other in relations of tense but intelligible harmony. In this structure of themes the figure of the citizen is crucial: emerging from the household to confront his sovereign in respectful independence, he is the mediating link between the plurality of social life and the unity of the public realm (1.6).[2]

The coherence of this picture depends inescapably on the conception of order that Bodin accepted. It is that of a 'great chain of being' (1.1), of a graded and hierarchical universe to which the principles of dignity and subordination are essential: each part is placed in relations of relative dignity to others and thus enfolded in order. Not only that, but in each component of the universe the structure of the whole is reproduced in its essentials. What have been termed 'multiplane correspondences' are therefore possible:[3] the ordering proper to the Commonwealth may be inferred from the ordering of God and man, reason and passion, husband and wife, father and child. Social and political hierarchy is thus part of the chain of creation itself and is cosmologically underwritten. It is his insistence on correspondences that leads Bodin to one of his principal objections to Aristotle, who had seen household and *polis* as different in character: Bodin insists that they display the *same* order (1.2) and, as if to make the parallel good, demands shortly afterwards that the power of life and death over children be restored to fathers, the family thus becoming indeed a miniature sovereignty. But while the implications are in the first instance hierarchical in their obvious tendency, they are also more than that: the thesis involves, too, an implication of necessary diversity. Everything that exists must exist, or else order would lack 'plenitude' and the chain of being would be discontinuous, as it cannot be. In a political context the conclusions are apparent: the sovereign is set above the components subjected to him but cannot dispense with them or annihilate their essential qualities. The sovereign's realm is composed not of individuals but of families (I.2), within which there is, as in his own realm, an ordained structure of authority; to this structure the ownership of property is essential, and the sovereign cannot undermine this principle of ownership without annihilating the essential components of his own realm. In brute political terms this argument concerns the right of taxation: can the sovereign draw upon his subjects' property without their consent? The idea of sovereignty, abstractly viewed, might seem to indicate an affirmative answer: but Bodin insists on a negative one (I.8). An unqualified right to tax his subjects at will would imply the sovereign's right to extinguish the very institutions that constitute the material basis of his own authority, and would thus imply a contradiction. In Bodin's argument for the necessity of consent to taxation it is made abundantly clear that his conception of political life is one that insists upon the necessity of partial rights no less than it does upon the right to command. Here we should have no doubts about the distinctness of Bodin's position from the (later) Hobbesian argument, in which (in principle at least) all such alleged partial rights are described in unflattering terms and in which the right of sovereignty can admit no rival. Those partial associations – 'corporations' – which Hobbes was to see as worm-like parasites, are viewed by Bodin as essential constituents of political order: they embody relations of 'friendship' (III.7) – reverting, once again, to Aristotle – without which, despite their partiality, no political order can subsist. 'Guilds, estates and communities' are no more assimilated by sovereign power than the family is: rather they confront the sovereign in full confidence of their rights, and political life is constituted by the mutual adaptation of private and public rights rather than by the extinction of one to the advantage of the other. What Bodin offers is a picture well described as one of the 'co-existence' of society and state.[4]

There are indeed conceptual tensions here.[5] The principle of hierarchy requires that subordinate parts should offer no resistance to the ordering imposed by the superordinate agency, just as, following up the organic analogy, instrumental parts of the human body can properly offer no resistance to the imperatives of its directing centre. Yet at the same time, what the centre can properly direct depends upon what its peripheral agencies are instrumentally adapted to perform. One penetrating account has suggested a solution to, or an easing of, this dilemma.[6] As Bodin describes the sovereign, that agency is empowered (as in Hobbes) to do anything that its own political conceptions dictate. But it is also imagined to be constrained – as Hobbes's nominalism does not permit – by its own proper definition. What Bodin's thought points to is not at all the mechanistic cosmology of Hobbes but a teleological cosmology within which all agencies are constrained by an end that defines what they essentially are. True, the absolute right to command may collide with the institutional rights of participation that Bodin also admires, and thus make citizenship impossible; but law expresses not only the right to command but also *right* command; and if we posit a standard of right that accommodates all the requirements of civil life, then sovereignty is in no necessary conflict with either pluralism or citizenship. The sovereign, representing the whole, must respect parts of the whole no less than they respect him (II.3); and the citizen, spanning the gap between whole and part, must be at once deferential and independent. There is no contradiction between his deference and his independence, for both spring from and are justified by one and the same order, within which part and whole are mutually indispensable.

Rousseau's question – How can I defer yet retain my independence? How can a will be both mine and sovereign over me? – is far from being raised. And it is not raised, essentially, because citizenship does not have to bear the sort of weight in Bodin's account that it had to bear later; perhaps this is why Rousseau says that neither Bodin nor 'any other French writer has understood the true sense of the word *citizen*.'[57] For Bodin citizenship is a feature of order and is not called upon to constitute it: it is sovereignty that constitutes political order (I.1) and the acceptance of sovereignty that defines citizenship itself (I.6). But for Rousseau it is citizenship alone that can bring a political order into being, and the existence of sovereignty depends upon the presence of citizenship. Political order is called upon to be self-sustaining; and while Bodin may have seen citizenship as one token of a well-ordered commonwealth, as a feature distinguishing kingly from tyrannical rule, citizenship is now required to supply the principle of legitimacy itself.

The movement of ideas from Bodin to Rousseau is complex, and not susceptible to brusque treatment. But if we focus upon the transition sketched above, some general reasons for it may be suggested. With little if any pretence to originality we may note three factors that together were to render citizenship problematic and at the same time to impose upon it severe burdens of legitimation. We may associate these with the names of Montaigne, Pascal, and Montesquieu, who in different but sometimes related ways placed political thinking in a new context of a very much more precarious kind. To sketch what they said, however briefly, may help to suggest why Rousseau said what he did and also to articulate some themes and problems to which political thought even after Rousseau was often to revert.

To understand a theory such as Bodin's we must adjust ourselves to a view of the world that is distinctly pre-modern in several respects, notably in its resting upon final rather than efficient causality. To read his contemporary, Michel de Montaigne, is – as has often been pointed out – to step into a world of astonishing familiarity. At the very time that Bodin was completing his backward-looking *Summa*, new conceptions of the human self were emerging, conceptions that we have made our own and that distance us effectively from the assumptions of cosmological argument. What is striking there is not so much the emergence of a new cosmology – which would be the case, later, with Hobbes – as the detachment of the human sciences from a cosmological foundation. Montaigne's radicalness is not in challenging any cosmological thesis but in declaring its irrelevance. There may be an order, such as had traditionally been posited, but it is beyond our reason to know it. It may be reasonable to accept an authoritative definition of what it is (III.2),[8] but it is not reasonable to expect our knowledge of man, or of his social and political relations, to find guarantees in knowledge of an objective and universal context. 'Those people who bestraddle the epicycle of Mercury and see into the distant heavens make me grind my teeth' (II.17). Moreover, apart from being essentially limited in its scope, reason is inherently prevented by its own nature and direction from grasping a common and objective order: 'I freely state my opinion about all things, even those that perhaps fall outside my capacity and of which I do not for a moment suppose myself to be a judge. What I say about them, therefore, is meant to reveal the extent of my own vision, not the measure of the things themselves' (II.10). And 'Things in themselves perhaps have their own weights, measures, and states; but inwardly, when they enter into us, the mind cuts them to its own conceptions' (I.50).

The consequence is not the rejection of a God-centred world for a man-centred world but, rather, the rejection of a centred world. The world has as many centres as it contains selves; and in place of the revolutions of the spheres or of the planets, an imagined cosmic orderliness within which human life could be supplied with a context, we have the *internal* 'revolutions' of each individual self (II.17). Here we have but one example of a process of transference that is so well-marked a feature of Montaigne's *Essays*: images and concepts are taken from a realm of public knowledge and installed in the private interior of the self. It is political language that provides the most striking case: in place of a self located in a political order Montaigne describes a self that has become a kind of polity. The mind becomes a 'ruler' (I.50), sometimes a 'tyrant' (III.3); and while Montaigne accepts without reservation the right of authority to direct and limit behaviour, nevertheless 'I have my own laws and my own court to judge me, and I refer to these rather than elsewhere' (III.2). This citizenship in oneself, so to speak, necessarily detracts from our literal citizenship. Each self is not, it is true, in a condition of isolation from other selves: there are experiences of 'friendship,' which Montaigne values highly, in the Stoic manner (I.28, III.3); but such friendship is no longer the public friendship that Bodin, like Aristotle, had valued as a political bond, but is of value as a rare item of private experience.

Montaigne appears to envisage three kinds of order, none of which is identical to the cosmological order of medieval and Renaissance thought. One is the order that each individual puts into, or finds in, his own life, or that an observer can see there: 'Every action reveals us. That same mind of Caesar's that is apparent in the ordering and direction of the battle of Pharsalia can also be seen in the ordering of his idle and amorous intrigues ... Any particle and any occupation of a man betrays him as well as any other' (I.50). If order is a certain agreement between part and whole, it is found, then, not in the cosmos but in the relation between act and character, Montaigne himself providing here, interestingly, an example of what he means, his point 'revealing' his own disposition to transpose public images to private life. This self that we carry with us is largely opaque: we do not will it into being; it governs our will, and it is a 'tyrant' in the sense that we have made no voluntary agreement with it. What it is may indeed be discernible only at the end, for no individual decides, by a series of wholly deliberate sequential choices, what his self is, and its nature may be revealed only in the pattern that governs its initiations and its ending. There is, in short, an *individual* order, determinable by inference from a pattern of successive choices, a pattern experienced rather than made by the individual in question.

There is, secondly, the order or regularity arising from agreements, possibly voluntary, more likely habitual and imitative, among those who occupy a certain limited phase of space and time: the order of 'convention.' 'We are all convention,' Montaigne writes (ii.17); and if we are *all* convention, it follows that we must abandon as absurd any project, such as Bodin's, to determine the essential and universal features of collective life. It is the familiarity of institutions, rather than their demonstrated rationality, that lends them force (i.27). In one of his best-known essays Montaigne notes that the European's horror of cannibalism is matched by the cannibal's amazement at the gross inequalities that European man can tolerate (i.31). The theme was, of course, to be given classic expression by Pascal – 'Three degrees of latitude reverse all jurisprudence' – who saw in Montaigne's scepticism a compelling revelation of the true scope of human reason.

There are, finally, 'unintended orders,' patterns of relations that are traceable to no conscious design. Of the three sources of order that Montaigne distinguishes, 'nature, chance, and art,' the third is the most imperfect. Nothing man can produce by art can match in perfection the regularity of the bird's nest or spider's web (i.31); and there is in human physiology itself an ordering that not only is not conscious but is ruined by self-consciousness (ii.17). In human relations what is due to chance is much more important than what is due to art: 'Whatever position you put men in, they pile up and arrange themselves by moving and crowding together, just as assorted objects, put in a bag without order, themselves find a way to unite and fall into place together, often better than they could have been arranged by art' (iii.9). Hence Montaigne's valuing of custom, of the 'fixed shape' of patterns that we have accumulated but have not made: art is more capable of destroying such shape than of creating it. But there is no sort of providential guarantee that order *will* thus spontaneously construct itself; on the contrary, the signs are that decay rather than progress is to be expected. 'Our morals are extremely corrupt, and have a striking tendency to grow worse; many of our laws and customs are monstrous and barbarous; nevertheless, because of the difficulty of improving our state, and the danger of collapse, if I could put a drag on the wheel and stop it here, I would gladly do so' (ii.17). Montaigne did not embrace the Stoic (or any) cosmology, but he embraced their pessimism and their notion of inherent decline; and while he denied that politics could create anything decisively better, he thought it could stave off the still worse and should be assisted in doing so. But if one assists, one must do so with a certain (very Stoic) detachment; Montaigne did not confuse himself with 'the mayor' (iii.10), echoing Marcus Aurelius's injunction that one distinguish between Antoninus and the man.[9]

None of these kinds of order, it is important to note, is equivalent to the order by which the value of citizenship was sustained. They do not hold out the promise of self-realization and equilibrium in public life, a promise underwritten by cosmic guarantees; they represent no more than contingent occurrences. They are things of which we must take account but not things into which any meaning can be read. It is no surprise to find, therefore, that citizenship, deprived of its legitimating order, is radically undermined as a value. As a fact it is absorbed into the realm of private experience – 'we only feel public calamities in so far as they affect our private interests' (III.12). Nothing is uncoloured by such interest, least of all an imagined public spirit, which is coherently explained only as the expression of vanity. We come close indeed here to a world – soon to become more familiar – in which the notion of a public good is displaced by complex networks of private advantage and in which each of us seeks 'profit' in the 'loss' of others (I.22), interest displacing friendship as the principle of association.

Montaigne's relativism, and a good deal else, was to be absorbed by Pascal in his development of a view of the human condition that was to have a forceful and complex influence. From a moral and spiritual point of view, of course, Pascal found Montaigne pernicious: 'We are not satisfied with the life we have in ourselves' (806),[10] and the love of worldly diversion that Montaigne had also observed is no more satisfying, merely a vain attempt to escape. Neither wry self-inspection nor frenetic business are solutions for the human mind, only symptoms of the problems that it encounters in evading truth. It is indeed as something brilliantly if morbidly symptomatic that Pascal reads Montaigne's work. What it illustrates is, above all, the limits to human reason. Reason does not reveal to us a natural order in which we can feel at home and through which our ends can be justified; it is not through the understanding of nature that the meaning and ends of life can be revealed (3,463). Here Pascal the theologian and Pascal the scientist are at one, in condemning both metaphysical apologetics and the suppression of scientific truth by dogma.[11] Dogma can settle questions of science no more than theories of the natural world can supply religious truth; they belong to different orders. As for the social and political world, here reason merely deceives itself in discovering 'natural' principles, as Montaigne had rightly said and as Pascal stresses with bleak rigour. 'Larceny, incest, infanticide, parricide, everything has at some time been accounted a virtuous action. Could there be anything

more absurd than that a man has the right to kill me because he lives on
the other side of the water, and his prince has picked a quarrel with
mine, though I have none with him?' (60) If we knew what was just by
nature rather than by mere convention, 'true equity would have
enthralled all the peoples of the world with its splendour, and lawgivers
would not have taken as their model the whims and fancies of Persians
and Germans in place of this consistent justice. We should see it planted
in every country of the world, in every age, whereas what we do see is
that there is nothing just or unjust but changes colour as it changes
climate.' Are there, even, laws common to the various conventional
codes? 'The joke is that man's whims have shown such great variety
that there is not one.' But it is necessary for us that laws should be
obeyed, and hence necessary that they be thought just (525); and so
conventions take on the force of nature, our 'second' or habitual nature
taking on the dignity of a 'first' or inherent one. 'What are our natural
principles but habitual ones?' (125).

Though his account of convention owes much to Montaigne, Pascal
has in advancing it an overriding purpose that is not Montaigne's at all.
'Custom is our nature. Anyone who grows accustomed to faith believes
it, and can no longer help fearing hell, and believes nothing else' (419).
Reason can show us the necessity of belief; what we stand to lose is so
small, what we stand to gain so great, that to 'wager' on faith is
inescapably rational. But we can achieve belief, as opposed to
conviction of the necessity of belief, only by 'taking holy water, having
masses said, and so on. That will make you believe quite naturally, and
will make you more docile' (418). It is not 'l'esprit' but 'la machine,' the
force of routine and habit, that sustains religious belief just as it sustains
the authority of law. Here Pascal's psychology, as well as his objective,
differs from Montaigne's: for Montaigne had believed that routines
were without a hold on the stubborn interior of the self and that one
could 'bend the knee' without submitting the mind.[12]

The Jansenists, whose most distinguished convert Pascal was,
described themselves as 'les défenseurs de saint Augustin.'[13] It may
well be true that Pascal's knowledge of Augustine was neither thorough
nor direct, but he was thoroughly Augustinian in taking as his central
stress the radical break between the earthly and the divine, or being
without and with God. In place of the two cities, though, Pascal devises
three orders, and the contrasts he draws are correspondingly nuanced.
Augustine's 'civitas terrena' recognizes no distinction between the carnal
and the intellectual, for it is important to the argument that it should

collapse together the distinctions valued by pagan philosophers; anything unillumined by God, including the so-called best or philosophic life, is as carnal as anything else. Without disputing Augustine's point Pascal restores a distinction between carnal and intellectual (308), interposing 'l'ordre de l'esprit' between the orders of 'la chair' and 'la charité.' L'esprit, by means of the logic of the wager, can bring us to see the rationality of belief, and it is only la chair and its passions that impede us once we have been brought to this point. Pascal also says that it is in reasoning that man's characteristic dignity is to be found. The crucial divide, therefore, appears to be between the first order and the second and third. But Pascal says the opposite: 'The infinite distance between mind and body symbolizes the infinitely more infinite distance between mind and charity' (308). So the crucial divide is where Augustine had placed it, between the third order and the first and second. That conclusion is reinforced by the treatment of knowledge as simply one of the three ends of 'concupiscence,' 'libido sciendi,' the others being 'libido sentiendi' and 'libido dominandi' (545) – a treatment for which Pascal cites St John, though conceivably it also owed something to the more occasional influence of Hobbes. What explains this different stress is, once again, the theory of habituation, the view that belief is achieved only by the whole organism and with the collaboration of feeling, grown docile through its submission to ritual and routine.

Social and political life is placed decisively within the carnal realm, and it is simply beyond question that it is Augustine and not, as in Bodin's case, Aristotle, who is recalled. Politics belongs to l'ordre de la chair, not to l'ordre de l'esprit – let alone to that of la charité – for its very existence precludes rational understanding. It is a compound, merely, of force and opinion (97). Force, which is the basis of political existence, wins opinion over by clothing its instruments in such a way as to strike the imagination. When imagination is brought into play, a legal order can take on the image of a just one; if reason were brought to bear upon this image, it would dissolve at once. It is a practical necessity that some source or other of political authority should be obeyed; it is a rational truth that any proposed source can be fatally questioned. 'Merely according to reason, nothing is just in itself; everything shifts with time. Custom is the whole of equity for the sole reason that it is accepted. That is the mystic basis of its authority. Anyone who tries to bring it back to its first principle destroys it' (60). It is 'the art of subversion, of revolution ... to dislodge established customs by probing down to their origins in order to show how they lack authority and justice ... There is no surer way to lose everything; nothing will be just if weighed in those scales ... That is why the wisest of legislators used to say that men must often be deceived for their own good.' In the social and political context, then, reason, on rational grounds, must be self-denying; just as it must recognize that there are questions of faith that transcend its realm, so too it must recognize that in practical matters it will be merely 'subversive' if it does not recognize its limits. 'Reason's last step is the recognition that there are an infinite number of things that are beyond it' (188). Belief is beyond it, in that reason is inexhaustibly inventive in manufacturing objections; practice is beyond it in that, in a political context, practice depends upon the acceptance of some framework of obligations that, if subjected to rational inspection, will always fail or prove inconclusive. So it is reason itself that sets reason aside. If it is reason that constitutes man's dignity, dignity and worthiness consist in the recognition of ends of which reason is not worthy, or which are not worthy of reason.

To philosophize about politics, Pascal says, is to 'lay down rules for a madhouse' (533). He says this not only of Plato but even of Aristotle, and this sharply reveals his radical lack of sympathy for any philosophy in which political life is valued. He does not even share Augustine's view of political life as a sort of preparatory metaphor for spiritual life, the admirable civic devotion of the Roman prefiguring the religious devotion of the Christian. The closest he comes to that is in viewing the Jews' belief in national salvation as a prefiguring of universal salvation – but that, he says, had been only a *mis*reading of the salvation actually offered by biblical prophecies. None of this, of course, touches the question of obedience. To call the polity a madhouse is not at all to undermine the authority of its rulers but, on the contrary, to show that obedience is essential, that no more rational alternatives are available. Pascal's man, like Augustine's, will be a loyal and punctilious citizen, even a conscientious ruler if it is demanded of him, although – unlike the providentially mystified carnal man – he will not confuse what is necessary with what is just. But this is citizenship only in a minimal sense: we obey not because of any values that can be called civic but because political subjection is included as a duty in a scheme of things in which value is located elsewhere. Like Augustine, too, Pascal displaces the reference of civic language in such a way as to empty the city itself of its own meaning. Just as the *civitas* is displaced by the *civitas Dei*, so too *la république* is displaced by what Pascal calls 'la république chrétienne,' the community of those who seek God. It is to this community that the themes of unity and devotion are applied; it is 'a body of thinking members' (371, 372), an organism whose parts are conscious and willing and in which the harmony of 'individual' and 'primal' will is achieved. Here alone, not in the political context, Pascal permits the use of correspondences between body and society such as Bodin had deployed in explaining the commonwealth. This degrading of politics, along with the denial of political use to political concepts, was to exercise distant and often surprising influences in French thought as political discourse itself was diffusely penetrated, and sometimes overwhelmed, by a mode of thinking in which political life is no more than something to be tolerated.

Here the impact of Augustinianism converged in part with that of Stoicism, for Stoicism too had taught that civic duty has only a secondary or provisional status, that it is a condition that one accepts although one's essential loyalty lies elsewhere: before Augustine, Seneca too had said that there were 'two republics.'[14] But Stoicism, as in its Roman phase, was noticeably more open to assimilation by civic life. The Stoics too discriminated between man and citizen, but in the thinking of both Roman patricians and French republicans the duties of man and citizen became curiously similar and the space between general society and particular society became small indeed. It was not the distinction between man and citizen but the more radical distinction between man with and man without truth that was to keep the space open and to set obstacles to notions of immanent order.

A second long-term influence on French thinking was different, though not contradictory – that is, the influence of Pascal's conception of *esprit*, and particularly of its scientific accomplishments. The world is, after all, a created world, and while it is idolatry to worship it, it is not right to despise what good it contains. Augustine himself had singled out human knowledge as 'the chief ornament of this mortal life.' 'Man shows remarkable powers of mind ... and those powers are evidence of the blessings he enjoys ... How abundant is man's stock of knowledge of natural phenomena! It is beyond description.'[15] Whatever tension Pascal may personally have felt between his scientific and his spiritual endeavours, the Augustinian doctrine of wretchedness does not inherently exclude a belief in progress such as Pascal had sketched in the preface to his *Treatise on Vacuum*. In the scientific community as in *la république chrétienne* a correspondence between part and whole is allowed; because knowledge of the world is cumulative, we may imagine the generations of those who contribute to it as 'one single man,' their knowledge maturing in the manner of an individual mind – 'the same thing happens in the succession of men as in the different ages of single individuals.'[16] Ancient science is thus rejected no less categorically than ancient politics, Pascal looking back in neither case to classical authority or a vanished ideal – in the case of science because there has been progress, and in the case of politics because there is nothing to return to. Although from a scientific point of view he is on the side of the moderns, the dynamic character he ascribed to science was to contribute, in the following two centuries, to an aggressive spirit of modernity that we can scarcely imagine him to have approved. Paradoxically, this spirit was itself to reinforce that despairing view of politics that Pascal recommended: for to the extent that theories of progress were to restore notions of a value immanent in human history, they often located this value not in the political madhouse but in realms of life where to speak of progress is less inherently implausible.

While Bodin's importance to the origins of social science is sometimes urged, it was in many ways the position advanced by Montaigne that contributed more than Bodin's mammoth comparative enterprise. Nor is there any paradox here, for the concept of *social* relations is more intimately connected with the idea of private than of public interests. A society, as opposed to a *république*, is constituted precisely by networks of private relations; and there can be a 'science' of it, moreover, only to the extent that the order it displays is distinct from the order of nature itself. While there is no intention here to trace the very complex historical threads involved or to claim any special influence for Montaigne, it is surely noteworthy that the three kinds of order springing from his individualism are precisely those that were to preoccupy the emerging social science of the eighteenth century. What Montesquieu was to attempt in *Spirit of the Laws* may have owed more to Bodin than its author was willing to admit; but what made his work different from Bodin's was, in broad outline, just those features that it owed to Montaigne.

That 'there is nothing like tempting the appetite and the interest,'[17] that what individuals can be led to do must somehow figure in the personal shape of their desires and tendencies, was a point that was to receive extended elaboration in later thinking, notably in a much-quoted passage from the *Persian Letters*: 'I have often tried to decide which government was most in conformity with reason. I have come to think that the most perfect is the one that attains its purpose with the least trouble, so that the one that controls men in the manner best adapted to their inclinations and desires is the most perfect.'[18] Here we have, of course, the whole complex phenomenon of a moral, social, and political theory founded upon the concept of *interest*.[19] In place of the ancient model of the repression of passion by reason, a new model emerges, one in which the self accepts direction only by those stable and central desires termed 'interests,' which must, in Montaigne's terms, be 'tempted,' or engaged. The self cannot be governed *de haut en bas* – nor, indeed, can the polity. These two considerations may provide a hint of Montesquieu's reasons for thinking as he did about the republic on the one hand and despotic regimes on the other. Demanding 'virtue,' the ancient republican ideal may demand too much by way of self-denial, too much austerity (v.2), and may allow too little space for the natural shape of human desire. Montesquieu was close enough to classical sources to find the ideal admirable, but he certainly is sceptical about its plausibility, though to an extent about which commentators disagree.[21] At the same time, despotism relies excessively upon external repression, ignoring rather than engaging the desires. Montesquieu's classic statement of this point – transformed by a sexual metaphor – is in the *Persian Letters*, where it is eventually revealed that the lordly rule of the seraglio has been a sham thoughout and pretended obedience has merely disguised the covert satisfaction of desire. If virtue and despotism were exhaustive alternatives – as classical models had implied – our condition would indeed be desperate. But between self-repression and despotic repression there are other alternatives, neglected in ancient thinking, notably Montesquieu's category of *monarchy*, precisely a system in which order provides satisfaction for motives of self-enhancement (III.7). This category corresponds to an aristocratic view of French government to which Montesquieu subscribed, a view in which there is diffuse (though non-democratic) participation in the process of government;[22] and again the *Persian Letters* is most revealing, offering as it does a brilliant critique of rule by neutral bureaucratic (or clerical) instruments – 'black eunuchs,' in the seraglio metaphor – which was exactly the means by which successive French monarchs had sought to displace the aristocracy from its governmental role.

Montesquieu's critique of despotism is plainly somewhat in tension with the second theme at issue here, that of conventionalism. He cannot bring himself quite to treat despotism as simply one system among others, as (his typology implies) he sets out to do. It is, he says, 'corrupted' from the beginning (VIII.10), and his use of the term here is evidently not the same as in other cases, where corruption is strictly relative to the system in question. With that exception, however, Montesquieu follows up the relativistic thrust of Montaigne and Pascal. Political orders are classifiable into types, each type corresponding to a complex of social, geographical, economic, climatic, and demographic factors. Each type has its own 'principle' or spring of operation: virtue is thus relativized as the principle of but one type, the republic (democratic or aristocratic), another principle, honour, being attributed to monarchy, and a third, fear, being assigned to despotism. The notion of corruption, therefore, is not a moral or universal one but political-sociological in character: only in the republic is the corruption of virtue a fatal occurrence – the monarchy can live without virtue, its fall deriving from the corruption of its own principle, that of honour. We have, then, a conception of political life in which the conventional or local character of imperatives is recognized and in which no system can claim the sanction of a universal guarantee. The relativism is not necessarily thorough or complete: there are 'laws of nature' (I.2), and it may be by virtue of these that despotism is declared corrupt from the very start, denying as it does the minimal conditions of human reciprocity.[23] But the limits set by these laws of nature are generous, and within them political sociology must respect the relativities of a much broader spectrum of systems than the political science of virtue had admitted.

The third kind of order, that of causality rather than design, is still more amply developed in Montesquieu's argument. It is a kind of order that has been proposed, contentiously, as nothing less than the essential object of the social sciences. Such an order was noticed by Montaigne, given its most vivid and paradoxical expression by Bernard Mandeville – with whom its origins are sometimes associated – and received a mature formulation at the hands of Montesquieu and Adam Smith. While the order in question is often seen as fundamentally economic and as political only by extension, it is Montesquieu's political thought that takes precedence here: his picture of monarchical order, in which 'each individual advances the public good, while he only thinks of promoting his own interest' (III.7), antedates Smith's 'invisible hand' by some twenty years. Nor is it only the case of monarchy that exemplifies such a model. It is exemplified too, though in a different version, in that curious but inescapable model of order supplied by the English polity, to which Montesquieu attached so much importance but which cannot easily be fitted into his doctrine of social types (XIX.27). We have here an order that is admirable in its respect for freedom. Its ruling or animating passion is neither the virtue of the republic nor the honour of monarchy nor the fear of despotism. Here 'all the passions' are unleashed, yet an effective order is constituted by institutions that permit the balancing of one passion by another. Since England's polity rests upon an essentially commercial society, it enjoys, too, the balancing of passion against itself: the commercial motive requires the postponement of gratification, thus requiring something in some respects functionally comparable to virtue: frugality valued for the sake of future gain. Such a commercial motive, together with the channeling of interest supplied by political institutions, provides a socio-political order in which individuals enjoy more personal freedom than in any other known system; and such a system, together with the (idealized) French monarchy, constitutes one of the two real alternatives open to eighteenth-century man. We cannot, it seems, sacrifice ourselves to virtue; but we can adopt motives that, though self-interested, lead causally and in an unintended manner to political orders for which there is much to be said and that provide working alternatives to despotic rule.

The virtue of the citizen and the freedom of the person are thus distinguished; and to the extent that order is seen as springing from the central desires and voluntary actions of persons, order is in some cases counterposed to citizenship, not, as in Bodin, connected with it. There may be no need to press the point further than that, and there certainly is no need to do so in the present context. Whether Montesquieu intended us to prefer freedom to virtue or whether (more consistent, surely, with his catholicity of vision) he wished simply to set out a range of systematic alternatives is a question that requires no answer here. Nor need we ascribe to Montesquieu any rigid dualism of freedoms such as has since become familiar but that, in the French context, is often exceedingly hard to apply. The older *equation* of freedom with civic participation is indeed abandoned for a conception in which freedom depends upon the security enjoyed by interests; but freedom thus understood is scarcely *detached* from participation, for in both the English and the French models sketched by Montesquieu participation of one kind or another is a requirement of the regime as he defines it. All that is claimed here is that such participation is no longer citizen-like in the sense once understood.

The sense in which it is not citizen-like shows what Montesquieu's contribution, viewed in the broadest context, had in common with those of Montaigne and Pascal. In the French or English polities the order that is achieved does not find its microcosm in the orderly self-discipline of citizens; the supremacy of the general over any particular good is not matched by the supremacy of reason or virtue over passion in the individual soul. The order that is achieved, called 'social,' does not call for such severe moral inhibition but accomplishes general objectives through rather than against particular interest. In this respect, too, theories of elegant sustaining correspondences are thus demolished, just as Montaigne could find the features of order only in patterns of biography, Pascal only in *la république chrétienne*. Consequently, or concomitantly, political society is stripped of teleology, its explanation becoming efficient-causal, outcomes lacking symmetry or congruence with the forces that bring them about. Good, indeed, can come of bad – 'admirable order,' as Pascal said, from 'concupiscence' – just as general ends can come from particular ones, a sort of economy of sin working market-like transformations upon the outcomes of human action. It was of course in its moral aspect that 'society' thus understood was to offend Rousseau; in its explanatory aspect, however, it was to find in Rousseau its most determined exponent.

The relationships, institutions, and wants that civilized man has imposed upon himself, Rousseau contends in the *Discourse on Inequality*, do not correspond intelligibly to the needs of human nature or of human freedom. There is indeed an order of a kind in the situation of civilized man, an order that imposes itself with terrifying necessity; but it is an order of only a causal kind, not one in which we can see our intentions or our needs reflected, nor one in which a larger intelligible purpose is inscribed. Its causes Rousseau outlines with a realism that, though conjectural in its form, was sufficiently sociological in spirit to win Durkheim's praise.[24] His praise was qualified, for Rousseau could not wholly escape the individualist assumptions of his age: but he clearly grasped that society, far from expressing individuals' designs, imposes itself, that there are social facts that are experienced but not intended. The development sketched in the *Discourse on Inequality*, especially, occurs in and through a series of unintended consequences, of devastating effects that are neither in proportion to nor continuous with the human efforts from which they spring. Central to the theme of the *Discourse* is a critique of what may be called rationalism, or the expectation that institutions will meet pre-existing needs in the way that instruments are contrived for use: on the contrary, Rousseau contends, institutions impose our ends upon us. The family is the effect of building shelters, not the reason for it; technology creates wants rather than satisfying them; and above all, society itself creates sociability, of a kind, rather than responding to sociable desires. We are here far indeed, with such a picture of civilization as an opaque and self-generating process, from any cosmological vision in which the social world, like the natural, bears the stamp of coherent purpose.

The order of human institutions can be known, it follows, only a posteriori. Following up here a point urged by Montesquieu and also by Hume, Rousseau complains that political theory has ascribed to man the prospective knowledge of the maker, as opposed to the merely retrospective knowledge of the historical patient, or victim. 'The philosophers' have ascribed to man as he began the civilizing process knowledge that he was to have only at the end. For this reason, while they have tried to depict man as he is by nature, they all have abjectly failed, and their views are, in the literal sense, preposterous.[25] In any essentially causal account, after all, 'the time that must elapse' is an indispensable medium of understanding, for it is only over time that causes can display themselves as such if causation is taken to be a matter of succession; we cannot, as in an intelligible order, make inferences from part to part, or predict by assuming rational correspondences; we can know only after the event, and when it is too late. But that is not even to say, by way of comfort, that experience inherently brings knowledge: for causes do not merely open themselves to our inspection; they act upon us, and in such a way as to constrain our knowledge of how we came to be what we are. Hence the need for radical conjecture, for 'setting aside all the facts,' for the facts about what we now are merely conceal what we once were, and conceal, too, the heterogeneity between hidden cause and visible effect. The same goes for the theological schemes by which men interpret the world to themselves: these too – like the apparent facts of human nature – must be 'set aside,'[26] for they are merely evidence of the need to imagine a divine world in correspondence with what the human world has contingently come to be. Theology and philosophy, in short, are essentially rationalizing in their tendency; they both seek to demonstrate the fitness of beginning and end, and hence disguise the unfitness of what we have to what we are.

Nor is there in the civilized order any essential harmony of a kind remotely comparable to that of musical intervals or mathematical proportions, the symbols of order favoured by Renaissance theorists such as Bodin. The whole point of Rousseau's account is that there are tensions and dissonances that amount to virtual contradictions. In particular there is the paradox of goodness and morality – the 'Rousseauan moment,' as it has been called.[27] Natural man, though a creature of limited abilities and cramped horizons, has 'natural goodness' and bears no ill will to anyone. He lacks, however, moral goodness, because he acts with complete spontaneity and without the sense of making choices. To acquire this sense he must become self-conscious, and also conscious of himself as a being with temporal identity; he must acquire 'general ideas,' permitting him to compare and contrast situations and thus to identify principles of right and wrong; he must also, of course, acquire a social context, for without this moral choices do not confront him. All these things he acquires as individuals are compacted together into increasingly elaborate social formations, which give them a language, the means of moral discrimination, conceptions of relative merit, and a sense both of relatedness and distinct existence. But the very same processes that create the potential for moral behaviour also prevent its realization. For the development of human powers is connected inseparably with the sophistication and extension of wants, and the development of social formations is connected inescapably with the rule of vanity as the overriding motive of behaviour.[28]

All this stripping away of philosophical and theological illusions and this harsh insistence on relentless paradox in the human condition have one objective: to present man as a creature who, by nature, has no context and who, if he is to be understood, must be deprived of the comfortable but illusory contexts that are offered him. And when man is identified by these means, he turns out to be, if not wholly unattractive, a frighteningly vacuous creature, offering little if any leverage for moral argument or for the construction of anything orderly. His nature Rousseau pieces together conjecturally from various discrete sources – what we know of 'savages,' of children, or of ourselves in moments of introspection, or the curious evidence of 'wolf-children' or accidental social isolates. Rousseau does not mention another revealing possible source – the *Essays* of Montaigne.

Montaigne had believed that by a process of sustained, unblinking self-reflection he could discover in himself a *moi* enjoying only tenuous relations with his social and civil persona. That is Rousseau's point too: the self engaged in the intricate reciprocities of vanity is not the authentic self. To recover that, we must set aside what we take for granted and grasp the original movements of the self in relation to others. In doing so we understand that self-absorption is our natural state: there is a fundamental distinction between the self that we can know directly and the others who are knowable only by complex processes of inference. The imperative need of one sex for another, the maternal instinct, and the natural distress on the part of one living creature in observing another in suffering scarcely amount to significant exceptions. They sustain temporary indiscriminate liaisons and do not immediately bring a society into being. A society comes into being only through 'a slow succession of things' that cumulatively destroy the circumstances in which self-absorption is possible. The original self is overlaid and can be recovered only with difficulty. But when we do recover this displaced self, it turns out to have much in common with Montaigne's *moi*. Its most fundamental distinction is between what it finds to be meaningful and what others require of it. Naturally perceiving itself as its own centre of experience, it can ascribe no meaning to claims to direct its behaviour. It has no reason to distinguish degrees of importance on some external objective measure and thus cannot concentrate on one thing at the expense of another. It has no sense of the publicly prescribed dimension of time; its memory is weak, and it takes what once happened to be barely connected, if at all, with what will happen again. Unable to adapt things to its own wants, it adapts itself to things. All these features of the self are those described in Montaigne's *Essays*: and in the *Discourse on Inequality*, Rousseau generalizes these features and presents them as the original properties of the human self. Rousseau's natural man is, in outline, Montaigne, as Montaigne describes Montaigne: a self-preoccupied and indolent being for whom time is merely puzzling, society merely problematic, and escape from isolation only fitful. And Rousseau sets himself the astonishing task of transforming this creature into a citizen and of ascribing to him those virtues that Montaigne and others had radically undermined. It is as daunting a task as Pascal's attempt to make Montaigne's readers into Christians[29] and not wholly dissimilar in its techniques.

While the *Discourse* leaves us in no doubt as to the limitations of natural man, he is described there in somewhat affectionate terms; in *Social Contract*, however, he is described brusquely as a 'lazy and stupid creature' awaiting transformation into 'an intelligent being and a man,'[30] his intelligence and his humanity both being inseparable from his acquisition of citizenship. What requires to be imposed, evidently, on his sunny if dumb particularity is a universal: a conception of shared properties and ends that obliges him to see his actions in relation to the experiences and actions of others. He must learn, in Rousseau's phrase, 'the art of generalizing'[31] – that is, the habit of seeing himself not as discrete nor as privileged but in a typical light – and thus to make comparisons and parallels between what he does and what he is willing others should do. This is an 'art,' or something acquired, of course, for the same reason that language is acquired: the formation of 'general ideas,' on which both language and morality depend, is painfully learned, and does not spring spontaneously from desire or from experience. But the possible sources for such a universal, as we have seen, had been drastically limited. There could be no taking refuge in cosmological order, in 'the sacred precepts of the various religions' or in any sort of teleology that offered an illusory exit from a rigorously efficient-causal view of history. We should, then, take seriously Rousseau's 'C'est de l'homme que j'ai à parler':[32] a universal, if any is to be found, must be conjured out of man and the relations of men to one another.

There is no need at all to exaggerate Rousseau's originality here, and it has been quite rightly stressed that in outline what Rousseau attempted owed much to 'the political science of his time.'[33] For the natural-law jurists of the seventeenth and eighteenth centuries, whether or not a moral universal could be generated out of the structure of human relations was a central question as well as a crucial ideological one, for it was connected with the bases of political legitimacy. According to the rival school of *droit divin*, whose last great representative was Bossuet, the obligation that attaches to the state requires divine ordination. While the boundaries of states are indeed determined by strictly secular factors (military, diplomatic, dynastic), the *sovereignty* of the state, its right to demand obedience, rests upon divine will. 'La majesté est l'image de la grandeur de Dieu dans le prince':[34] in such phrases, of course, we may see a late though vigorous flowering of the argument from correspondence, and an effort to return political society with its internal hierarchy to its place in cosmic order. Against such claims theorists of *human* right contended that the human origins of government provided a sufficient constitutive basis for its sovereignty and that human association stood in need of no further (divine) authorization or legitimation. Even though it would be the 'utmost wickedness,' as Grotius said, to suppose that there was 'no God,' no god is needed to sustain those rules of 'mutual aid and reciprocal service,' perceived by human reason, that lead men to make and keep agreements. [35] It is evidently this argument that precedes and also explains Rousseau's proposal to argue from 'the nature of man by the light of reason alone, and independent of the sacred dogmas that give sovereign authority the sanction of divine right.' [36] Rousseau took the further step, to be distinguished clearly from the political caution of the natural-law jurists, of identifying not only the *origins* of sovereignty but also its *exercise* with the reason of the associated people; [37] it was this that led him from the familiar notion of general rules of conduct, sustained by human reason, to the notion of a general *will* enjoying legislative force.

But before we can approach the topic of the general will, a second context must be noted, one that brings to light both what Rousseau could accept and what he could not accept in the argument from *human right*. That 'mutual aid' and 'reciprocal service' were inherent requirements of human reason was accepted by Diderot in his *Encyclopaedia* article on 'Natural Right'; [38] and this is an important text here, for it evidently was written, in part at least, in rebuttal of Rousseau's argument in the *Discourse on Inequality*. Without mentioning Rousseau by name – probably without needing to do so – Diderot denounces as 'mad' or 'evil' the 'violent reasoner' who cannot grasp that there are principles of justice inherent in the relations of one human to another. 'At every moment the unjust and passionate man feels inclined to do to others what he would not have done to himself.' What can we say to him? That he has 'no legitimate authority' to require others to accept a situation in which he is privileged and they are disadvantaged; that there is in each individual 'a general will' that is 'a pure act of understanding that reasons in the silence of the passions about what man can demand of his fellow men and about what his fellow man can rightfully demand of him.' Simply to reason, then, according to Diderot here, is to grasp the necessity of mutual obligation and to be led to claim for oneself only what can be consistently or 'legitimately' granted to others; in this sense, a will that obeys reason rather than passion is inherently general.

This is a notably ineffectual objection, and Rousseau's argument – or that of Diderot's *Rameau's Nephew*, which wholly subverts the case presented in 'Natural Right' – makes very much more sense. To set the violent reasoner for judgment at the bar of the entire human race is simply to neglect the fact that, for each member of the human race thus set in judgment, the violent reasoner's case recurs. From the fact that I do not wish something generally to be done it does not follow that I ought not to do it: for while its being generally done would produce unacceptable consequences for everyone, including me, it is not the case that my doing it will produce significant consequences for anyone, let alone me – and in *my* case the benefits of doing it wholly outweigh the minimal costs incurred either for others or for myself by my doing it. Moreover, my doing it, in a case in which benefits to me far exceed costs to me, will not necessarily cause others to do it, a case in which costs to me will exceed the benefits of my doing it. On this issue modern theorists of rational choice are very much on Rousseau's side.[39]

Two themes, above all, appear to have led Rousseau to this 'violent' if wholly satisfactory reasoning. One is what may be termed his sociological realism, influenced deeply by Montesquieu, among others, which led him to see in institutions and *moeurs* the primary formative conditions of moral belief. We conceive of obligations, he insists, only when we experience solidarity. A solidarity founded upon reason alone is sporadic and conditional; effective solidarity is achieved only in the interior of communities, where it is reinforced by sanctions and by a sense of common identity. A 'general society' of all mankind, actuated by a 'general will' whose content is that of natural law, is a mere projection, an abstraction that philosophers can make once the solidarity of national communities has been haltingly achieved; it cannot, then, precede social obligation, and to offer it as the basis of social obligation is again to fall victim to a retrospective fallacy. The second theme is that of the Montaigne-like *moi* that Rousseau sees in pre-civil man, a *moi* that insistently refers all issues not to rules or principles but to itself. This *moi* is clearly to be found in the 'independent man' with whom Rousseau confronts the 'philosopher' in the draft version of *Social Contract*. The philosopher, quoted verbatim from Diderot's article on 'Natural Right,' recommends a pure act of understanding, which will reveal the necessity of following general rules and the inherent reciprocity between what we can expect and what we can give. The independent man does not seek to deny the philosopher's logic but simply declares that it is without any hold upon his own motives: 'I admit that I can see in this the rule that I can consult, but I do not yet see ... *the reason for subjecting myself to this rule.*'[40]

Now Rousseau's objections, it should be noted, occupy the plane of social and individual psychology. They relate to the conditions under which moral obligations can be acquired, and involve no challenge to the philosopher's view of the substance of moral obligation. No one, Rousseau says, would deny the logic that; what Diderot called a 'universal motivation, which makes each part act for an end that is general and relative to the whole,' is, after all, to occupy a central place, and under the same name of the 'general will,' in the completed political model of *Social Contract*. It is not a new argument that is offered – no amount of argument can overcome the egoist's view that he has no *interest* in acting as he would wish others to act – but, rather, 'new associations,'[41] which will practise upon the egoist what is best described as a form of social, moral, and political therapy. The egoist, like Pascal's sceptic, is to be made docile.

There is no natural causal connection between the egoist's doing something and others' doing it, such that if he had an interest in others' refraining from it he would also have an interest in refraining himself. But as a first step an artificial causal connection can be supplied. He can secure a system of enforcement, obliging others to act as he wishes, only at the cost of becoming subject to it himself, for the others, obviously, will not agree to such a system if he is exempted. He may consider this a bargain that he has an interest in making if the damage he expects from others' unrestrained behaviour exceeds the advantages he expects from his own being unconstrained. It is necessary, further, that the rules that are to be enforced be both general in form and also generally agreed upon by those who are to be subject to them: for this gives him an assurance that others will not seek to oppress him, the rules that they make bearing also upon themselves. At the same time, of course, these requirements will make clear to him the impossibility of making good any privileged claim on his own behalf, for the others will never agree to that; and here we have the beginning of the art of generalizing, of the understanding that particular claims are self-defeating and that claims upon others must rest upon a shared or typical interest. But this still will not be enough to make the independent man content. He still would prefer a situation in which others obeyed and he did not: he still may hanker after Gyges' ring, and its impossibility does not make it any less ideal. We cannot say that we are forcing *him* to be free in compelling him to obey; we can only say that doing so is a necessary implication of others' being compelled. In terms of the logic of interest there is no rational escape from this point. But perhaps the impossibility of the independent man's ideal will eventually prove wearing, especially if the design of institutions works systematically against any possible reinforcement of it. We can imagine that repeated demonstrations of the futility of privileged claims will make the consultation of shared rather than special interest habitual. We can imagine that each will include himself in the all whose behaviour he wishes to be regulated. We can imagine that in this way a self considered in a particular light will insensibly be replaced by a self considered in a typical light; and if so, we can imagine that interest and justice eventually will merge, the pursuit of shared interests being identical to the rule of justice that requires that claims be generalizable. We can imagine that the initially independent man will in this way come to see himself as the author of the rules that he obeys and of the sanctions attached to them.

There can be no decisive objection, then, to classifying Rousseau as a theorist of 'conditional natural law,' as one commentator has proposed,[42] for it is, after all, only in terms of the *conditions* of moral obligation that Rousseau takes issue with the natural-law theorists. Whether or not a theorist belongs to a natural-law tradition is sometimes obscure, and the terms upon which an answer can be arrived at so unclear that the question is not always worth asking. But there is at least one important reason to stress the natural-law dimension in Rousseau. He was no moral relativist, even if he was in some sense a cultural one:[43] there is for Rousseau a rational and universal core to morality, even if – men being what they are – it can exist only within the penumbra of an exclusive and distinctive national identity. National identities are celebrated, and the cosmopolitan is despised; but national identities domesticate, in the political sense, the cosmopolitan general will. The political community becomes a moral community, and its principle of legitimacy is to be found in the structure of moral thinking itself, that is, in the art of generalizing.

Whenever a teleological moral scheme is abandoned, Alasdair MacIntyre has suggested, some version of Stoicism tends to be substituted for it.[44] This is illuminating with respect to much Enlightenment thinking, to which Stoic reminiscences were often important.[45] In a teleological moral scheme society is understood to occupy a natural or divine order, which permits us to ascribe immanent purpose to roles and relationships within it and to establish a hierarchy of the virtues. When such a scheme is lost, undermined, or challenged beyond plausible defence, a morality of law or rules or principles, no longer tied essentially to the moral agent's social place nor ascribing meaning to it, is the most natural recourse; and Stoicism is indeed the model for such moral transitions. But whatever the merits of MacIntyre's suggestion, there are in Rousseau's case independent grounds for noticing the importance of Stoicism for him, whether through the mediation of Montaigne or Montesquieu or through his evident debt to Stoic writers themselves, perhaps most especially to Seneca.[46] The critique of sophistication, vanity, and luxury; the loss of original 'humanity' under the weight of artifice; the corrupting consequences of knowledge; the critique of 'imitation' or fashion as a form of slavery; the identification of reason with the capacity for autonomy; the appeal to 'man, of whatever country you are': all these are Stoic themes. The last mentioned, of course, poses a problem, for it is in obvious tension with what Rousseau also says about the (archetypically Stoic) cosmopolitan, whose 'love for the whole world' can only be shallow.[47] But we already have seen how this apparent contradiction might be, if not exactly resolved, at least notably eased. For reasons deeply embedded in human psychology, the society of reason and autonomy can be realized only within the frontiers of an exclusive society; only by first becoming citizens do we then become men, and while Rousseau's *humanité* retains many of the connotations of the Stoic *humanitas*, it stops short – like that of the Romans, Rousseau says – at the borders of the republic.[48]

While even the unlikelier of Rousseau's views may thus be illuminated by Stoic reminiscences, Stoicism is here put to a very paradoxical use. The Stoics' concern, after all, had been to show that the community of all men, or of all rational men, had some of the essential attributes of a city; to describe the universal community as a 'city' of the world was to employ the term that, to the highest degree, then expressed the obligation that attached to it, and the solidarity and fellowship among its members. Rousseau, however, does exactly the opposite. He takes the attributes of a universal society, 'la société générale,' and transposes them to the smaller and exclusive territorial community; for it is no longer the political notion of the city but now the moral notion of *humanité* that carries the highest degree of obligatory force. The polity is, as it were, a *cosmopolis* in miniature, for Rousseau's task, unlike the Stoics', is to contract rather than to expand the scale of obligation. But Rousseau's diminished *cosmopolis* is not a *polis*. The patterns of thought and image relating *polis*, *cosmopolis*, and Rousseau's polity are too highly mediated to be reducible to differences of scale alone. While the Stoic *cosmopolis* may have been imagined as a large city, Rousseau's conception of the city derives its essential features not from the original but from its enlargement. It has become, as he revealingly says, a *means* to the realization, on a local scale, of a 'universal justice.'[49] Physically delimited for merely contingent reasons, it is a local fragment of an order that is in principle universal, though in practice not so. It is a 'subdivision of humanity.'[50]

In Seneca's *cosmopolis* 'we do not see things from this or that standpoint, but consider only the ends of our city.'[51] Nothing could better express the principle that Rousseau regards as essential to his ideal republic, in which the exclusion of 'this or that standpoint,' the primacy of shared inner perceptions over public contestation, is precisely what is demanded by his idea of a general will. Rousseau does not, as has been claimed, combine a Stoic morality with a classical politics.[52] His conception of politics is very distant from Aristotle's. He sees no inherent value in public action; 'communication' actually impedes the possibility of autonomy, and 'long debates and discussions' are signs of the decline, not of the fulfilment, of association.[53] Nor is the polity to be distinguished qualitatively from the other associations within it or beyond it. The *polis* had been regarded as something different in character from household or village or from the associations of friendship or society: Rousseau, however, while admitting only a partial identity between family and city, explicitly regards all associations as, no less than the city itself, bearers of a general will, plainly following the Stoics, not Aristotle, here.[54] As for associations beyond the city, ancient political theory had scarcely recognized them at all; but Rousseau's argument, as we have seen, depends upon a relation of fundamental similarity between the city and the *société générale* of man. And it is here that the central problems of legitimation begin to emerge.

In Rousseau's argument there is an intriguing but perhaps ultimately paradoxical balancing of two competing principles. On the one hand the force of an attachment is in inverse ratio to its scale. The cosmopolitan's love is too diluted to be real; the sentiment of humanity 'evaporates' if extended too far;[55] the philosopher of 'society' covers his ears as a passer-by is murdered beneath his window.[56] Attachments of any degree of extensiveness require to be fostered in smaller schools of experience – just as the general society is imaginable only as an imaginary enlargement of the *patrie*, so too patriotism can thrive 'only in the soil of that miniature fatherland, the home.'[57] On the other hand considerations of a moral kind dictate generality of concern. There is a direct proportionality between the justice of a will and the scale of the context of consideration in which it is formed. As Rousseau had written in his *Encyclopaedia* article on 'Political Economy': 'Particular societies always being subordinate to those who embrace them, one must always obey the latter in preference to the former; the duties of the citizen precede those of the senator, and those of the man precede the citizen. But unfortunately, personal interest is always in an inverse ratio to duty, and increases to the extent that the association becomes narrower and the commitment less sacred: incontestable proof that the most general will is always the most just.'[58] This passage displays not only the inversion of considerations of scale but also a fundamental tension between the requirements of ethics and of psychology. The 'proof' that the more general will is more just is precisely that it involves to a higher degree the suppression of 'personal interest.' It is intriguing to note that even Rousseau's earlier doctrine of goodness as innocent spontaneity does not survive the requirements of this argument: as the conception of an ideal association takes shape in the draft of *Social Contract*, the idea of goodness is no longer satisfied by unreflective innocence but demands the conscious attachment to an association to whose needs one submits one's own. Without that, our 'similarities' do not 'unite us.'[59]

Arguments of ethical and psychological kinds, one might convincingly argue, occupy different planes, and hence there is no contradiction in embracing an ethics of generality and a psychology of particularity. We may perhaps then locate political association at a point of equilibrium between the two: it is the product of a compromise or balance, small enough to engage loyalty, large enough to provide that generality of consideration that is essential to duty. Such a compromise may in principle be possible; and certainly it was Rousseau's effort to fuse these two arguments together that lent such radical force to the democratic ideology that was derived, in part, from his thinking – as Tocqueville and others have stressed.[60] The *patrie* takes on all the moral attributes of *humanité*. A trend of thought that, in its Stoic origins, had sometimes served to diminish or qualify the political attachment now serves to justify it: while the Stoic idea of nature had ascribed to the city of one's birth only a conditional importance, Rousseau's adaptation of *droit naturel* ascribes only conditional importance to particular associations within the city and thus erodes their claims. In this way the argument from generality protects the city from the claims of partial groups within it, while the argument from particularity protects the city from the claims of a hypothetical association beyond it.

But how can this be true? A state claims unique authority; but if, as Stoic theorists such as Seneca and Marcus Aurelius had observed, all associations are fundamentally homogeneous in character, there is at least a *prima facie* implausibility in ascribing a unique status to any one of them. The point is well put by Plutarch, whose importance for Rousseau has also been urged: 'Now say that thou dost not dwell and live in Sardis: what matter is that? Surely it is just nothing. No more do all the Athenians inhabit in the boroughs or tribe Colyttus, nor the Corinthians in the street Cranium.'[61] Household, street, borough, and city differ in scale alone; ideas of proximity and distance allow of an indefinite number of gradations, and anything can be declared near or far, depending on what it is contrasted with. Such a conception is adopted by Rousseau himself to the extent that he declares 'political society' to be 'composed of other smaller societies,' each of which has a will that is 'general' with respect to its members and 'particular' with respect to a larger association encompassing it.[62] Hence the possibility, noted by Rousseau, that an action that is admirable in conforming to the general will of a relatively small group may be condemned as particular with respect to what is required by the general will of a relatively large one: 'An individual may be a devout priest, a brave soldier, or a zealous senator, and yet a bad citizen.' And since the more general will is always the more just, the devotion of the priest and the zeal of the senator must be subordinated to civic duty. Rousseau, it is true, says only 'may be,' and to that extent we may feel some sympathy for the view that he did not see the 'smaller societies' as *necessarily* malign:[63] but however much we may wish to pluralize his conception of the polity, he leaves us in no doubt as to which will is to triumph when the wills of smaller and larger societies collide. To the extent that he does admit less general wills, he does so only on condition that they be subordinated to more general ones.

Here we may contrast Rousseau's view that it is 'the good man, the good husband, the good father who makes the good citizen' with the terrifying picture of the citizen offered in *Emile*: the Spartan asks about the outcome of the battle before considering the fate of her sons. To be sure, the two views are not incompatible: we may at once trace the roots of civic loyalty to family feeling *and* imagine the former, once developed, to override the latter. But this is to abandon the image of tiered or layered or nested circles of association for a model in which the largest circle wholly absorbs those within it. We must take seriously Rousseau's remark that the relations among citizens must be as weak as possible, their relation to the state as strong as possible;[64] and it is doubtful that we can take this seriously without introducing a conception of generalization that differs radically from the conception that figures in those trends of his thinking that we may identify, however broadly, with the traditions of natural law. In these traditions it is precisely the relations among individuals, governed by their perceived generic properties as creatures of God or bearers of reason, that constitute justice; Rousseau, however, substitutes for this a conception of justice governed by one's relation to a general object, general not in a distributive but in a collective sense: 'It is in the fundamental and universal law of the greatest good of all, and not in the particular relations between one man and another, that the true principles of the just and unjust must be sought.'[65]

The patriot must feel less for the foreigner than for his compatriots, just as the *patrie* must do more for its citizens than for those of other countries.[66] But Rousseau has two views as to why this should be so. It is one thing to say, as he does in *Political Economy*, that there is a sense of *humanité* that, however, stops short at the frontiers of the city; it is something else to say, as he does in discussing the same topic in *Emile*, that to the patriot foreigners are 'only men.'[67] More important than the fact that the two explanations are directly contradictory is the point that they carry with them two opposed theories of citizenship. In the former conception, a sense of respect and attachment is broadened through successive tiers of association until it reaches its maximum (effective) scope: the notion of the *man* retains its force up to that point, and each individual's life is contained within a number of zones or realms, in each of which the requirements of human respect are learned and applied. They are applied, Rousseau claims, following Diderot and more distant sources, even within a band of robbers. In the latter conception, however, the notion of the man becomes empty, perhaps deprecatory: a man is what is not a citizen. And the idea of the citizen is not achieved by the progressive expansion of an attitude of sympathy or respect, which in principle could be universal, but by way of a notion of shared membership in a community, which is, by its nature, exclusive. Such a conception, moreover, not only relegates non-citizens to the status of men but also, in distinguishing men from citizens, effectively denies that status to the inhabitants of the city; for to be united by shared *membership* is not the same thing as to be united by common *representative* qualities, recognized in one's relations at various levels of association. The chilly Spartan mother makes the point: it is as members of the city, not as persons bearing representative human features, that she thinks of her sons. And can such a notion of civic or public duty be derived in any way from a picture of obligation that rests upon the recognition of shared or general properties? Here two distinct visions of association appear to confront one another, one only contingently exclusive and in principle (though not in practice) universal, the other exclusive by its very nature. Human *society* is indefinite in its range: a *city* necessarily confronts other cities, and loyalty to it is defined by preference for its concerns.

One kind of problem posed by the concept of the general will results from the effort to locate it in terms of the categories of moral philosophy. Some commentators, impressed by Rousseau's intuitive grasp of issues in the theory of rational choice, insist that the general will is a post-Hobbesian or proto-utilitarian construct. Others, sustained by Kant's glowing tribute to Rousseau, are no less insistent that the construct is not a utilitarian but a Kantian one.[68] While this is not an issue to be pursued here, it should be pointed out that the obstacles that stand in the way of either reading are considerable. For reasons sketched above, Rousseau's central concern was to overcome the egoist's reservations and make him susceptible to the claims of moral duty; he thus sought a point of coincidence between utility and justice.[69] But if utility and justice can be said to coincide, they cannot be equated, as in the utilitarian thesis; while if justice depends upon its coincidence with utility, it cannot require that wholly disinterested willing of the good that Kant requires.[70] If there is no rigorous separation in Rousseau's argument between interest-centred and duty-centred arguments, that may be because he was intent on blurring the differences between them, for persuasive reasons; or it may be that the distinction is anachronistic in its application to Rousseau, whom we need not assume to have made distinctions that later moral philosophers quite rightly find crucial.

The relevant difficulty here, however, is one that permits this issue to be bracketed out: for it concerns not the conceptual location of his moral philosophy but rather the relationship between those of his views that we may call moral and those we may call political. As a moral doctrine the ideal of generalization requires the actor to consider the possibility (in either the Kantian or the utilitarian sense) that an action of the kind he proposes to perform will be performed generally. This is evidently different from the question of the general consequences of an action's being performed. To ask 'What would be the consequences of x's being generally done?' or 'Could x be universally willed?' is not the same as to ask 'What will happen, viewed generally or overall, if x is done?' Yet it is the latter question that most naturally comes to mind when a political action or a proposed law is being considered. Moreover, it is the latter question, Rousseau says, that is the question to be asked by the citizen before voting: the proper criterion is that of 'advantage to the state.' This is clearly not a criterion of a hypothetical kind, in the way that 'What would happen if everyone did x? or 'Could x be universally willed?' are hypothetical questions. What is involved is a prediction and not a hypothesis adopted in a spirit of moral self-reflection.[71]

In both cases, it is true, the individual is required to step outside his immediate circumstances, as it were, and to consider a question in a less immediate or more general context. But what he is required to step *into* is not the same in the two cases. Either of the moral arguments mentioned above requires the actor to consider what is representative or typical: an action can be said to be just if it is possible for it, in one or the other sense, to be a typical one. But a policy or law is to be prospectively evaluated not by its typical effects – if indeed the idea of the typical has any meaning here at all – but in terms either of some balanced judgment of its differential effects or of its consequences for the survival of the community as a whole or the survival of some valued general feature of it. A state, as Rousseau insists, may perish even if none of its members does; and clearly, therefore, the notion of 'advantage to the state' is not always reducible in Rousseau's thinking to any summation of particular or typical advantages.

Here an attractive but misleading possibility presents itself. What is typical and hence morally relevant may be taken to include the fact that fellow citizens are, typically, members of a city. In this way we could arrive at the criterion of advantage to the state by proposing that each citizen should see himself as having only the typical status of citizenship, thus disregarding particular and exclusive statuses that he may also have. The logic of the generalization thesis could then be followed, in that each man would have to see himself as a citizen if he wished that to be the status given weight by others in considering laws or policies. But what cannot be shown, surely, is that the moral principle of citizenship must take precedence over all other principles. The process of generalizing will presumably generate a range of principles, of which seeking the advantage of the state will be only one among many; and while there is no problem at all in pulling the rabbit of civic duty out of the hat of moral obligation, problems most certainly arise if we are arbitrarily prohibited from putting any other creature into it.

The central difficulty here is that to the extent that Rousseau's argument is a moral one, of whatever moral type is favoured, it serves to define an *attitude* of a certain kind: the good man is disposed to respect the concerns that he shares with others in preference to those concerns of his that are merely particular. But Rousseau also sees the general will as supplying an *object*. It brings about not (or not only) a shift of attitude but also a displacement of attention: public affairs, he says, will preoccupy the citizen to the exclusion or near-exclusion of private ones.[72] Now, while we may indeed speak of 'political things' as a special, restricted class of concerns, we cannot in the same sense speak of 'moral things,' for morality is not constituted by a special class of events or concerns but by a disposition to approach any event or concern whatsoever in a certain manner. While we can recommend public affairs to his attention, we cannot say that the good man will attend to this or any class of concerns in preference to any other.

What Rousseau introduces here is a consideration that is hard to square with either of the two principal readings of *generality* in the context of moral philosophy. He tries to sustain the shift of attention that he favours by proposing what is nothing less than a redefinition of the self, thanks to which each individual will see himself not merely as *having* citizenship – as one among several possible statuses – but as *being* a citizen. If this were achieved, the moral question of the relation between self and others would literally vanish, simply because the two entities whose relation is in question would no longer be distinguishable. Speaking again of the desirability of men's consciousness of 'common life' to the exclusion of private concerns, Rousseau attributes this condition to 'good social institutions' that will 'make men unnatural' by virtue of the fact that they 'merge the unit in the group.'[73] Elsewhere this process of merging is connected with the idea of patriotism, to which Rousseau attributes 'the greatest miracles of virtue': 'This sweet and ardent sentiment, by combining the force of egoism with all the beauty of virtue, gains an energy which, without disfiguring it, makes it the most heroic of all passions.'[74] How are we to reconcile this with the view, noted above, that virtue is accomplished only in the transcendence of egoism? Simply by recognizing that the ego, for Rousseau, is mobile and elastic, a field of emotive identification as attachable to the group as to the self. The attachment of egoism to the private self makes one non-virtuous; the attachment of egoism to the group does not, apparently, 'disfigure' the virtue of civic devotion. I can, it seems, regard *our* things as 'mine' no less easily than I can distinguish my own things from others; and if I can manage to do this, then I will enjoy more 'sweet and ardent sentiments' than if I identified what is mine with what is particular to me, as I will do without the support of 'good social institutions.' Not only that, but the juristic and moral (distributive) rules governing relations among men, to the extent that men continue to perceive themselves as particulars, are actually *derived* from the (collective) notion of the greatest good of all: 'Hence *cuique suum*, because private property and civil freedom are the bases of the community. Hence *love thy neighbour as thyself*, because the private self extended to the whole is the strongest bond of the general society, and because the State has the highest possible degree of force and life when all our private passions are contained in it.'[75]

Here the duties of citizenship are not things to be (problematically) derived from an idea of interpersonal obligation but are the very bases upon which interpersonal obligation is to be grounded. We may thus seem to have come full circle. As a theorist of *droit humain*, drawing upon trends of thought originated by the Stoics, Rousseau appears to be attempting to derive political duty from obligations of a moral kind: as a theorist of the *patrie*, however, he appears to be attempting the opposite. The claims of the general interest in a collective sense are not derived by extension from, or as a case of, the rightful claims that individuals generally make upon each other; on the contrary, one's claims as an individual are rightful only because of their bearing upon a collective interest, their contribution to a valued common life.

Here we may feel much sympathy for a third model, one that is neither Kantian nor utilitarian but belongs to what has been called a different 'paradigm' altogether.[76] Both the Kantian and utilitarian arguments belong to what has been called the paradigm of 'obligation,' establishing (in their different ways) rules of conduct or criteria of choice that are binding upon moral actors. They have been distinguished, accordingly, from the older paradigm of virtue, which holds up, on the contrary, a picture of an admired way of living. If indeed *Social Contract* begins with what looks like a question about obligation, its answer is cast in what is at least in part a framework of virtue, proposing not (or not only) a set of reasons for obedience but an ideal conception of how life should be; it proposes to mould or form individuals according to a pattern of community in which the question of obedience no longer arises. That this is in fact the central tension in

Social Contract has been argued vigorously and at some length.[77] The difficulty is revealed, it is argued, in the very notion of general will; for while 'will' introduces the notion of voluntary obedience, the assent of autonomous individuals to rules of association and behaviour, 'generality' introduces, rather, a reminiscence of classical virtue, of cohesiveness and public devotion, and of the thorough absorption of the individual by an admired community. As the bearer of will the individual *obeys* the requirements of citizenship; as a bearer of the spirit of generality he *is* a citizen, and conformity (rather than obedience) to a common good is simply the medium in which he lives.

For reasons outlined above, it is not possible to accept the identification of Rousseau's 'generality' with cohesiveness of the kind exemplified by some image of the ancient city-state. For one thing, the very notion of generalization is connected essentially, in Rousseau's argument, with the phenomenon of will: it is the art of generalizing that leads the individual to will those rules that common interest, or mutual respect, or (perhaps) the very logic of moral concepts requires. It is not the exclusive polity but, on the contrary, the general society that is the root of the general will, even though the general will severs itself from its root in its eventual growth. For another thing, Rousseau's classical image of the *polis* is juxtaposed with and highly modified by themes and images that he draws from the late classical period: the Stoic is at least as important as the Spartan, and the city is imagined in a way that may draw more from *cosmopolis* than from *polis*, its principle of life resembling an inner conscience much more than it does a process of public interchange. What has been suggested above is that the difficulties in Rousseau are internal to the notion of generality rather than occurring between generality and will. But that said, there is much in this interpretation that can be accepted here – in particular, the important perception that the 'common good' as Rousseau sometimes uses that term figures in an idiom different from that employed in Rousseau's voluntarist picture of individual autonomy. While autonomous man can indeed generalize, in a non-civic sense, the art of generalizing that he may acquire cannot lead him to a common good of the kind that Rousseau wishes him to respect; or at least, it cannot lead him to assign primacy to *this* good over the other goods to which moral reflection may lead him. The *primacy* of political obligation – the shift of attention that Rousseau favours – requires a specific paradigm or idiom of civic virtue that is not derivable from the self-reflection of individuals, whether individuals are imagined on a Hobbesian or a

Kantian model, and that, in an age of *social* morality, lacks any secure justification.

Among the elements belonging prominently to Rousseau's 'classical' idiom, two deserve attention, for a special reason, here. One is the figure of the 'Legislator,' introduced in chapter 7 of book 2 of *Social Contract*, the other the concept of civil religion, which, as manuscript evidence shows, was added to the body of the text as something of an afterthought and appears as chapter 8 of book 4. Both notions have, of course, a distinguished classical pedigree, and both relate very directly to that strand of Rousseau's thinking that led him beyond those rules of conduct to which a rational man would agree to the vision of a way of life that men were to be led to adopt by the force of public education and of *moeurs*. The great Legislator – who might better be termed the 'Lawgiver,' for he has no legislative powers – presents to the people a set of institutions that will, over time, 'transform each individual,' 'take away man's own forces,' and produce circumstances in which each individual regards himself as a citizen. The civil religion that the good republic should institute adds to whatever obligations may be rationally derivable an obligation to subscribe to certain religious beliefs that Rousseau holds to be indispensable to the republic's life. The Lawgiver, too, we may note, relies upon a religious appeal. He can rely neither on force nor on reason, for he has no force, and the requisite powers of reasoning are not an antecedent but a consequence of his laws; so 'he must necessarily resort to another order of authority, which can win over without violence and *persuade without convincing*. This is what has always forced the fathers of nations to resort to the intervention of heaven and to attribute their own wisdom to the Gods.' He seeks 'to convince by divine authority those who cannot be moved by human prudence.'[78]
    Here we are led back almost to the beginning of the argument. Rousseau, as we have seen, set out to argue from 'the nature of man by the light of reason alone, and independently of the sacred dogmas which give sovereign authority the sanction of divine right.' He had further written, 'Let us ... set aside the sacred precepts of the various religions, whose abuse causes as many crimes as their use can avoid.' We should, to be sure, distinguish clearly between what Rousseau calls 'right' and 'fact': at no point is divine authority employed in arguing for the *de jure* legitimacy of political association; its role is purely in establishing its *de facto* effectiveness, the argument of divine-right

theories thus being precisely inverted. But all the same we may well wonder why an argument that is so forthrightly secular in its beginnings should come to rest, politically, upon an appeal to the divine. In a context broader than that of interpreting Rousseau, we may be reminded of Hannah Arendt's remark that the 'enlightened' men of the eighteenth century were driven to 'plead for some religious sanction at the very moment when they were about to ... separate politics and religion once and for all.'[79] Why should such religious sanctions have been retained when the argument for the legitimacy of the state had become essentially 'human,' or secular?

Rousseau requires the Lawgiver to depend upon religious appeals because, as noted above, the acceptance of the human argument depends upon the completion of political education and thus cannot precede it. Such an argument is surely less compelling in the case of the civil religion, which, unlike the Lawgiver, is intended as a permanent feature of the ideal republic. Here another argument, which is not offered by Rousseau and to that extent is only speculative, suggests itself. The proposed civil religion contains five essential points of doctrine: the existence of God, the afterlife, the happiness of the just, the punishment of the wicked, and the sanctity of the social contract and the laws. The first four of these are the common coin of the eighteenth-century doctrine of natural religion. Their function is evidently to act as an adjunct to a secular morality and to add further sanctions to rules of conduct that (short-term) self-interest might tempt the citizen to flout. But the fifth is more surprising. Referring as it does to a human or conventional act, it obviously cannot figure among the minimum articles of a natural religion. Moreover, it appears redundant: since the social contract is a promise, its 'sanctity' is guaranteed by the sanctity of justice itself, for promise keeping is essential to justice. Since Rousseau says that the articles should be 'few in number,' we may perhaps wonder why there seems to be one too many.

The chapter on civil religion bears a special relevance to a theme stressed in this discussion: the relation between universal and exclusive loyalties. The objection that Rousseau makes against Christianity as a universal religion is precisely that it has 'no particular relation to the body politic.' It is the 'religion of the man,' not, that is, a religion in which citizenship has any place of special dignity. 'I know of nothing more contrary to the social spirit.' The Christian, Rousseau continues, 'does his duty, it is true, but he does it with profound indifference to the good or bad outcome of his efforts'; in this respect the Christian is, he implies, like the Stoic: the man whose 'homeland is not of this world' is, we are thus led to think, rather like the man whose homeland is 'the whole world' – each refuses to the *patrie* the special loyalty that it requires. Indeed, it was thanks to Christianity (rather than to Stoicism) that ideas of 'natural right and the brotherhood of all men' came to be diffused in the world. To some extent, then, the critique of Christianity recapitulates the abandoned critique of the general society in the first draft of *Social Contract*; and we should regard the proposed civil religion less as an adjunct to morality in general than as a defence of the exclusive society against the claims of the general one. The fifth article, from this point of view, is crucial.

In the published version of *Social Contract* Rousseau had complained that Christianity, as a religion of the man, 'leaves laws with only their intrinsic force, without adding any other force to them.' In the first draft, however, he had written: ' ... leaves *political and civil laws* with *only the force that natural right gives them*, without adding any other force to them.'[80] When Rousseau first decided upon the need to add a civil religion to his ideal republic, it seems, he had in mind the deficiencies of 'natural right' as well as those of Christianity. And the deficiency of natural right, as we have seen, is precisely that it cannot establish the priority of civic obligation over those other obligations that a natural or secular morality may dictate. It is not only the *force* of obligations that the civil religion sanctions but the hierarchy among them. If the first four articles are directed at the egoist who cannot otherwise see the necessity of moral behaviour, the fifth seems intended, rather, for the moral man who cannot otherwise accept the ordering of values required by citizenship. The civil religion is, therefore – as its pagan origins alone may also suggest – a means of closure; and some means of closure is required because the natural and secular argument fails to supply the state with the unique and morally terminal character that its sovereign status apparently demands.

The independent man, then, or the recalcitrant *moi* that Rousseau detected in human nature, cannot be argued into accepting moral obligations. But although he cannot be (rationally) *persuaded*, he can be (therapeutically) *convinced* by the experience of institutions that bring home to him his interdependence with others and encourage him to substitute for his wholly discrete self a typical self subject to general rules. By this means he can be brought to respect obligations that, if they cannot be rationally taught to someone unprepared to accept them, are rationally defensible in terms of the necessities of human life and are appreciated as such by those who have had experience of their benefits. But disguised in this therapy is a second transition in self-identification. The egoist is first made vulnerable to the claims of morality; in addition, however, the claims of morality are collapsed into the requirements of political obligation – and for this transition, no good reasons are given. Nor is it easy to see what reasons could be given; for if, in the moral framework adopted, such things as 'mutual aid' and 'reciprocal service' define the structure of duty, that structure is not confined to political relations. It cannot demonstrate the supremacy of political obligations over other kinds. We may agree with Rousseau that 'no one can deny' that there is a force to human right: the mistake, however, is to suppose that human right can perform the same functions as divine right, can license vertical relations of authority and obedience that override the horizontal relations of reciprocity. When such vertical relations are no longer sustained by an order that lends natural or divine status to hierarchy, all that is left to sustain them, Rousseau's argument ultimately implies, is the state's superior power to convince. That may be a good point at which to end, for what Rousseau's critics were to urge, from their varied standpoints, was precisely that he had justified power without right.

In many respects they were anticipated by Rousseau himself, here as elsewhere his own severest judge. Against the Rousseau of civic virtue we have to set the Rousseau of the *Discourse on Inequality*, who sees in political order as it is a cruel sham; the Rousseau of *Emile*, who pursues the theme of defensive self-cultivation rather than of political liberation; above all, the Rousseau of *Perpetual Peace*, who admits that political society may, after all, represent a bad bargain – 'we have put an end to private wars only to ignite national wars a thousand times more terrible.'[81] It was not, however, the sceptical Rousseau who would be remembered by French political thinkers but the author of *Social Contract*, a book that, according to Auguste Comte, 'inspired more trust and reverence than the Bible or the Koran.'[82]

2

God and the State:
Maistre and Proudhon

When Proudhon said that Rousseau was the first to conceive of government as 'a human institution,'[1] he identified – at the cost of some exaggeration – a crucial feature of modern views of citizenship. In common with other theorists of *droit humain* Rousseau derived political legitimacy from the structure of social relations themselves in order to free it from any dependence upon divine sanctions. And extending this logic from the juristic to the political plane, Rousseau placed the concept of citizenship at the centre of questions of legitimation. Valid laws – or, in his terms, 'laws' *tout court* – can be prescribed for a community only by members of the community themselves, respecting as they do so the essential mutuality of human association. Only where there are citizens, then, can there be legitimate order. Since government is distinguished from law making, legitimacy thus viewed does not require a particular kind of political regime, the suitability of one regime rather than another depending upon contingent and empirical factors, as Bodin and Montesquieu had said. But what it excludes, along with the divine ordination of political right, is any proprietorial regime in which political right is monopolized by its rulers, for such regimes could not be the product of human agreement and are incompatible with the reciprocity on which any claim to justice must be based. It is in this sense that we may read Rousseau's remark that, 'before examining the act by which a people elects a king, it would be well to examine the act by which it becomes a people.'[2] What makes a people can only be the recognition of mutual association and, hence, the generalization of principles of conduct. It is in the same sense that we may take the insistence, in the revolutionaries' Declaration, that the king is king not of France but of *les Français*.[3] Political society is a community and not an item of property.

Now the revolutionary ideologies, not to mention the revolutionary state or any of the regimes that succeeded it, are obviously to be distinguished from what Rousseau said and what he proposed. But in looking back at the revolutionary crisis, French political theorists of the earlier nineteenth century, and even much later, fixed upon Rousseau's thinking as the central expression of the changes that had transformed the political world. Whether they were right to do so is largely beside the point, for their reading of Rousseau's meaning and significance entered the history of ideas as a fact independent of the facts of what Rousseau said or did. That is not to say, however, that the Rousseau who was read was a simple travesty of the Rousseau who wrote. While he was often read with intentions more polemical than sympathetic and while causal attributions were often made with little regard for historical evidence, there is, in the broadest outline, some real continuity: the shape of the discussion, the manner in which problems and solutions were offered, was governed largely by what Rousseau had done to the topic of political legitimacy. In particular, the problems of legitimation that were detected were just those problems that Rousseau's concept of citizenship had posed.

Two core problems may be sketched. The first concerns the principle of political authority. Authority is in some sense a restraint upon those subject to it, and respect for it implies limitations to what one does; Rousseau, however, had represented it in terms of *will* and by this means had substituted the citizen, who prescribes rules to himself, for the subject whose task is only to obey. Now Rousseau believed that in the very logic of willing, in the context of association, principles of restraint could be discovered, for to will without restraint is to will something to which no one else will accede. This may be true, and Rousseau's critics in the post-revolutionary period may be faulted for neglecting this crucial feature of his argument; but even if it is true, political authority may still lack a foundation, for one may perfectly well doubt whether the restraints identified in moral reflection inherently coincide with political restraints, or that moral generalization corresponds substantively, and exclusively, to a general good in its political sense. The problem, in the context of Rousseau's own discussion, may be negligible, for the state he describes in *Social Contract* is buttressed by special persuasive devices that convey the 'sanctity' of its requirements. But his sense that these buttresses were needed may be significant; and the vulnerability of his argument in this respect was to be vigorously exploited, from diverse points of view, by theorists of the post-revolutionary period. Yet intriguingly, even his critics were unable to escape the paradox that Rousseau may have installed as the central problem of modern political theory:[4] that the state is at once made by us and an order that imposes itself upon us, the product but also the determinant of human association. That this was a problem for Rousseau but not for Bodin was suggested in the previous chapter, and some reasons for its being a problem were offered: but a Bodin-like order, containing both states and citizens as indispensably complementary components, was no more available to Rousseau's critics than to Rousseau himself. And in some of the fiercest critiques of the Rousseauan republic, it will be argued below, it emerges that order cannot be satisfactorily represented as either made *or* given.

A second problem, which, however, overlaps significantly with the first, concerns what may be called the definition of loyalties. In the context of theories of *droit divin* the scale of loyalty is simply not raised as a possible issue. While the status of kings is divinely ordained, the scope of their power is determined by brutally empirical factors: a king is to be obeyed, but *who* obeys him is a historical, military, or dynastic question. An indefinite number of people can be *subjected*, for it is the extent of patrimonial or conquered territory and not the differentiation of political communities that fixes the scale of the king's authority. The power of an office is indefinitely extendable or contractable in spatial terms. But when political authority is taken to be a property of human associations, its scope becomes an issue because associations rest on consent, because they are multiple and often overlapping, and because they are of different kinds. Citizenship obviously involves a claim to privilege; political associations override other kinds. But there is nothing in the concept of human association itself that explains why this should be so. Secular political thought may succeed in justifying authority on no less compelling grounds than *droit divin*; but in also inheriting the ambition to justify the priority of one association over another, it may have set itself an impossible task.

These problems are very abstractly stated. But the point has been to suggest that what was left by Rousseau, read in the light of revolution – or perhaps by the revolution, as viewed in the light of Rousseau – was a structure of issues that imposed itself on political and social theses of very disparate kinds. The issues were taken up by counter-revolutionary thinking on the one hand and by anarcho-socialism on the other: by Joseph de Maistre, who regretted Rousseau's very existence, as well as by P.-J. Proudhon, whose regret was that Rousseau, and the revolution, had gone only half-way. If their arguments converge at what may be unexpected points, that is because the Rousseauan and revolutionary citizen was their common object of criticism; and though they had different reasons for finding that figure objectionable, they had somewhat similar reasons for finding him impossible. Above all, they accept the alternatives of theocracy and anarchy and refuse to believe that there can be a *political* order that rests upon the logic of human association alone.

Maistre, like Proudhon, saw in the conception of government as a human institution the key to what the revolutionaries had attempted. 'One of the great errors of this century is to believe that the political constitution of peoples is a purely human work.'[5] Like Proudhon, too, he saw Rousseau as the principal author of this delusion – 'Everywhere he inspired distrust of authority and the insurrectionary spirit. It was he who outlined the code of anarchy'[6] – although, when he quotes Rousseau, it is surprisingly often in order to agree with him.[7] Not only did Maistre share more with the Enlightenment than he liked to give the impression of doing, but where he despised the philosophes, he did so for much the same reasons as Rousseau had done. But Rousseau's own critique of *philosophisme* is mentioned by Maistre only to be set aside; for his highly polemical mode of argument required him to present Rousseau, and Voltaire, as uncomplicated and unqualified symbols of a delusion that had gripped the French mind, with consequences that had been, in an equally unqualified way, appalling. It is wholly a matter of conjecture whether his own reading of Rousseau was so lacking in sophistication or whether he could expect little by way of discrimination from the émigré readership for which he wrote.

Maistre's reading of Rousseau, selective though it is, does bluntly confront one centrally Rousseauan theme: that of the 'obedience to oneself' that is the key element in his idea of citizenship. 'It needs discussion,'[8] Maistre says, and we may entirely agree with him, especially as, for once, the expression is nicely understated. Self-government implies both that one commands and that one obeys: but what is the relationship between the self that obeys and the self that commands? Rousseau offers an answer: the generalizing self commands, and the particularizing self obeys. Maistre, however, gives no sign of recognizing this answer, for he is bent upon making a point that is much less intricate but that is not for that reason inherently worthless. Whatever the relationship between the commanding and obeying selves, it is clearly not the same as a relationship between distinct persons who command and who obey.[9] To that extent the notion of popular sovereignty can only be a kind of metaphor, one that depends for its force upon analogies with systems of hierarchical sovereignty. *I* obey *us*, in Rousseau's republic, and since I am included in us, I also command: but Maistre's implied point is that 'us' can also be decomposed into 'I' and 'you,' and that there is no inherent reason why I should include myself in the 'we' that adopts political ends. Maistre's reading here is wholly unsympathetic in failing to note that Rousseau, too, found this inclusion very problematic. But he is on strong or at least plausible ground in claiming that such an inclusion is achieved only by a sort of transfer of deference, that popular sovereignty makes sense only in relations of analogy to other forms of sovereignty, and that what I can obey is not something that I see as *mine* but something that I see as imposing a legitimate obligation *upon* me. I must see it as a duty and not as a mode of self-expression. Popular sovereignty created – in Proudhon's phrase – 'à l'image de l'homme-roi'[10] is incoherent.

Now Rousseau himself had despaired of deriving political duty from self-expression and for that reason proposed both a Lawgiver, who would convince individuals of their duties without persuading them of their rational necessity to the self, and also a civil religion, which would impose upon social man the priority of law. With regard to the former proposal, Maistre's objections to what Rousseau had said are either carping or inaccurate, while with regard to the latter he is in undisguised agreement. And since Rousseau had adopted these proposals exactly at the points at which the argument from reason could go no further, Maistre himself can hardly be faulted for seeing in them the essential limits of human reason. But what Maistre insists upon is something much more categorical than Rousseau had in mind, for authority, he wants to say, is inherently extra-human, or divine. 'Men never respect what they have made,' he writes,[11] and he applies this principle not only to the respect for political authorities but also to respect for constitutions: 'The essence of a fundamental law is that no one has the right to abolish it. For how could it stand above *all men*, if *some men* had made it?'[12] If there is a logical point here, as opposed to a psychological view, it is in connection with fundamental laws that it is to be found. For what Maistre attempts to do, in a manner comparable to but more impressionistic than Kelsen's, is to show that regressive questioning must lead eventually to an ultimate norm that cannot be derived from any other, and certainly not from human agreement. Law is precisely *not* that 'uniting of wills' that theorists of a social contract propose, but must rest on something antecedent to the uniting of wills. 'Law is only truly sanctioned, and properly *law*, when assumed to emanate from a higher will ... This is why primitive common sense, which fortunately precedes sophism, has always sought the sanctions of laws in a superhuman power, whether recognizing that sovereignty comes from God or in worshipping certain unwritten laws as given by him.'[13]

More prominent than any logical point about sovereignty, however, are repeated and quite harshly expressed judgments about the political incapacity of masses. Authority cannot spring from their will, for they can will nothing – 'The mass of the people plays no part in political events'[14] – or, if they will anything, cannot will anything good: 'It is an affectation of Providence, if I may be permitted the expression, that the efforts of a people to obtain a goal are precisely the means that Providence employs to keep them from it.'[15] This incapacity to choose, or to choose well or effectively, obviously disqualifies masses from exercising the political rights of citizenship, and the attribution of political citizenship to them is very largely a sham. 'When Rousseau tells us, in the introduction to the *Social Contract*, that, in his capacity as a citizen in a free state, he is himself *sovereign*, even the most benevolent reader feels a laugh coming on ... The simple citizen counts for nothing.'[16] 'Citizen' is for Maistre an honorific term, rightly earned by deeds of patriotism and civic spirit;[17] but the revolution 'dishonoured' the term, applying it to the 'vilest of humans.'[18] To apply it universally is to misapply it, for the lot of most men is not to win public glory but to labour in the 'obscurity and happiness' of productive life, as 'bon laboureur, artisan laborieux.'[19] They are better called 'subjects,' a term that, moreover, is better suited than 'citizen' to convey that kind of equality attainable, unlike equality of power, in political society: 'The ordinary man who feels insignificant when he measures himself against a great lord, measures the lord against the sovereign, and the title of *subject* that brings both of them under the same power and the same justice is a kind of equality that stills the inevitable pangs of self-esteem.'[20]

The sense in which the origins of law are divine is not perfectly clear. Reasons of various kinds are given for supposing them not to be human in the sense of a deliberate human creation, but it does not follow that they are not human in some other and less restrictive sense. To make it follow, Maistre deploys several arguments. That hereditary kings rule by *droit divin*, he says, is evident from the manner of their appearance. Royal families take their place in their societies with a naturalness, a suddenness, and a sense of fitness inexplicable except as signs that they have been prepared by God. But Maistre is not a theorist of the *droit divin* of kings alone, for the right of all governments is divine. Despite a strongly stated preference for monarchy – which does not, however, preclude an obvious admiration for republics – Maistre recognizes that different kinds of governments are appropriate for different societies and times. 'To ask, then, absolutely, what is the best government, is to ask a question that is as unanswerable as it is indeterminate; or, if you like, there are as many good answers as there are possible combinations in the absolute and relative situations of peoples.'[21] But this is not to imply that there is a choice of regimes: 'All peoples have the government that suits them, and none has chosen its own.'[22] It is in this fitness of institutions to circumstances that one sees the hand of God. And if God has apparently made special provisions for monarchies by preparing rulers for them, he also has made appropriate if less generous provisions for all political societies in impressing upon them constitutions that suit their natures. When nations *try* to choose, they choose badly.

The 'general order'[23] that Maistre sees in the political world is not, as in Bodin, cosmologically underwritten. Though there are analogies between the natural and social worlds, they are not analogies of patterned correspondence: interestingly, where he employs the Bodin-like analogy with musical intervals, he finds there not an absolute rule of proportion that institutions reflect but an essential dissonance that institutions must moderate or 'distribute.'[24] And this is part of a general argument of great importance for him. We must judge things not by the perfection of their genesis but by the appropriateness of their consequences. Order is not immediately apparent to man: no multi-levelled harmonies impress themselves upon his mind; man perceives 'disadvantages,' which affront his pride and his desire that institutions should correspond to his will and reason.[25] Only over time is order displayed beneath the disorder that we are prone to see: not a cosmology of a Renaissance kind but a historical providence (of, by way of contrast, a somewhat Augustinian kind) is revealed to us by the hidden ordering of events.

Few theorists can have had so pervasive a sense as Maistre had of 'unintended consequences,' or of the 'heterogeneity' between ends sought by men and ends achieved in history. Few can have carried so far the stress upon the human incapacity to shape events, to create things in foreseen ways, or to determine anything at all by reasoning. Reading of the Americans' plans for a new capital city, he comments:

'There is too much deliberation, too much of mankind in all this, and it is a thousand to one that the town will not be built, or that it will not be called *Washington*, or that Congress will not sit there.'[26] A similar implausibility is found in the proposed revival of the Olympic Games.[27] Maistre, clearly, ignored the limits to unpredictability in human affairs. But this kind of emphasis did not lead him, as it led some eighteenth-century writers, to a social science: it led him to a theodicy. Or perhaps it led him to a social science as well: 'Movement has its laws, and observing it carefully over a certain span of time one can draw certain enough conclusions for the future'[28] – here he is a mediating link between Condorcet and Comte. But such passages are in the last resort misleading, for the objectivity of social processes was viewed by Maistre not as material for social science but as evidence of a latent intention. If man does not intend the course of things, it does not follow that history is explicable by social causes but that it is explicable only as God's intention. 'Suppose that handfuls of printed characters thrown from the top of a tower should on landing make Racine's *Athalia*. What could one infer? *That a mind had directed their fall and arrangement.* Common sense will never find another answer.'[29] In particular common sense rebuts any notion that what we can infer from the intelligible patterns of history is any chance interrelation of causes.[30]

What are these intelligible patterns? Two striking patterns are offered, one negative, one positive, but both salutary. The negative example, strongly Augustinian in spirit, concerns the working of evil against itself in the course of the French Revolution. Maistre sees in the logic of events a sort of economy of sin in which criminals bring about their own punishment and contribute unwittingly to the creation of order out of disorder. The 'crime against sovereignty' committed by the revolutionaries was 'a national crime, for it is always more or less the fault of the nation if any number of rebels can put themselves in a position to commit a crime in its name.' This crime is punished by the logic of the revolutionary process itself: 'One could name by the thousands the active instruments of the Revolution who have died a violent death.'[31] It would have been beyond the impartiality of the king himself, and even beyond his coercive powers, to punish so thoroughly, just as it would have been beyond the powers of a legitimate ruler of France to punish the 'national' crime as it has been punished so terribly by the excesses of tyranny and civil disorder. Moreover, once the Revolution had made war on French sovereignty and on all the legitimate sovereignties of Europe, the integrity of France was placed at risk; it was not from the coalition of France's enemies that the exiled king could expect to be restored to full possession of his father's realm. But here the 'infernal genius' of Robespierre played its part. With a rage and contempt for life inspired by the Terror, the revolutionary armies hurled themselves at their nation's enemies and vanquished them. 'All the monsters born of the Revolution have, apparently, laboured only for the monarchy. Thanks to them, the lustre of victories has won the admiration of the world and surrounded the French name with a glory that the crimes of the Revolution can never entirely eclipse.'[32] The king will recover his throne as ruler of a chastised yet strengthened nation.

The positive example of intelligible pattern concerns the political consequences of religious belief. 'Look at history and you will not see any institution of any strength or duration at all that does not rest on a divine idea.'[33] Here, of course, Maistre returns to the theme of the weakness of human power, his critique of *philosophisme* and of that species of political rationalism that represents institutions as things to be created by design. 'The more human reason trusts in itself, the more it tries to rely only on its own resources, the more absurd it is, and the more it displays its impotence.' In contrast, 'the true legislators have all sensed that human reason could not stand alone and that no purely human institution could last.' A list of examples is offered in confirmation: Moses, Mahomet, Lycurgus ('He imagined nothing, he proposed nothing, he prescribed nothing, except on the word of oracles'), Numa;[34] Loyola is added a few pages later, and of him it is (interestingly) said that 'no one succeeded more perfectly in obliterating particular wills in order to establish the general will and that common reason that is the generating and conserving principle of all institutions whatever, large or small.'[35]

In all this, however, one may begin to wonder about the importance of divinity, as opposed to 'a divine idea.' In his example of the ways of providence in the revolutionary process Maistre also introduces miraculous interventions of special providence; to his claim that God arranged the winds to protect French grain ships from convoy raiders, or obligingly abbreviated the lives of Gustavus III and Catherine the Great, or conveniently trapped English ships in North Sea ice, there is very little that can be said.[36] But what is claimed about the beneficent 'interlacing' of religious and political authority belongs strictly to the realm of political sociology and could as well have been said by Rousseau; in fact, much of it was said by Rousseau. All that is claimed is that a political society needs 'a large, profoundly rooted belief.'[37] 'It does not matter what kind ... for there is no entirely false religious system.'[38] More strongly still, 'whether one laughs at religious beliefs or venerates them does not matter: true or false, they nevertheless form the basis of all durable institutions.'[39] Now in Christian or even in Catholic theology there is no doubt a range of views as to whether other beliefs are false or not entirely false, but it would plainly be odd to suppose the Catholics' God to have made special exertions on behalf of those who held any religious beliefs whatsoever, whatever degree of partial truth may be seen in all expressions of a religious sense. It is hard, then, to escape the conclusion that Maistre's argument here is wholly pragmatic and that, if the truth or falsity of religious belief is irrelevant to its consequences, then the causal mechanisms involved are political-sociological in nature and not providential.

This conclusion is strongly reinforced by Maistre's use of the comparative in a passage quoted above – 'The more human reason trusts in itself ... the more absurd it is.' We are dealing here with relative levels of human capacity. More clearly still, he says elsewhere: 'As soon as man separates himself from divinity ... his action is false, and his agitation is only destructive ... But as soon as the idea of divinity is the principle of human action, this action is fecund, creative, invincible.'[40] Maistre's commentators have understandably been worried by the question of the relationship between humanly induced and divinely induced causation: does he attribute any degree of causality to human intentions, or is human action merely epiphenomenal?[41] The answer, surely, is that he writes as though both accounts were true, and he can do so because a political distinction supervenes over the theological question of human freedom. 'The more' human reason trusts itself, the less the causal force of human action; while 'as soon as' human reason recognizes the limits to its power, action becomes 'creative.' This is a point that could perfectly well be expressed, and has been expressed, in strictly secular terms. There are different political situations in which policies are successful to different degrees. Abrupt and radical projects are more likely to meet insuperable obstacles than are cautious ones. A contestatory policy is more likely to meet fatal resistance than a conciliatory one. We are bound by a 'chain' that restricts us, despite our freedom, within the confines of 'universal order': but this chain, Maistre says, is 'abruptly shortened' in revolutionary periods, when, confronting obstacles not familiar to us from our regular experiences, we are driven to use means that 'deceive us.'[42] If in an ultimate sense man can create nothing, nevertheless there is a crucial *political* difference between policies that *are*, as he says, 'creative' and policies that are doomed to create nothing because they depend on deceptive means lacking any basis in political experience. There is no general theological answer to the question of the status of man's freedom because the argument belongs to political science and not to theology.

It is in Maistre's concept of sovereignty that this perhaps unexpected ideal of a creative politics is best expressed: for the term 'sovereignty' comes to be used in an essentially political-sociological sense. Sovereignty in the sense of legitimate rulership comes from God; but what discloses its existence or, even more strongly, what it is that God gives is a certain kind of political experience, and it is, in effect, by a substantive criterion that we infer its origin. Consider, for example, what Maistre says about the French Republic: 'Open your eyes and you will see that it does not *live*. What an enormous machine! What a multiplicity of springs and wheels! What a fracas of pieces in collision! What an immense number of men employed to repair the damage! Everything shows that there is nothing natural in these movements, for the primary characteristic of the creations of nature is power accompanied by an economy of means. Everything being in its place, there are no jerks or bumps, friction is low, there is no noise, and the silence is august ... *Therefore sovereignty does not exist in France.* Everything is artificial, violent and all announces that *such an order of things cannot last.*'[43]

It is not, then, the fact that the republic *has not* lasted that demonstrates its rulers' lack of sovereignty but the fact that it 'cannot last.' Time confers sovereignty not *by* duration but *because* duration is a sign of good order; and good order is defined exactly as Montesquieu had defined it in the *Persian Letters*, in terms of an 'economy of means.' Like Montesquieu, Maistre views monarchy in the light of *la thèse nobiliaire*, as a regime of co-operation between king and nobles, in which consensus, mutual respect, and willing accommodations smooth away the bluntness of coercion – a view in which Maistre persisted despite a certain understandable coolness on the part of the exiled king.[44] It is because there is no such spirit of mutuality, because institutions, being merely imposed, are clumsy and wasteful, that 'sovereignty does not exist in France'; and to such an argument divine ordination is functionally dispensable, although, of course, it is perfectly possible to maintain that this happy state of affairs termed sovereignty is willed or desired by God, or that it is by following God's commands that it is attained.

But the more formal treatment of sovereignty shows how far Maistre's theocratic argument has departed from the theses of divine right. 'There have been heated disputes about whether sovereignty comes from God or men,' he writes, implicitly recalling the pre-revolutionary debates between rival views of *droit*. But the answer he offers is not Bossuet's. 'Sovereignty,' he says, 'is founded on human consent: for if any people suddenly agreed not to obey, sovereignty would disappear, and it is impossible to imagine the establishment of a sovereignty without imagining a people that consents to obey.'[45] Human consent, however, is the instrument that God employs to establish sovereignty, 'not having thought it appropriate to employ supernatural instruments.' But too much is given away here. The distinction between sovereignty, a divinely ordained status, and power, which depends upon factors of human history, is abandoned, and sovereignty *itself* is said to disappear when human consent is withdrawn. And in his appeal to the French people, Maistre gives almost everything else away: 'Do you want to accomplish a sovereign act? ... Recall your sovereign.'[46] While the king in exile retains the name of sovereign, the nation's choice to return power to him would be a sovereign act, and here, for a moment, we glimpse an implied theory of sovereignty as ascending, or as being conferred upon rulers by subjects. It is only a glimpse, and the expression is more rhetorical than cautious. But is is clear that, within a formally theocratic framework, sovereignty has effectively become a descriptive political concept and denotes a relationship of a bilateral rather than a unilateral kind.

This willing and unforced concurrence that constitutes sovereignty is to be found, too, in republics, though not of course in the so-called French Republic. In republics it takes the form of a spirit of 'association,' which, no less than the 'love' that binds together a monarchical system, is 'divine.'[47] But association is more demanding than love, for it is not sustained by that search for personal honour that, as in Montesquieu's monarchy, at once binds subject to king and rewards him for his subjection; nor does association provide subjects with as 'palpable' an object of loyalty as does a monarch. In a republic, Maistre says, sovereignty is 'purely moral'[48] – as Rousseau had said, the sovereignty of a moral person is substituted for that of a real one. For such reasons the glory of a republic may be more brilliant than that of a monarchy but, as a sterner and more rigorous achievement, is also less durable. The natural place and original model of the republican spirit, Maistre suggests, is to be found in the 'voluntary associations of men who have united for some end of self-interest or charity. These men have voluntarily submitted themselves to certain rules ... But these regulations have no sanction other than the will of those who have made them and, when there are dissidents, there is no coercive force among them to restrain them.' When this model is expanded, however, to the scale of a political society, even a small one, the rule of the whole people over itself – even if theoretically imaginable – is inevitably displaced by the rule of some over others. The purely moral sovereign cannot rule, and the model of the association is not transferable to the state. On that subject another French theorist, of the next generation, was to express equally decided views at very much greater length, though in ways that are not wholly dissimilar.

Proudhon's ambivalence towards Rousseau is quite as obvious as Maistre's. Rousseau was 'the apostle of liberty and equality,' but 'the Revolution, the republic, and the people have never had a greater enemy than Jean-Jacques.'[50] As these terms make plain, neither Proudhon's admiration nor his hostility rested upon the same grounds as Maistre's. If Maistre's objection was that the Revolution, inspired by Rousseau, had tried to sweep aside the inherent limits to human reason, Proudhon's was that the Revolution, bewitched by Rousseau, had not swept aside nearly enough, having been deflected from its immanent purpose. If Maistre's objection was that the Revolution had tried to make citizens out of the 'vile' individuals in whose name it was made, Proudhon's was that the Revolution had culminated *merely* in the political equality of citizenship; it had not advanced to the real equality to which its own logic committed it. Looking backwards to left-wing revolutionaries such as Babeuf and forwards, beyond Marx, to 'revisionists' such as Bernstein, Proudhon saw social revolution as a necessary extension of political revolution, as an elaboration of its true and essential principles, and as a winnowing out of the false and accidental in what it had come to be. What was living in the Revolution was to be preserved, and what was dead in it – its rigidities or arrests – was to be buried. And citizenship, as a political value, was merely an arrest of the spirit of liberation, whose ends were not political at all.

In some of the most unpleasant pages in his writings Maistre contended not only that war was the 'habitual state of mankind' but that it is good that it should be so.[51] Proudhon, however, drawing upon the pacific and industrial vision of Condorcet and Saint-Simon, believed that progress carries with it the eventual substitution of work for war as the generative source of values. Combat was once the source of *droit*, and it fulfilled an indispensable historical role in bringing home to men the rigours of both justice and virtue. But war 'has said its last word' and has nothing further to contribute. 'Travaillez à présent, nous dit la Guerre; vous avez assez combattu.'[52] It is no longer combat but contract, the typical resource of the producer, that is the founding model of *droit*; and contract carries with it the elimination not only of combat but of the essential combatants, states, and with them political oppression. 'The problem of the universal republic is resolved, the dream of Napoleon is realized, and the chimera of the Abbé Saint-Pierre becomes a reality.'[53] It was for this reason that Proudhon's condemnation of Rousseau was so severe. Rousseau had put contract to use in legitimizing the *state*; he had enclosed men irrevocably within so-called sovereign territorial units and thus had foreclosed on the promise of liberation. Contract is the enemy of authority, the germ of an order in which subordination and hierarchy would be unknown; by a supreme and vicious paradox Rousseau had transformed it into an instrument of political authority that was to license not only an intensely centralized government but also the social and economic despotism that flourished under its protection. To this critique the notion of *humanité*, and its interpretation, are crucial. For Rousseau the state was the means by which the 'lazy and stupid' animal became an 'intelligent being and a man,' for it was only in recognizing the humanity of others that he could attain his own; generic humanity, 'the general society,' being a mere abstraction, it was only in states that this recognition could be achieved. For Proudhon, however, a general society or 'universal republic' is attainable, in the network of contractual ties that human work brings into being. *Humanité* is an essentially economic conception that Rousseau had misrepresented as a political one; but what it licenses is a nest of attachments, communal, regional, and global, not the moral privilege of the state; and in introducing it as the foundation of the state, Rousseau had perversely undermined the state's moral legitimacy.

Why, though, is the state incompatible with a human order or with the 'becoming human' of right? Proudhon's answer is the same as the answer given by Maistre, who had written: 'Government is veritably a religion: it has its dogmas, its mysteries, its ministers; to extinguish it, or to submit it to discussion by each individual, comes to the same thing.'[54] Proudhon wrote, likewise: 'Government is by divine right or it is nothing.'[55] And he too believed that its essential divinity was incompatible with what he called 'human' premises. In part he meant that political and religous institutions are inseparably linked and are 'in coalition, against the Revolution.' Since 'their ends are the same, their principles, methods, dogmas absolutely identical, government must be shared between them.'[56] In part, though, he also meant – as did Maistre – something much more fundamental: that, whatever the institutional connection between politics and religion, authority is by its very nature 'a mystical principle'[57] and that men will obey only what they regard as 'natural or divine.' Here Proudhon introduces themes of both religious and political alienation. God is only a fantastic repository of human powers – 'This God whom you adore, O Man, is you yourself'[58] – and in deferring to God man defers to what is really his own power in alienated and mystified form. Likewise, in deferring to government he defers to an agency to which he has alienated what are properly his own powers to act. In both cases, as Proudhon puts it, he creates 'intermediaries' between himself and his own powers, assigning to others what is inherently his, alienating his own 'faculties.' The ideas of God and of the state, precisely as in Maistre, stand or fall together, Proudhon differing, of course, in hoping that they *will* fall together, that the 'free man' will 'hunt the idea of God out of his mind,'[59] just as he will dispense with obedience to states. It is not only attachment to certain institutions that is at issue but attachment to a way of thinking. All 'absolutes,' as Proudhon calls them, or 'criteria,'[60] as he also calls them, are to be abandoned, as things that require to be accepted on trust and thus require us to stop thinking for ourselves. *Humanité* especially is not to become a new absolute. In German humanism Proudhon detected an insidious theism in which all the absolutist errors were perpetuated under the guise of dispensing with God. Though he does not appear to know anything about Max Stirner, his objections, in *System of Economic Contradictions*, are quite parallel to the argument of *The Ego and Its Own*: humanity, simply, is not *men* and is no less external to any given individual than is God. The point is not to divinize man but to de-divinize thought. True, the idea of divinity is nothing but a metaphor for human power, but the humanity that has exercised this power can be thought of as an active subject only if the experience of men is denied. It can be represented as a subject, and venerated, only in the (essentially theological) mode of the everlasting now, which collapses the distinct expriences of men of different times and posits a man who can be represented as his own creator and thus become an object of worship. But all this merely evades the fact that nothing is to be worshipped, that nothing – not even humanity – has authority, that nothing is to be treated as an absolute, and that a *human* life is one that recognizes only transactional or horizontal relations among free human individuals.

What Rousseau had attempted was the impossible task of resting the 'mystical' principle of authority upon 'human conventions'[61] or, in different terms, of combining a vertical principle of subordination and deference with the essentially horizontal device of contract. For what Proudhon meant by human conventions reverts beyond the contract of Rousseau's political man to the contracts of civil man, in which natural-law jurists had seen the model of *droit humain*. What Grotius had called 'mutual aid through reciprocal service' now becomes the defining principle of anarchism, not the basis for a theory of sovereignty. It is not a hypothetical, original, or tacit contract *of* society that is posited, but real, repeated, and personal contracting *in* society, in that mutual satisfaction of need that, behind the 'phantoms' of politics, constitutes what society is. It is 'society' – as Grotius had stressed, explicitly following Stoic models – not polity, that flows immediately from human nature: and society, Proudhon contends, is not only different from a governed order but is 'ungovernable,'[62] for it is complex and multi-centred, and inherently incapable of direction from a single centre. It is constituted by a 'fluid relationship, and economic solidarity' among individuals who 'circulate freely,' by turns 'approaching one another, joining together, and separating.'[63] The rules proper to it are 'transactional' and relate together individuals, enterprises, and localities without the mediation of governmental imperatives: 'The political idea, the ancient notion of distributive justice, must be contradicted through and through, and that of commutative justice must be reached.'[64]

Since the Revolution did not achieve this substitution of commutative for distributive justice, 'it has plunged us into economic chaos. In place of a natural order, conceived on the basis of science and work, we have had a factitious order, in the shadow of which have emerged parasitic interests, deviant morals, monstrous ambitions, prejudices departing from common sense ... '[65] In calling the order of mutualist justice a *natural* one, Proudhon qualifies somewhat his view that ideas of natural order, as of divine order, are coercive mystifications and that the eighteenth century merely abandoned God in order to transfer divine attributes to nature – a view that Proudhon might have owed to Comte. His fierce onslaught on any limit to autonomy is also moderated significantly by the rules of mutualist justice. Exchange, he contends, implies a common measure, which he calls 'value'; and the value of a good or service is constituted by the average labour time required by its production or performance. This rule of exchange, as he interestingly says, is an 'absolute,'[66] a concept that, of course, he elsewhere holds in disfavour. Value thus constituted may well be inconsistent with a strict libertarian position, as one critic has pointed out.[67] It would reward the efficient worker who produces faster than the average, while requiring the less efficient worker to accept a penalty derived from a standard not of his own making. True, Proudhon sometimes writes of value as though it rested on agreements – it is 'the contract of contracts'[68] – but this poses the same problem of binding future generations that Proudhon insists on regarding as fatal to Rousseau's argument. Moreover, we cannot imagine agreement to be free, since presumably those who refused to agree would be unable to enter into exchanges and so would be excluded from 'society.' It is not altogether clear, however, that Proudhon *held* a strict libertarian position or that some of his case for autonomy is not more exaggerated than precise. For alongside what is offered as an argument for unqualified autonomy is another well-marked trend of thinking, one that requires the qualification of autonomy: this is Proudhon's stress upon objectivity, on 'science,' and on the recognition of necessity.

To contrast 'authority and faith,' termed 'divine,' with 'individual and social reason,' termed 'human,' is clearly not to contrast obedience with autonomy but to contrast one kind of allegiance with another. In this respect Proudhon is a theorist of autonomy only in the sense that all rationalists are, in insisting that it is demonstration, not authority, that concludes judgment. Moreover, 'individual and social reason,' when consulted, can yield only one outcome, the criterion of value being derived necessarily from the most elementary principles of moral reflection; and it is clear that what Proudhon admires in it is precisely not that it is chosen but that it imposes itself. It 'has only to be explained and understood to be affirmed by everyone.'[69] It 'does not depend in any way on human arbitrariness'[70] and is 'of all human things that which most resists any kind of regulation.'[71]

The contrast between association on political principles and association on economic principles is above all a contrast between factitiousness and objectivity. The various bases of political rule, 'generation, force, faith, primogeniture, lot, number, are all things that are equally unintelligible and impenetrable,'[72] a point that Maistre too had made – and before him Pascal – in order to show that government was not founded on *reason*. But Proudhon differs in offering in place of government an economic logic that is 'necessarily [*fatalement*] the same all over the world, does not depend on the convenience of men or nations, and does not submit itself to anyone's caprice.'[73] It constitutes, Proudhon says – bringing his argument full circle – 'a *divinity*, little understood, that rules the world.'[74] This is a line of thinking premised upon rationality, not autonomy. Proudhon is attempting to discover in the structure of human relations themselves rationally grounded principles that, being inherently compelling, will in securing obedience 'unite' without 'chaining' individuals.[75] The bonds among them will not be chains because, precisely as in Rousseau's argument, they represent no one's will but are immanent in association itself; but they are immanent in the life of the producer, not of the citizen.

These twin but somewhat competitive themes of autonomy and reason, of freedom as self-making and freedom as the recognition of the given, are nowhere better displayed than in Proudhon's view of historical process. 'While the individual only obeys or imagines himself only to obey motives that he understands fully, of which he is master and can refuse or give his compliance; while, in a word, he judges himself to be free, and all the more free to the extent that he knows himself to be more reasonable and better informed: society is subject to impulses in which, at first sight, nothing permits one to see deliberation or any project, but that gradually seem to be directed by a superior design, existing outside society, and driving it with irresistible force towards an unknown end.'[76] Of this force Proudhon says, as did Maistre, that its effects but not its origins are open to us. Like Maistre, too, he calls it 'divine,' though his purpose in doing so is quite different: for this 'superior design' is nothing but the unco-ordinated, unwitting, objectively collaborative force of men. The society in which they collaborate is 'a being that has its own functions, foreign to our individuality,'[77] and since it has its own individuality we imagine that it cannot be ours, and call it God. But it is, Proudhon says, really ours, and it only *seems* to be 'outside society.'

Maistre had written, 'Because man acts, he thinks he acts alone,'[78] and his point, of course, was that those unanticipated and unwished-for outcomes that flow from human action display the intervention of providence. In Proudhon's reading of history individuals believe that they 'act alone' without taking account of the ways in which the outcomes of their actions are governed by the actions of other *men*. But while the outcomes of multiple interwoven human actions are what we call God, we cannot infer from that, as we have seen, that humanity is god-like. The humanity that can be said to have made this history is only a construct, a fictitious humanity composed of successive human generations and that thus escapes the historicity of the human mind and the subjectivity of individual experience. It is not 'made' in the sense in which a craftsman makes something – it is not the 'work' of anyone. But this objectivity, the resistance of historical processes to calculated or capricious intervention, is valued, for it provides human action with a foundation that the vanished absolutes of natural or divine order no longer supply. What Proudhon calls 'revolution' is the prime and central example, for he sees it not as a political event but as an immanent social process to whose logic normative power can be ascribed. 'Leading men more than men lead it,' as Maistre had put it[79] – though he had in mind a political rather than a social process – revolution has the same inexorability as natural forces. But not only is it folly to oppose it; it is also, Proudhon says, 'a crime,' thus making strikingly clear the juridical function that revolution plays.[80] Overturning the conservative argument yet emphatically retaining from it the notion of historically grounded objective order, he ascribes to revolution a sort of prescriptive right: 'LA REVOLUTION,' as he writes in emphatic capitals, 'EST AU-DESSUS DE LA REPUBLIQUE.'[81]

But to make this mode of thinking normatively compelling, Proudhon modifies, and perhaps confuses, his earlier careful distinction between men and humanity and seeks to implicate men as individuals in what the 'superior being' of human society is said to achieve. This being, as he had rightly noted, is as alien to men as is God and exists only from a contrived perspective, from which actual human experience is derived; to take this projection as 'true' man is to suppress 'real' man.[82] The Pascalian model of humanity as a 'single man' whose historical stages are moments of a single life, forthrightly rejected in *Economic Contradictions*, reappears, and in a strongly positive light, in *Political Capacity*: 'Society must be considered as a giant with a thousand arms ... A single mind, a single thought, a single will animate him; and in the interrelation of his works the unity and identity of his person is revealed.'[83] It is from this, rather than from any individualist model, that the principles of justice are here derived: as 'parts' of a single 'person,' individuals' tasks are all indistinguishably significant and hence are to be rewarded on a common scale. Very much as in Rousseau, then, two pictures of obligation are juxtaposed: a model of autonomy and moral generalization, in which individuals grasp the dependence of their own dignity upon their respect for that of others; and a picture of parts and wholes, of social membership and of general loyalties.[84] According to the former conception, *we* do not make our own history, for we distinguish our own individuality from the being of that opaque entity constituted blindly by the interrelation of our forces. According to the latter, we make it, for we identify ourselves as members or parts of a collective order, constituting itself over time.

If there is a bridge between these distinct conceptions, it may perhaps be found in Proudhon's *Philosophy of Progress*. Written shortly after the advent of the Second Empire, it reveals a certain bleakness typical of much political writing of that time, and no longer do we find any serene faith in the ineluctability of revolution or the immanence of progressive change. 'France has exhausted the principles that sustained it,'[85] and 'spontaneity' is no longer to be relied upon. What was once immanent must become purposeful: 'Humanity, aspiring to know and being unable to believe, must write history in advance of the facts!'[86] What Proudhon has in mind emerges, though only obscurely, in a remarkable passage in which he suggests that, by analysing the range of interests and attitudes in society, we will be able to predict a 'general tendency' of development. This tendency, he says – once again transferring political and juridical notions to a historical plane – will have the status of a 'social contract,' a composition of diverse interests into a whole with a single direction that, however, expresses the 'will of no one' but of all collectively.[87] This will, once inferred, we are to adopt as our own and thus aim to produce a future in which the proper tendencies of the present will be realized. Here the competing requirements of objective order and human will are brought into formal harmony by a procedure that intriguingly if irrelevantly anticipates later French theories of 'indicative planning.' But the harmony is only formal, as one well-qualified commentator, Georges Sorel, was to note in criticizing this passage: 'When the historian speaks of a *general tendency*,' Sorel objected, 'he does not deduce it from its constituent elements but constructs it by means of the results revealed in the course of history.'[88] We cannot contemporaneously have the knowledge of the historian, for that is inherently retrospective, and so we cannot 'write history in advance.' Not only is the point quite proper; it is fully in the spirit of Proudhon's own historical conceptions, in which the heterogeneity between cause and effect is so vigorously stressed.

But even where Proudhon outdoes Rousseau in discovering unity of will among multiple interests, it is not in the political life of citizens that this unity is expressed. Even though the *tendance générale* is to do everything that the *volonté générale* is to do, supplying individual judgment with a criterion that is that of 'no one,' it resides in social and economic collaboration. It is politically unrepresented, for political life does not represent anything. It is, as Maistre too had put it, a 'fracas.'[89] It is not in the 'fraternity' of revolutionary citizens but in the reciprocity among producers that unity is to be sought. Nor is it in the sharing of uniformity of status as citizens that unity is found but, precisely to the contrary, in the diversity of skill and situation that, in making individuals complementary to one another, also makes them co-operative.[90] Like Maistre, then – though in a different spirit – Proudhon recommends to men that they content themselves with the status of 'bon laboureur, artisan laborieux'; and even though the spirit is admiring rather than condescending, the reasons are not wholly different, for Proudhon took as dim a view as did Maistre of the political capacity of masses. It is not under the political status of citizenship that the people display capacity; all universal suffrage yields is 'the fantasy of the moment erected as an absolute.'[91] As citizens, people are required to give 'general answers' to special questions, to make or approve legislation on matters about which they are wholly ignorant.[92] Knowledge is nowhere summed up and readied for central application, in a popular majority no more than in a king or cabinet. Central decisions will always be made, therefore, in ignorance, and for the illusory notion that there is, somewhere, a representable 'sum' of knowledge that can guide policies correctly, we should substitute the model of a 'resultant' of local decisions.[93] Only when powers are decentralized, or, rather, returned to their proper bearers, can special questions be matched with the special capacities they require.

This unrepresented human collaboration in which labour is divided and labourers united by shared rules, rather than commands, is what Proudhon calls 'collective force,' as opposed to the 'public force' of the state. The philosophes, he complains, did not see this force, for they saw society as a juxtaposition of individuals united by law and reason, wholly neglecting the increment of force due to association itself, which does more than the sum of what its members are individually capable of.[94] The eighteenth-century mind fell victim to the confusion of power with government; it was deflected by the lures of 'visible authority,' identifying power with its public trappings, and liberation with equality in the public realm.[95] But in thus demanding a society of citizens, engaged with one another only through a shared public status, the revolutionaries missed altogether that invisible power that rests in human exchange and the shared understandings that govern it. Perhaps, to exaggerate a little – but no more than Proudhon was inclined to do – they had missed the point that a society, as such and properly understood, has no place for citizens, for it is distracted, not fulfilled, by public questions, to which it always gives the wrong answer.

To be a citizen, Rousseau believed, is above all to be a legislator and to prescribe to oneself, through public and non-exclusive institutions, the rules by which one is to live. It is these rules that to the largest extent possible are to define one's relations to others, and it is these rules that above all display the people's sovereignty. For Maistre and Proudhon legislation is a sign of disorder and much legislation a sign of great disorder. If his subjects were better, Maistre says, the legislator would need to speak only once;[96] if we could follow the rule of justice, 'ne faites pas à autrui,' Proudhon says, we would need no laws at all.[97] (They thus outdo Pascal, who had said that two laws were necessary for the 'Christian republic.') Citing the same figures, Maistre and Proudhon express amazement and scorn at the fifteen thousand laws passed by the National Assembly, the Legislative Assembly, and the National Convention in six years. Geologists of the future, Proudhon remarks, will identify the revolutionary age as a papyrus stratum.[98] 'Any false institution writes voluminously,' according to Maistre, who indeed offers a critique of the *written* as the central theme of his essay on 'The Generative Principle.' Drawing a parallel with theology, he notes that written dogma is only a belated and defensive expression of faith, that the living core of faith is in what is sung, not in what is read. What is written has meaning only in pointing to something that transcends writing; it is wholly insufficient in itself. In politics, likewise, what matters is a 'spirit': 'what is written is nothing.'[99] Clearly, it is the presence of such a spirit that distinguishes a constitution that (as he said) 'lives' from one that consists of words and force. Though seeing the conditions for it in very different terms, Maistre could have accepted Proudhon's conception of order as 'une unité profonde et tout intellectuelle.'[100] They agree in seeing this intellectual unity as historically rooted, the product of repeated and dispersed experiences, and as something that can be neither generated nor replaced by formulas or dogmas. And they agree in seeing citizenship as a political ideal that rests too much on what can be articulated, too much on what can be judged, as opposed to pre-judged. When unity is sought by political means, they both believe, it runs up against the impossibilities that confront all action inspired by an exaggerated conception of human reason. Only when unity is achieved in 'quotidian' reality and not sought in a distinct public realm shall we see 'collective and individual spontaneity evolving without obstacles.'[101] Only when political life draws upon prejudices and symbols that *give* it unity can action be 'fecund, creative, invincible.' What Maistre attributes to the achievement of sovereignty has much in common with what Proudhon attributes to its abolition or its dispersal.

For Proudhon unity is to be found in the spirit of reciprocity by which producers can maintain their independence while securing their interdependence; its material condition is social and economic diversity, which allows a society to draw from its own internal resources the means to satisfy all its needs. It is in this sense that the project of 'making right human' is to be realized, in freeing human *society* from dependence upon anything external to it. For Maistre unity springs, in the last resort but one, from a nascently Romantic principle of national identity. A society cannot choose, whatever the scope of its choice in other respects, the principle that makes it one society. Its character is given. 'It is the same with nations as with individuals. All have a character and a mission that they fulfil without realizing it.'[102] Nations have 'souls,' 'national minds' – hence what may be Maistre's best-known remark: 'There is no such thing as *man* in the world. In my life I have met Frenchmen, Italians, Russians, etc ... but as for *man*, I declare that I have never met him in my life.'[103] To create institutions for man is to create institutions that are not for the Frenchman, for they have no roots in his distinctive history. So vigorously is this organic conception advanced that orthodoxy is sometimes brought into question, as when the bishops of France are said to have inherited the theocratic role of the Druids:[104] France's national character is made antecedent to its Christian character. What is also brought into question is the view, advanced by theorists of *droit divin*, that the identity of a political society is defined by subjection to its king: while Maistre may give verbal allegiance to such a view – 'The *patrie* of a man is the entire country subject to the domination of his sovereign'[105] – it is clear that for him there are differentiated national communities, distinguished from one another by nature and history. His is, irrevocably, a post-revolutionary theocracy, in which nations can no longer be understood as items of patrimonial property. It is a critique of Rousseau that cannot escape Rousseau.

Rousseau too had of course said that there should be 'très peu de lois,' and also that 'the most important of all laws' are those 'engraved ... in the hearts of the citizens.'[106] He too had called (in his book on Poland) for 'a distinctive national education'; and his writings may yield a doctrine of cultural identity that is at least as strong as his doctrine of political identity. But this was not the Rousseau who was important to writers of the revolutionary and post-revolutionary period in search of a doctrinal symbol for that astonishing explosion of power in which the political status appeared to eclipse every other; and Rousseau had, after all, said that 'everything is rooted in politics.'[107] It was for this that Maistre and Proudhon criticized him, for this above all was the assumption upon which, they believed, the Revolution had produced such devastation. Their response was to insist upon replacing the political definition of community with a definition of a different kind, nationalist in the one case and economic in the other. *Le citoyen* is displaced by *le Français* and by *l'ouvrier*.

We can ask the historical question of whether their views of Rousseau were sound; the answer, either way, would have to be highly qualified. But we also can ask the conceptual question of whether Rousseau's conception of citizenship can withstand either of these twin assaults: and here the answer must be, fairly clearly, a negative one. To the extent that citizenship rests, in Rousseau's account, on moral generalization, on the adoption of general principles as motives of conduct in place of exclusive interests, then no level of generality is terminally privileged over any other. Proudhon's advocacy of nested layers of unity (or nested 'sovereignties'), in which moral respect operates at successive levels from the personal to the global, is if anything a more natural position to reach than that of the moral supremacy of the state. Yet, to the extent that citizenship rests, in Rousseau's account, on empirical views about political education or the formation of consciousness and loyalty, it cannot claim any moral distinctness at all. It rests upon fact rather than right, the fact, that is, that some institutions have more power to convince than do others; and there cannot be much doubt that the power of nationality to secure loyalty and to induce self-sacrifice is quite as impressive as that of republicanism and can sustain hierarchy no less effectively than it can sustain equality. Maistre's empiricism is quite as good as Rousseau's; in fact, it is often much the same as Rousseau's, though its normative use is very different.

If, then, citizenship in its political sense can be rescued from nationalism on the one hand and anarchism on the other, it is not on

Rousseau's terms that it can be done. And perhaps a question worth raising is that of the sense in which it *is* political, a question to which Rousseau gives so deeply unsatisfactory an answer. To conceive of the political in terms of the creation of moral community is necessarily to render its central concepts indistinct, for there are both moralities and communities at once more vivid and more consistent than civic ones. We may then want to ask whether what is civic can be identified, without mediation, with what is either moral or communal.

PART II: RECOVERING POLITICS

3

Alienation, Corruption, and Freedom: Proudhon's Federalism

It is to Proudhon's contemporary, Tocqueville, that one would first look for a defence of political citizenship that is as adamant and sustained as Proudhon's critique of it, though less confident of success. *What Is Property?* was published in the same year as the second volume of *Democracy in America*, in which Tocqueville laments much of what Proudhon recommended: the vanishing of a public realm, the substitution of economic for political life, and the dissolution of political power under conditions of social equality. Unlike Proudhon, Tocqueville identified freedom with political tension rather than with the tranquillities of economic exchange, and wished above all to preserve the sense of a realm of action beyond the interests of productive life. Unlike another contemporary, Auguste Comte, he greatly feared the substitution of administrative for political rule, and the loss of independence that would follow the rise to power of managers and priestly social therapists. In that remarkable generation of theorists – who took so little interest in one another's work – the alternatives of anarchy, politics, and bureaucracy are forcefully demarcated and advanced: the producer, the citizen, and the functionary confront each other as rival typical models for post-revolutionary man. But there is another source for the model of citizenship as an ideal, more occasional and fragmentary than Tocqueville's defence of it but all the more compelling for being unexpected: and that is Proudhon's own adhesion in his later writings to what he called 'the principle of federation.' For we find here a vision of civil and political life to which the values of citizenship are quite central; if Proudhon had once found 'government' incompatible with 'society,' he now finds *anarchie* 'scarcely likely ever to be realized.'[1] He now identifies freedom with a certain active relation between the governed and those who govern them, and thus emphatically rejoins a political tradition to which such a relation was crucial.

What brings Proudhon into this perhaps surprising conjunction with Tocqueville is their distaste for the administrative regime that Comte and, before him, Saint-Simon so much admired, a regime whose subjects are immured in socially defined tasks and are refused a say in their own self-definition. Under such a regime, Proudhon says – and Tocqueville is in complete agreement here – 'The citizen has nothing to do but perform his little task in his little corner, drawing his little salary, raising his little family, and relying for the rest upon the providence of government.'[2] The citizen can enjoy what is due to him, Proudhon contends, only in a state of a kind that Proudhon calls 'federal'; it is no longer the demise of the state but the radically new ordering of relations within it that will issue in civic freedom.

One should not, however, exaggerate the novelty of Proudhon's later writings, for the continuity with what he had said before is very clear, as Proudhon himself rightly insisted. For one thing, what he had called 'anarchie' depended for many of its themes upon political traditions, putting to new use the notions of human right and social contract and extending to its furthest limit a critique of despotism that owes much to Montesquieu and Rousseau; it was, as it were, an immanent critique of the state, exploiting the state's own criteria of legitimacy in order to demonstrate its impossibility. Moreover, the political formations that Proudhon recommends in his federalist writings are radically trans-formed states and are certainly not equivalent to the states of modern European experience; they, in turn, have absorbed many of the themes and demands of *anarchie* itself. Before, Proudhon had thought in terms of producers' associations, whose relations were to be commutative and unmediated by government; now he thinks in terms of groupings of governed territories; but it is still a strictly commutative vision, in which, as before, the focus is upon contract, exchange, and mutual obligation.[3] Proudhon now finds a place for authority: this is no longer, though, the divine or mystical authority derided in his earlier critiques but a bounded and rational authority of a kind that had had no place in Proudhon's thinking before, reason and authority having been strictly counterposed.

Some commentators go too far, however, and insist too much on continuity, in denying that the federalist Proudhon was thinking in terms of states at all.[4] He uses the word 'state' without embarrassment and, what is more to the point, ascribes to the state enoromous importance; it is 'prime mover and general director,' 'the highest expression of progress,' and 'the spirit of the community.'[5] Nor is it at all clear that the larger formations that he had in mind are confederations rather than federal states, a semantic distinction not available to him but one that obviously marks an important difference. On the precise legal question of sovereignty Proudhon is very unclear, and he does not tell us enough to enable us to judge whether this property resides at the provincial or federal level. On the question of jurisdictions, however, what Proudhon proposes, fairly abstractly viewed, is more like a federal state than a confederation. If in the latter arrangement the central organs have no direct jurisdiction over the citizens of constituent states, while in the former each citizen is subject to a dual jurisdiction, then we have to say that it is a federal state that Proudhon is recommending; for the whole point of his federalist scheme is that jurisdictions should be dispersed among levels, that loyalties should be divided, and that no one political identity should be absolute. If he wishes to abolish the 'indivisible will' of the unitary state and to substitute a federal dispersal of power, he has no wish to set the unitary province in its place; just as states are to be opened to the interests and demands of provinces, so too their provincial components are to be opened to the common interest embodied in states. If Proudhon is unclear on matters of legal status and erratic in his use of the word 'state,' that is because questions of sovereignty are rather distant from the centre of his concerns. What he has in mind is a political process in which the authoritarian spirit of commanding and conquering is replaced by a co-operative spirit of arranging and bargaining; and he seeks to achieve this by 'leaving nothing undivided,'[6] by dispersing jurisdictions in such a way that consent must always be won and can never be assumed.

This proposal carries with it and depends upon the ideal of an invigorated public spirit, the citizen no longer being a mere object of administrative 'providence' but stepping beyond his 'little' concerns to engage in the responsibilities of public judgment. For Proudhon's objection to that ideal, it now transpires, arose only from the political context in which it had been advanced. The possibility of civic capacity depends upon the scale and mode of the institutions through which it is solicited. It is vain, and also dangerous, to solicit participation in mass constituencies. Here – as Proudhon had argued earlier – one meets everywhere with radical incapacity, and also – as he now stresses –

with brutal, violent, and regressive popular beliefs of a magical and barbarous kind. They are myths that lead to intolerance: 'The people imagine themselves, in their obscure manner, as a huge and mysterious entity, and their language serves to reinforce this notion of indivisible unity. They call themselves the People, the Nation, the Multitude, the Mass; they are the true Sovereign, the Legislator, the Power, the Ruler, the Country, the State; they have their Assemblies, their Votes, their Assizes, their Demonstrations, their Edicts, their Plebiscites, their Direct Legislation, sometimes their Judgments and Executions, their Oracles, their Voice, like thunder or the voice of God. The more they imagine themselves to be infinite, irresistible, immense, the more horrified they are by divisions, splits, minorities. Their ideal, their fondest dream, is of unity, identity, uniformity, concentration; they condemn, as affronts to their own majesty, everything that may divide their will, break up their mass, create diversity, plurality, divergence within themselves.' Their myths lead also to political idolatry: 'Every mythology requires idols, and the people never lack them.'[7] But in a federal system, in which powers are dispersed among a pyramid of communities, local communities retaining the preponderant share of them, the masses are not 'inert' and not 'mere voters' led to self-destruction by myths and idols; local communities will have 'learned to live their lives once more.'[8] Communities, in which responsibility is learned and exercised, replace masses, and local powers replace that centralization of power that lends masses their devastating potential for destruction. 'Let Paris make revolution within its own walls. What is the use, if Lyon, Marseilles, Toulouse, Bordeaux, Nantes, Rouen, Lille, Strasbourg, Dijon, and so on, if the departments, masters of themselves, do not follow? Paris will have wasted its time.'[9] The argument is precisely that of Tocqueville in *The Old Regime*, published seven years earlier, and it is one that clearly assigns determining significance to political institutions, which make the difference between repressive self-deception and true self-government.

While the logic of federation is clearly parallel to the logic of mutualism – and while federation, as a political arrangement, must be accompanied by economic mutualism ('agro-industrial federation')[10] if it is to survive – it is not in terms of either economic or moral argument that Proudhon seeks to justify it. He justifies it by means of an exercise in political science. Federation is, he says, the 'necessary conclusion' of 'the theory of government in general.' 'Politics,' he says, 'though infinitely flexible as an applied art, is an exact science in its regulative principles, no more or less so than geometry or algebra.'[11] He discovers the 'inescapable logic' of politics in the interplay of authority and liberty, two principles whose interrelation determines the character of any regime. At once indispensable and exclusive – 'their reconciliation, separation, or elimination seem equally impossible' – authority and liberty have hitherto found no stable point of equilibrium and will do so only when the principle of federation has generated an authority that liberty can accept: an authority resting on freely given consent. Despite his claim, Proudhon's argument is scarcely 'exact,' and the authority that he finally reconciles with liberty is not the same as the authority that he had initially counterposed to it; it is not 'familial, patriarchal, magisterial, monarchical, theocratic,'[12] but something that, established by consent or contract, is simply a product of liberty and not of a principle inherently opposed to it. Proudhon's new political science, however, is not displayed to best effect in his careless argument about authority and liberty. It is the language he adopts and his choice of descriptive terms that belong essentially to a tradition of civic thought.

In presenting federation as the 'necessary conclusion' of his theory of government, Proudhon claimed for one political principle what Marx had claimed for another when he wrote: 'Democracy is the resolved mystery of all constitutions.'[13] Marx meant that democracy reveals what was always true but always concealed: that institutions are the work of man himself, that their power is *human* power in alienated form and will cease to be alien only when human society achieves deliberate control over its own organization and circumstances. Democracy – provided that it is understood not merely as a political but as a social principle – expresses this achievement, in returning power to human society itself. Now Proudhon, as we have seen, had developed a parallel argument without any debt to Marx and, indeed, with only the slightest acquaintance with German thought of the period.[14] He too had seen in the state an alienation of human powers, a process by which what belongs to human association is taken from it and presented to it as its authority; the *System of Economic Contradictions* is contemporaneous with the *German Ideology*, and its central thesis in this respect much the same. But in the *Principle of Federation* it is no longer alienation that is the object of Proudhon's critique. What he is concerned with is *corruption*; and that term places his argument in a quite different context, one in which Marx took no interest at all. It is a context to which political categories are crucial. Alienation belongs above all to a historical scheme in which identity is lost and regained, and it lends itself to themes of qualitative transformation; Marx, taking alienation as the problem, imagines an eventual mode of society that, in laying bare its own nature, 'differs from all past movements.'[15] Proudhon, adopting now as his topic the traditional notion of corruption, stresses the continuity of political science and the presence in all political societies of dangers that it is the task of institutions to avoid.

The link between federalism and the theme of corruption is supplied in a classic though brief discussion by Montesquieu, to which Proudhon's argument is deeply indebted. In *Spirit of the Laws* Montesquieu contends that 'it is natural for a republic to have only a small territory; otherwise it cannot long subsist,' for only in a small polity is the common good 'within the reach of every citizen.'[16] But small polities are militarily weak, and Montesquieu wonders if there is a solution to this dilemma – 'If a republic is small, it is destroyed by a foreign force; if it is large, it is ruined by an internal imperfection.' The solution is a 'confederation.' and of this Montesquieu remarks: 'Cette sorte de république ... peut se maintenir dans sa grandeur sans que l'intérieur se corrompe.'[17] Proudhon is concerned likewise with *grandeur* or scale: the idea of federation comes into its own when the nation-state brings into play relations of interdependence that are incalculably more vast than the ancient city experienced.[18] Federation, for Proudhon, is the (partial) disaggregation of massive social and political entities, not the (partial) aggregation of miniature ones. Still more significantly, Proudhon is preoccupied with Montesquieu's two linked concepts of *maintien* (maintenance) and (its opposite) corruption. This preoccupation virtually displaces – without, of course, suppressing – Proudhon's more characteristic concern with justice. Justice is given an honourable mention on page one, as one of the four cardinal political virtues, but afterwards almost disappears from view, Proudhon simply referring his readers to his earlier writings for an account of his thinking. Two of the other cardinal virtues, order and stability – together with the fourth, liberty – bear the weight of his discussion.

Corruption is the opposite of maintenance by virtue of the definition established by Montesquieu and, before him, Machiavelli. A polity is held to have a 'principle' essential to it, a principle that was present at its founding and that must be maintained if the polity is to retain its identity. Corruption is the loss of the founding principle. No less than three chapters in the first part of Proudhon's text are devoted to this theme. He seeks to show that no existing regime can remain faithful to the principles that it claims as its own: 'since arbitrariness enters necessarily into politics, corruption soon becomes the soul of power, and society is led without rest or reprieve along the path of incessant revolution.'[19] The corruption that especially concerns Proudhon is the corruption to which 'civic spirit' is liable[20] – that is, the corruption of the republic, whose principle, according to Montesquieu, was that of 'virtue.' What corrupts virtue is passivity, lack of responsibility, dependence, all of which undermine the engaged concern for a common good that the democratic citizen is required to have. This is the essence of Proudhon's critique of the grossly centralized nation-state, France in particular, in which the citizen has become a mere subject. Citizenship requires, on the contrary, the diffusion of a spirit of responsibility, of self-government, of local and individual initiative. As such it centrally involves a critique of professionalism: of military professionalism, a Machiavellian theme that Proudhon takes up in his rejection of mercenary armies and his advocacy of militia forces;[21] and of administrative professionalism, Proudhon's critique of bureaucracy strongly echoing the fear, prominent among classical theorists of civic virtue, of excessive executive power. The very existence of public functionaries, Proudhon says, is a threat to a self-governing society.[22] It is surely relevant to note here that, as Proudhon stresses at the outset, the *Principle of Federation* is intended above all as a popular book, readily accessible to a broad readership and designed to contribute to the diffusion of political prudence, and hence to civic responsibility.

It is the lack of prudence, the inability to take the long view, that lies at the root of corruption. Political orders are ruined by 'the succession of forgetful but endlessly renewed generations,' which, lacking awareness of the long-term constraints of order, endlessly 'follow the same path' and become 'exhausted in turn.'[23] This argument may be traced to the second chapter of Machiavelli's *Discourses*, where the endless cycles of change and decay are attributed to the fact that 'the children succeeded their fathers' and were 'ignorant of the changes of fortune.' Proudhon shares, too, in Machiavelli's ambition to master the flux of change that menaces political institutions; and he shares the conviction, said to be characteristic of the Machiavellian tradition, that the present or near future offers a 'moment' of fateful significance, when change will either be mastered or lead to total ruin: 'The twentieth century will open the age of federations, or else humanity will undergo another purgatory of a thousand years.'[24] But what sets the final seal of authenticity on Proudhon's republicanism is his call, at the beginning of part 2 of his book, for a return to 'ancient principle,'[25] a call issued by Machiavelli and by countless successors in that tradition. For although Proudhon sees the federal system that he admires as the culmination of a long development, he also believes it to have been foreshadowed in the political organization of barbarian Gaul. Liberty, the spirit of self-government, is thus indigenous; but it has been lost, or, rather, overlaid by alien (Roman) forms; the federalization of France is its recovery.

There is here a most interesting conjunction of two languages, or, as some prefer, two paradigms. On the one hand, federalism, as we have seen, rests upon a universalist argument: it is the 'necessary conclusion' of 'the theory of government in general,' the resolution of antinomies, the overcoming of contradictions, the achievement of a final equilibrium between universally necessary properties. On the other hand, the argument also draws upon a native and patriotic theme, the recovery of France's lost order, and thus the restoration of civic pride: 'the short duration' of the French constitutions, Proudhon writes, 'reflects so poorly upon our country.'[26] This conjunction is strongly related to another, the adoption in the *Principle of Federation* of two distinct conceptions of time in its political bearing. One view, more characteristic of the earlier Proudhon and of his century, is expressed in his view of federalism as a universal solution and historical culmination. It will be 'the greatest triumph of human reason' to have grasped, eventually, its necessity; but before it can be grasped, other forms must have accomplished, over time, their preparatory mission.[27] The view of time here is inflexibly linear and irreversible: there is a general and necessary order of succession, and the eventual resolution is definite and complete. The other view is characterized by the themes of loss and recovery. Societies have individual principles, which they can compromise, abandon, regain. The 'incessant revolutions' of which Proudhon speaks, which 'come and go like the seasons'[28] or, alternatively, reflect the rotation of a 'wheel' of fate,[29] obviously recall the early modern conception of revolutions as recurrent and cyclical events, connected in metaphor (at least) with cosmic or astral process. Such revolutions are not the revolution of nineteenth-century thought, an upheaval placed within a linear conception of progressive development and viewed as a decisive and irreversible transition from epoch to epoch.

Now Proudhon himself had once expressed this latter, linear view no less emphatically than, say, Marx. His *General Idea of Revolution* had been among the clearest expressions of that idea: 'Revolution' was an immanent process of change, rooted in social and intellectual necessity, to which Proudhon called the 'fracas' of politics was wholly irrelevant. The recurrent revolutions of which he now speaks represent the triumph of a political conception over a historical one, for they are traced wholly to contingent if regular political causes. Interestingly, Proudhon allows his earlier usage of the term to linger in the subtitle to *Principle of Federation*: *La Nécessité de reconstituer le parti de la Révolution*. Here is a strong implication, as before, that revolution is an immanent and progressive force capable of being sustained and extended. But 'la Révolution,' for Proudhon, turns out to be the French Revolution *prior* to 1793 and the Jacobin triumph.[30] What was authentic in the Revolution was the moment, before Paris reasserted its malign control, when the old provinces briefly regained their political voice and the dogma of 'indivisibility' was temporarily broken. It is here that Proudhon speaks of a return to ancient principle: for here Gaul at last reappeared, diverse, localist, and populist, from under the enormous weight of centralism artificially imposed upon it. What is contained in Proudhon's subtitle, then, is a remarkably elegant linkage between his earlier and later conceptions of time: there is a universal, *the* Revolution, an immanent and necessary trend of change, which is to be 'reconstituted': but its content, on closer inspection, is a particular and non-temporal principle of national identity.

Proudhon's federalism is thus sharply to be distinguished from that other 'federal principle,' as it has been called, of the Jacobins: a principle of mass mobilization by *sections*, linked by tiers of delegation to a national centre. Such a thing was to be admired by Hannah Arendt, who called it 'the federal principle';[31] it also was to be admired by Lenin, who, however, denied hotly that it should be called federal, for he wished to rescue it from any taint of (petit bourgeois) Proudhonism.[32] Lenin's distinction was sound, for this is not Proudhon's federalism at all, as his hostility to the Jacobins makes clear. His federalism is not even properly viewed as a revolutionary model: it is a model for a polity that seeks to preserve itself and to escape 'mortality.'[33] What concerns him is not intense participation valued either for its own sake or as a means of political mobilization, but the defence of regional societies, and their political life, against the encroachments of central power. The federal society he favours is valued above all for the restraints that it places upon change, which he views, in a thoroughly classical manner, as destruction.

In seeking in federation what he calls an 'unshakeable equilibrium,' in seeking to arrest those cycles of decline and decay to which in the past all orders have fallen victim, Proudhon turns to a new form of an ancient solution: that of creating some mixture or balance of powers so that they complement and restrain one another. Proudhon quite explicitly presents federation, the division of powers by area, as an extension of the constitutionalist principle of the division of powers by function. It is 'childish,' he says, to confine the principle of division to the distribution of powers at the centre; by implication, the 'mature' division of powers will be territorial in character, and powers will be divided among provinces and towns and between these regional units and the federal centre. Proudhon is faithful to the constitutionalist tradition, moreover, in seeing the principle of division as a check not only upon the ambitions of central executive power but also upon the 'people,' who are (as he interestingly puts it) 'one of the powers of the state, and one of the most terrifying.'[34] By dividing them, federation will save the people from their own folly: socialist decentralism joins hands with the federalism of Madison's Letter 10, the obvious difference being that Madison, with a confederation as his point of departure, seeks to extend association so as to *take in* multiple interests, while Proudhon, in the context of a unitary state, seeks to reduce associational scale so as to *create* multiplicity. But the object is in both cases to put an end to mass 'turbulence,' by setting institutional obstacles in the path of mass movements.

To link Proudhon's and Madison's names may at first seem odd, not only because Proudhon directs some venomous pages against the American constitution but also because of the very different economic concerns underpinning their respective systems. Proudhon's thinking is reputedly defined by the answer he gave to the question that forms the title of his best-known work, *What Is Property?* to which he had replied, 'C'est le vol.' For Madison, however, and indeed generally for the civic tradition upon which he had drawn and that Proudhon here silently revives, the institution was highly valued. It is the possession of property that, it was held, guarantees the independence of the citizen, supplies the material basis for his active political life, and also supplies him with an immediate interest in resisting excessive and arbitrary governmental power. But if it is paradoxical to set the great critic of property in the context of a property-owning theory, it is Proudhon himself who invites this paradox, for he explicitly adopts the standard argument that it is the absence of property that disposes men to tyranny. 'The people,' he writes, 'living from day to day, without property ... have nothing to lose under tyranny, and scarcely worry

about the prospect.'[35] Moreover, it is, he says, the property-owning
middle class that has always been the source of political liberty.

The difficulty is only apparent. The property-owning middle class,
the bourgeoisie in its original and non-Marxist sense, has, Proudhon
says, ceased to exist.[36] It has given way to the concentration of wealth,
to finance capitalism as it was later called, or to 'economic feudalism' or
'bankocracy,' as Proudhon calls it. And how, he asks, can a democratic
republic be created without the social base that it has always been
thought to require? It is here that Proudhon returns to the idea of
economic organization that he had favoured from the beginning, the
idea of self-governing producers' associations, trading with one another
according to a principle of just exchange or 'value.' Before, though, this
idea had rested upon ethical foundations; now it becomes a political
instrument. Now that the bourgeoisie has vanished, a society of
self-governing producers' associations is the only basis for a political
order in which the concentration of power can be avoided. The
concentration of wealth breeds political dependency, dividing society
into a class of passive wage-earners on the one hand and an elite of
financiers on the other.

Although Proudhon retains intact his long-established economic
proposals, they have come in *Principle of Federation* to acquire a new
significance and meaning: as weapons against the concentration of
power and as the means by which the political ideals once attached to
the possession of property may be rescued.[37] Property as the classical
theorists thought of it no longer exists; but an equivalent is to be found
in the joint property rights of producers' associations, which likewise
preserve their members from dependency. Like earlier theorists who
had stressed the civic rather than the juristic aspects of property,[38]
Proudhon examines property relations in the light of their political
consequences. The deconcentration of economic control gives life to
the region; and it is regional life that permits the values of self-
government to be realized, and supplies the only alternative to an order
in which 'power invades everything, dominates everything, absorbs
everything, for ever, for always, without end,'[39] in which, also,
'political life abandons the periphery for the centre, and collapse
overcomes a hydrocephalous nation.'[40]

The most provocative of Proudhon's large claims for federation is that it
maximizes and guarantees freedom, reducing authority to its inescapable minimum; for that claim has been sharply contested by political

scientists who wish to present federation as an arrangement of a wholly pragmatic kind and to purge it of any hint of immanent value.[41] This, of course, undermines not only the substance of Proudhon's account but also its enthusiasm. Federalism, critics allege, is thought to provide freedom because it divides power and because it provides effective local democracy; but the former claim is defeated by the argument, attributed to Bentham, that institutional pluralism is meaningless unless there is also social pluralism, the latter by the argument, attributed to Mill, that a unitary state with effective institutions of local government can do everything a federation can do. More strongly still, the division of power does not, it is objected, lead to freedom: by frustrating national majorities it may lead to tyranny; by protecting local majorities it may oppress local minorities. *Federation* may be in some circumstances a necessary expedient, attractive only in the sense that compromise is attractive if one cannot have one's way; to turn it into *federalism* is to create a mystifying ideology out of something that is only an institutional device.

Of these challenges there is a great deal to be said. The first is that such objections, while certainly serious, neglect a theme that Proudhon stresses and that indeed is implicit in the topic of corruption itself: he is concerned with the question of maintaining freedom over time. To be sure, Proudhon also tries to make a case that the conditions for federation and for freedom are identical, a case that is open to many objections and is also – as will be suggested below – interestingly if unsatisfyingly complex. But his claim to realism rests on the essentially temporal and dynamic argument he offers, which, while very much in the spirit of Montesquieu's political sociology, goes far beyond anything Montesquieu had said about confederation. For Montesquieu, the cause of a republic's corruption, or of the loss of its identifying principle, had been *grandeur*, or scale. Proudhon takes over that argument, as far as it goes, with little modification; he claims that a federation combines the small scale of the republic with a larger sovereignty and also restrains territorial growth by aggressive means. But he adds to this an argument in terms of what may be called *internal* growth – that is, in terms of an increasing density of relations and an expansion of activities requiring general management and supervision. 'In a properly organized society, everything must be in constant growth – science, industry, work, wealth, public health.'[42] Growth in this sense creates no less of an administrative burden than territorial growth. Much importance attaches, therefore, to the manner in which a society responds, *over time*, to new relations and circumstances, and to the kind of institutions it adopts for managing the additional burdens that its progress imposes upon it.

Now in a unitary state, Proudhon believed, there is a natural tendency for new responsibilities to accumulate at the centre. Moreover, he believed, an increasingly massive aggregation of central powers will also be increasingly impenetrable to the value on which a republic rests – that is, virtue, or civic responsibility. The argument for federalism, therefore, rests principally upon the claim that in a federation the trend towards central accumulation will be less powerful than in a unitary state. The acquisition of new responsibilities will be both legally and politically challengeable by 'jealous' provinces. The risk of corruption will therefore be smaller, in the sense that provinces will better be able to preserve their internal politics from central administration than if they were, legally and politically, creatures of central power. In preserving themselves from central accumulation, provinces in a federation will enjoy greater legal and political resources than subordinate jurisdictions enjoy in unitary systems. It is not predicted that an initial division of power between provinces and centre will survive the unanticipated circumstances that, over time, foster increased central responsibility: it is only predicted that as such circumstances arise, provincial governments will be able to exercise significant control over the growth of central powers. This is not a manifestly unreasonable case. Of course, empirical evidence may or may not support it; but whether it happens to be supported by evidence or not, it is a case that is rooted in a tradition of political inquiry to which the experience of time is central and in which freedom is identified with the maintenance of political capacity. As such, it is a case that largely escapes the objections of later critics of the claims of federation.

Significant difficulties are still posed, however, on other grounds, even if we accept Proudhon's case for federalism's tendency to conserve freedom: for he is far from perfectly clear about what freedom is. He thus opens his argument to the powerful objection that to speak of federalism as conserving freedom *tout court* is simply vacuous, for there is no such thing as freedom *tout court*: there are *freedoms*. These different conceptions of freedom are not only different but also, in at least some circumstances, incompatible; to conserve one requirement may to be foreclose on others, and even if Proudhon is right about the dynamics of unitary and federal states, his claim about the later is plainly lacking in discrimination. In attempting to make it more discriminating for him, however, we find woven together in his account several distinguishable kinds of freedom that are equally indispensable to him, and are connected with several distinguishable (if overlapping) images of the federal polity.

In part Proudhon identifies as freedom what Montesquieu had preferred to call 'virtue' – that is, political capacity, and the self-discipline necessary to its exercise. To be free in this sense is to rule oneself, as opposed to being subject to another's rule. In this respect the case for federalism as an agent of freedom hinges on the opportunities for participation that it affords; in turn, an argument from political scale is brought into play. In a large state the common good is not 'within the reach' of its citizens, whose engagement can be fostered only within the narrower and more familiar horizons of the relatively small territory or group. Here, it is argued, the level of information is higher, the sense of efficacy stronger, and hierarchical distance less extreme. Either because it provides sub-national contexts or else (or in addition) because in providing them it cultivates a political sense that is transferable to the national level, federation is to be valued. Thus conceived, it is composed of a tiered or layered nest of constituencies that make freedom possible by offering the largest possible number of opportunities for political action.

Secondly, however, freedom may be identified less as self-rule than as freedom from arbitrary rule, two values that, clearly, may rest on similar grounds but, equally clearly, are different. The latter is closer to the sense in which Montesquieu himself had thought of freedom, and he connected it not with republicanism but with constitutionalism. Here Proudhon's relation to Montesquieu becomes complex, for if he advances federation as an extension of the civic virtues of democratic republicanism, he also advances it, quite explicitly, as an extension of the constitutionalism that Montesquieu had offered as an alternative to virtue. For here the point is to provide security by 'setting power against power,' to divide and balance powers so that attempted abuses will be restrained. The doctrine of the balance of powers is admired by Proudhon as an immense advance in constitutional thinking, but it is only very imperfectly satisfied, he maintains, by a separation of powers at the national centre. 'At first,' he writes, 'the demand for a constitution will be heard on all sides: later the demand will be for decentralization.'[43] Only the territorial dispersal of power, balancing provincial against central government, can offer the security against abuses that constitutional theorists had sought. Thus viewed, federalism is a (territorial) version of conflict pluralism, and sub-national units are not valued, inherently, as arenas of political education but as agents of political balance. It is for this reason that Proudhon is not content merely with the devolution of power to provinces; any power is potentially oppressive, and central government, in its turn a counterweight to provincial government, acts as a guarantor of personal and civil rights against local oppression.

Thirdly, Proudhon's introduction of local and cultural diversity adds yet another dimension to his case for freedom. For a community, too, may wish to be free in the sense of being independent, its separate identity respected. There are, Proudhon contends, real and historic communities, small 'peoples' or societies within the mammoth nation-states, peoples who have retained a memory of their distinctive character despite the Romans and the Romanizing trends of royal (and democratic) policy. It was on this ground that he called for the federalization of France, as a means of giving political recognition to admirably stubborn local identities; it was on the same ground that he had opposed the unification of Italy, which, he predicted, would suppress the vigorous independence of its provinces. On such a view sub-national units are valued not primarily as political units fostering civic virtues, nor primarily as agents of conflict pluralism, but as institutional shells for local cultures; and freedom is attained to the extent that their borders obstruct the flow of homogenizing, Parisianizing influence.

Now there is no inconsistency in holding all three views, for some of the conditions for all three kinds of freedom are the same; a province may serve all three of these functions. But the political tensions that Proudhon has built into his picture of federalism are considerable. Political participation generates majorities; constitutional rule requires the protection of individual (and minority) rights; cultural diversity implies the existence of collective personalities: the possibilities of collision are obvious, and collision is all the more severe in that majorities, minorities, individuals, and local identities may all claim the sanction, in one way or another, of the federal principle as Proudhon constructs it. No hierarchy of values is offered – or, rather, different hierarchies are implied at different times, for Proudhon writes as though each of the freedoms were in turn indefeasible. In terms, strictly, of what Proudhon says, the case must be conceded, for Proudhon does not answer the questions that are posed by his equation of federalism with freedom. But if we are open to the spirit of what he was trying to do, his account suggests a different and more productive approach.

Whether there are different concepts of freedom or, merely, different conceptions of it is a severely contested issue.[44] To stress the security of rights, or freedom *from* interference, is clearly different from stressing the value of democracy, or freedom *to* participate in self-rule. Security may be provided by a wholly undemocratic system; a democratic system may not provide security. There are undemocratic liberals and illiberal democrats, and the liberal and democratic traditions, while often intertwined, can be distinguished. Given that freedom *from* and freedom *to* may be put to such different and mutually exclusively political uses, it is understandable that negative and positive concepts of freedom should be distinguished. Against this view, however, it is urged that all intelligible uses of the term, as well as referring to the freedom *of* someone, involve at least implicit reference to someone's freedom *from* some impediment *to* their doing something.[45] Whether the *from* or the *to* is stressed depends simply on the context, and what we observe, therefore, is no more than a range of uses of a single concept, whose variables are differently defined on different occasions, and not two distinct concepts.

So complex a general issue cannot be resolved here; but two considerations may help to clarify it. First, even if it is the case that all uses of the term *freedom* can successfully be brought under a single conceptual umbrella, their political meanings – in the sense of what they politically imply – are indeed wholly diverse and can involve the most intense rivalry. If that is what is meant by distinguishing between negative and positive freedom, the distinction is beyond challenge. Second, however, no conceptual gulf shelters one meaning from another or impedes their political interplay.[46] Positive freedom may be valued not only as a terminal end but as the indispensable means to negative freedom, self-government being, in some contexts, the only mode of governing that can exclude arbitrary power; negative freedom, likewise, may be valued because democratic processes are impossible unless some elementary rights are secured. Despotism may be hated because political servility excludes both personal security *and* the sense of dignity that impels people to demand a say in what they are required to do; in a society's demand for self-government, it may be impossible to separate the desire for collective self-determination from the desire to enjoy personal freedoms.

If freedom, viewed in its most general aspect, is the freedom *of* someone *from* some impediment *to* his doing something, then the range of cases that it covers is dauntingly indefinite. We cannot announce in advance whose freedom will be most severely jeopardized by what restraint with respect to which potential action. Some concept other than freedom may privilege one actor over another, license one end rather than another, but freedom itself cannot do so. Is it, then, impossible to speak of a 'free society'? Raymond Aron has illuminatingly suggested that we may apply that term to a society in which the ambiguities of freedom are respected and in which the meaning of freedom is monopolized by neither a liberal nor a democratic dogma.[47] A free society is one that publicly admits the indeterminacy of freedom and allows its meaning to be politically open. We are free to the extent that we can question what freedom means, and it is the process of questioning, not a privileged answer to the question, that discloses the presence of political freedom.

An answer as sophisticated as Aron's is not to be found, to be sure, in Proudhon's text. But the relevance of Proudhon's text to it becomes apparent if we consider the first and seemingly most innocent of the variables of freedom – the freedom *of* whom? For how one conceives of one's freedom – *from* whatever impediment, *to* whatever ends – plainly must depend upon what one takes oneself to be and upon the points of reference by which one's identity is established. 'It varies with circumstances whether it is to this group or that ... that the individual will have the sense of owing certain precisely defined freedoms.'[48] Whether or not I am free depends upon the identifications that are salient to me; these identifications will be different for different individuals, and may well be different for the same individual over time. No one identity can be prescribed a priori. It is not far-fetched to detect an important parallel in Proudhon's *Principle of Federation*. For while he often stresses the multiplicity of powers, valuing federalism as a system of balanced restraint, what is no less important to him is multiplicity of *constituency*; powers are territorially divided not only for the sake of securing checks and balances but also because different features of freedom bring different contexts of action into play.

We may define Proudhon's federation as a polity in which the question of priority of membership will be permanently open. He speaks, indeed, of provinces as natural communities, of central power as artificial; but he also speaks of the federal state, as we have seen, in quite unexpected language that leaves no doubt that the state, no less than the province, is a locus of identification. He wants to destroy the indivisible state without setting the indivisible province in its place; he wants, ideally, a set of systematically competitive loyalties of which neither province nor state enjoys a monopoly. The self-administering province substitutes civic freedom for the administered subject of the unitary state; but in another sense of freedom the state must protect individuals against their provinces; while in a third sense the state may again be a vehicle of freedom, in giving force to the will to act with respect to 'common things.'[49]

Theorists of federalism have often found clarity desirable in the separation of provincial and federal jurisdictions. Proudhon seems at times to be developing a different emphasis. It is not through clarity but through conflict, or at least through the possibility of conflict, that a federation can be said to make freedom possible. He does not suppose freedom to have an assignable primary location. He supposes that its location will vary in unanticipated and also in differently perceived ways. What he means by federation is a re-politicized society in which the location of new powers is subject to contestation and negotiation. He sees this as setting limits to the natural but corrupting tendency of politics to give way to administration. In the classical manner, he sees politics as requiring an active and widely diffused sense of a common interest; but he also believes that such common interest will become a mere symbol of tutelage, administrative 'providence,' if any one collectivity takes it uniquely as its own. He insists that if freedom is to be realized, questions of jurisdiction must be capable of being raised; and rightly or wrongly he values federation as a political order in which such questions can be more effectively raised than in any other.

We may, in short, read Proudhon's federalist proposals as an elaborate critique of Rousseau's central view that 'the most general will is always the more just.' It is not always the most just, Proudhon perceived, and there are different levels of generality at which people form wills; only federation admits this fact. We may see his federal principle, then, as an attempted solution to the outstanding problem of legitimacy that Rousseau's thinking had generated, a problem that Proudhon himself had vigorously exploited in his earlier writings: if legitimacy resides in human association itself, the state can claim no terminal privilege over other associations within which the same mutuality, the same reciprocities of obligation, are displayed. The larger association is not more just than the smaller; it differs in its objectives, and in all associations the formation of a common will and the undertaking of shared obligations deserve respect. Citizenship, then, is inherently multiple, and much of civic life, as Proudhon views it, consists in the definition of association, the choice among levels of action, and the weighing of different memberships. Such definition is not performed *for* the citizen, as in *Social Contract*, by a civil religion and by other institutions that tell the citizen who he is and which of his memberships is real; it is a definition that constitutes the primary task of citizenship itself. To be a citizen is, to be sure, to identify *with* something, but it is also, Proudhon implies, to have a choice about *what* one is to identify with.

Now this conclusion is here argued for Proudhon as much as by him. Such a conception of citizenship is implied and even required by the tensions so evident in his federal model, though how far he himself grasped these tensions is a matter for speculation. He thus hints at, but does not make his own, a conception of politics that marks a radical break with Rousseau's, a conception in which politics does not express a unity that is brought to it but that itself defines the scope, level, and mode of association and the degree and manner of unity. He does not make it his own, however, or explore its implications, because he is deflected by images of order that require politics to be given an external justification: reverting to ancient images of orderly correspondence, he finds 'an admirable accord between zoology, political economy, and politics' and insists on giving federation the sanction of familiar organic analogies.[50] Such images of essential harmony belie the sense of conflict revealed in *Principle of Federation* and the still more acute conflicts implied by its argument. Likewise, the suggested analogies between 'politics' and 'political economy' tend to conceal the distance between mutualism and federation, and the presence in the latter of modes of conflict that have no economic analogy at all. Here, much as in the case of 'sovereignty' and 'state,' the *Principle of Federation* seems to display ideas engaged in struggle with a language that is only imperfectly appropriate to their expression.

Interestingly, even the language of civic virtue is only an approximately suitable vehicle for what he wanted to say. It supplied him with the notion of corruption, which was well suited to conveying the debased and passive citizenship that he saw in the administered state. That notion carried with it a trail of images and associations, of which he made forceful rhetorical use; and it also served to detach his thinking from the historical theme of alienation and its overcoming, leading him to see the continuing need for political institutions to ward off *recurrent* threats to freedom. But the central trend of his federalism is pacific; it detaches political institutions from the classical theme of war, and its object is to disperse identification, not to concentrate it for military purposes. Only in *con*federation, in relations, that is, *between* republics, are there hints in classical thinking of the kind of republic that he had in mind, one in which the 'city' becomes a constellation of loyalties. What he had in mind was citizenship without a *polis*; what he borrowed from classical thinking was not the image of civic community but a conception of politics as a process of self-identification.

4

Tocqueville and the
Human Point of View

If Proudhon's position was to shift, eventually, in a somewhat Tocquevillian direction, Tocqueville's position was not wholly without analogies to Proudhonism. In terms of social and economic theory, indeed, Tocqueville lacked sympathy for any variant of socialism, and his failure to give it serious attention diminished the much admired predictive capacity for which he is famous. In terms of his most basic associative model, however, Tocqueville, like Proudhon, stressed and valued mutuality, regretting that unrelenting applications of central power had removed from society any co-operative capacity: 'The administration of the old regime had already deprived Frenchmen of the possibility, and the desire, of coming to each other's aid. When the Revolution arrived, one would have looked in vain, in most parts of France, for ten men used to acting in concert and looking out for their interests: central power was meant to do it for them.'[1] With sensitivities – no doubt class sensitivities – quite different from Proudhon's, Tocqueville did not see any connection between social equality and the spirit of mutuality; on the contrary, he tended to identify that spirit with an aristocratic society, with the old regime, that is, before royal policies had expunged co-operation in favour of obedience. He attributed to that society qualities that, needless to say, Proudhon would not have recognized there, that he would have attributed only to an egalitarian and as-yet unachieved order. Tocqueville finds in his remembered order, Proudhon in his anticipated one, reflections of an 'ancient constitution'[2] in which local association had a primary and honourable place: Tocqueville finds it (in the aristocratic manner) among the Franks; Proudhon finds it (in the populist manner) in Gaul, seeing Frankish feudalism as a corruption of Gallic federalism. But they are both on the barbarians' side against the Romans.

Above all, they are largely in agreement in their views of the Revolution, both regarding it as a centralizing rather than a liberating event, as a further assault on citizenship. And they see it in this way, moreover, because they both see in it a spilling over of religious sentiments and images into the political world. In creating mass constituencies, Proudhon says, the Revolution brought into play an obscure popular imagination with 'its incarnations, its messiahs, its divine emissaries.' For Tocqueville, likewise, it could be compared only to religious revolutions, such as the Reformation or the spread of Islam. It was cosmopolitan, proselytizing, contemptuous of 'local traditions, laws, and customs,' and aimed at 'nothing short of a regeneration of the whole human race.' In the manner of a religion it sought to identify 'men' rather than 'citizens,' and identified them in a 'universal' and 'abstract' way.[3] For their different reasons Proudhon and Tocqueville both found this political religiosity repellent, and they both criticized it from a point of view they called 'human' – one, that is, that they held to a true and not a mystified conception of the nature and limits of civil life. Here, though, there is a decisive parting of the ways, for while Proudhon's 'humanité' was atheist and implied the end of religious conceptions of order, Tocqueville's 'human point of view' implied only the distinction between religious and political orders.

In both volumes of *Democracy in America* Tocqueville speaks of a 'human point of view' in defining his approach to religious beliefs. 'Though it is very important for man as an individual that his religion should be true, that is by no means so in society's case. Society has nothing to fear or hope from another life; what is most important for it is not that all citizens should profess the true religion but that they should profess religion.' That it is important is, for Tocqueville, among the chief lessons of American experience, which displays so strikingly the dependence of political liberty on religious belief: 'Religion, which never intervenes directly in the government of American society, must ... be considered the first of their political institutions, for although it did not give them the taste for liberty, it singularly facilitates the use of it.' It does so by forming the individual's 'habits of regulating his opinions' or by teaching the 'habits of restraint' that a society that is to govern itself must necessarily have.[4] To consider religion from a human point of view is to bracket out the question of its truth and to examine its consequences for human life.[5]

The immediate point of Tocqueville's argument – its ideological point – is very clear and has been established beyond a doubt by recent scholarship.[6] Tocqueville looked at America, as is well known, with one eye upon France, and to draw attention to the role of religion in American democracy was to advance the centrist politics that he pursued – as theorist and, less effectually, as actor – in his own country. Here his position is in the mainstream of French liberal thought, and very comparable to Constant's.[7] For what he especially regretted in French circumstances was the polarization between a Catholic right and an anticlerical left; this, he was convinced, immobilized political life, and he was thus interested in showing that such entrenched mutual hostility was non-essential. Hence the point of his observations about religion in America: *there*, religious belief and democratic politics are not polarized but complementary, and to stress this fact – together with the deep affinities between democracy and specifically Christian religious belief – was to encourage Catholics and democrats to overcome their sterile opposition. Although it is pragmatic, Tocqueville's approach is not, it should be stressed, a pragmatism, for his whole point is to distinguish between questions of truth and questions of use, not to identify the two.

Now it is this duality that lends Tocqueville's position here what may be a still broader relevance. His distinction between religious truth and political use is suggestive of further distinctions, which relate clearly to the structure of his approach and explain, in part, its distinctiveness. As successive commentators' efforts have made amply clear, Tocqueville's political writings do not yield a clear and unambiguous commitment of what may be called an 'ontological' kind. His political analysis is shot through with the conviction that ontological *beliefs* have an explanatory role, the fundamental world-views of aristocrats and democrats generating profound consequences for their respective political societies; aristocracy and democracy are, he stresses, underpinned by rival visions. But what he himself thought of these visions is so reticently veiled, or else so finely balanced, that he can be represented as an aristocrat born out of his time, or as a democrat concealing his true views out of respect for the sensibilities of aristocratic readers, or, as Mill thought, as supremely impartial. It is here that his 'human point of view' may disclose a relevance beyond that of its initial context; perhaps the truth of social ontologies can be bracketed out of political science just as the truth of theologies can, and perhaps – as the conduct of his inquiry strongly suggests – there is a political or civic science that is independent of ontological commitments. That is the suggestion that will be pursued below.

There are, of course, 'many Tocquevilles,'[8] and comprehensiveness is scarcely to be sought, least of all in a discussion as brief as this. But the Tocqueville to be presented here is a theorist who insisted that what governs the nature of a political society is the manner in which its beliefs are mediated by institutions, and that what is of crucial political interest is not *what* is believed but *how* it is acted upon. Implicitly, he thus also insisted that politics is not derivative in any simple way from social visions or the moralities that flow from them, and that what decisively makes a polity what it is should be sought in the interactions that *compose* it, not in the cosmic or moral visions that are brought *to* it. If this is so, then the possible importance of his 'human point of view' is very considerable. It was in terms of what was human that Enlightenment and post-Enlightenment political theory sought a basis for political legitimacy; what Tocqueville contends is that the kind of legitimacy that a human point of view can supply is not only different from but is different in *kind* from the legitimacy of divine right. Like Maistre and Proudhon, then, he detects and criticizes a metaphorical displacement in the substitution of popular sovereignty for the sovereignty of kings.[9] For this reason, and along lines that occasionally converge with both the theocratic and the anarchist critiques, he finds in the democratic state a perilous sort of emptiness, a vacuum of authority that comes to be arbitrarily filled. But he also sees in America, and envisages in France, the outlines of a legitimate democracy; it is legitimate because it admits political mediation and, in doing so, makes citizenship possible.

What is distinctive about the human point of view may emerge if we make the contrast that Tocqueville makes, that is, with a point of view that he calls 'divine': 'God,' he writes, 'does not view the human race collectively. With one glance he sees every human being separately and sees in each the resemblances that make him like the others and the differences that isolate him from them. Thus God has no need of general ideas; that is to say, he never feels the necessity of categorizing a considerable number of analogous objects in order to think about them more conveniently.'[10] Man, as Rousseau too had argued in the *Discourse on Inequality*, must laboriously learn to detect universals in a world of particulars; but his efforts are irrevocably crude in comparison to a perfect understanding that can discern both identity and difference simultaneously. What lends this difference its political edge, as opposed to whatever epistemological interest it may hold, is that the categories of resemblance and difference supply the central points of departure for Tocqueville's political sociology. Resemblance is the ontology of democratic thought, difference the ontology of the aristocratic world-view; both, Tocqueville implies, are irrevocably partial. The democratic mind imagines unity to consist in likeness, in equality in the arithmetic sense, or in 'generalizing' in Rousseau's sense; it is the sharing of attributes that constitutes it, and the implications of shared attributes determine what it requires. The aristocratic mind imagines unity in terms of the complementarity that difference supplies: it is difference, not resemblance, that creates interdependence, and it is in grasping such interdependence that political unity is established, in the mutual indispensability of differently situated people.

Because the human mind is 'weak' and inherently partial in its understanding, humans must pick out resemblances or differences, and their conceptions are 'always incomplete.' Concepts of resemblance and difference lead to different associative principles, democratic society imagining itself in what may be called a 'metaphoric' fashion, seeing association in similarity, aristocratic society picturing association as 'metonymic,' as something established by contextual relations among dissimilars. The core image for the former is that of the 'flock,' an image with Stoic and (as Tocqueville stresses) Christian origins. In democracy, men have 'the same civilization, the same language, the same religion, the same habits, the same manners, and among them opinion takes the same forms and the same colours.'[11] Their sense of their own 'general similitude' governs their moral thinking and leads them to extend their sympathies broadly, 'for real sympathies can exist only between those who are alike.'[12] It enters into their system of inheritance, leading them to divide property among a father's children, a practice that has enormous social and economic consequences that themselves reinforce the idea of equality from which the practice springs.[13] It influences their notions of legal and political authority, for people who see themselves as alike are naturally disposed to expect uniform regulation by a single source.

The core image of aristocratic society, however, as Tocqueville repeatedly says, is that of the 'chain.' Diversity of rank and character is so stressed that 'the general tie' is scarcely perceived – indeed, 'man is scarcely perceived in the maze of special ties and dependencies which impose special and restricted obligations.' The point is not merely that there is diversity, but that diversity is associative, differences creating reciprocal connections: 'Amongst aristocratic nations all men are connected with, and dependent upon, each other,'[14] and they are connected precisely because they are dependent. 'Since in aristocratic societies all the citizens occupy fixed positions, one above the other, the result is that each of them always sees a man above himself whose protection is necessary to him, and below himself another man whose assistance he may claim.' But in picturing itself as a society of similar and independent beings, democracy eliminates this network of dependencies: 'democracy breaks that chain, and severs every link in it.'[15] Tocqueville isolates the revolutionary quality of this severing of the chain when he argues that democratic man can literally no longer understand the moral conceptions of the aristocratic age; identifying morality with 'the general tie,' he finds intolerable the exclusiveness of aristocratic sympathies and obligations. He quotes a letter in which Mme de Sévigné, a woman who 'passionately loved her children, and was very alive to the sorrows of her friends,' even 'treated her vassals and servants with kindness and indulgence,' engages in 'cruel banter' in reporting on the brutal repression of a popular revolt. Reading this letter, Tocqueville says, the most cold-hearted man of the nineteenth century shrinks from its callousness; no longer is so terrifying a blend of special love and general indifference comprehensible to him.[16] It is just such a radical shift of moral consciousness that amounts to one of the things that Tocqueville called a revolution.[17]

These two great organizing principles extend even beyond the social, moral, and political realms to supply aristocratic and democratic societies with their fundamental conceptions of the universe in which they live. 'Men in a similar and equal condition readily conceive the idea of one God, governing every man by the same laws, and granting to every man future happiness on the same condition. The idea of the unity of mankind constantly leads them back to the idea of the unity of the Creator; while, on the contrary, where men are separated from one another and very dissimilar, they are apt to devise as many deities as there are nations, castes, classes, or families, and to trace a thousand private roads to heaven.' Carefully avoiding a reductionist sociology of religion – adumbrated by Rousseau and elaborated by Comte – Tocqueville contends that the world was 'prepared for' Christian monotheism by imperial rule in Rome, 'which gathered a large portion of the human race, like an immense flock, under the sceptre of the Caesars ... they all obeyed the same laws, and ... every subject was so weak and insignificant in relation to the imperial potentate that all appeared equal when their condition was contrasted with his.' But with the re-emergence of distinct nations and, within them, 'castes,' layers of saints and angels were interposed between man and God so that heaven should reproduce the graduated hierarchies of earth.[18] What Bodin had called the chain of being was, in Tocqueville's view, a cosmic projection of the structure of feudal society: not a legitimating order but a rationalization.

What can be said, though, about the truth of these self-enclosed visions or paradigms of reality? If indeed they are, as Tocqueville's descriptions suggest, total, self-confirming, and incommensurable, each taking as real what the other denies, then the question of their truth is obviously vexed; there would seem to be 'two distinct kinds of humanity,' between which communication cannot take place. Tocqueville does not merely decline to pass judgment; he holds that 'no man on earth' can make such a judgment, not, at least, 'absolutely and generally.'[19] It is quite true that the aristocrats' belief that their social institutions belonged to 'the immutable order of nature' was false, for their society was in fact not only mutable but doomed. Here, it may seem, we find support for the view that Tocqueville was committed to the truth, or natural basis, of the democratic vision, and was prudently equivocal only in his expression.[20] But this consideration is scarcely decisive, for aristocracy was doomed because its conception of the world was only partial, and what it excluded – a sense of generic humanity and of universal justice – was eventually to destroy it. The democratic vision, however, is likewise partial, and what democratic man cannot see, or cannot easily see, threatens his own society as much as the aristocrats' selective blindness had threatened their own. We may take as literally as we wish the claim that 'providence' governed the demise of aristocracy and its replacement by democratic conceptions of justice. But providence has not guaranteed the success of democracy, and everything that Tocqueville wrote implies that democracy, like every vision, has 'natural defects' that are fatal to it if policy does not repair them.[21] Moreover, as that phrase implies, the concept of the *natural* is not used by Tocqueville in the way that is essential to a natural-law argument. What is natural to an order is what, unless prevented or deflected, will tend to occur *within* the set of institutions and assumptions that it has adopted. There are clear echoes of Pascal's 'second nature' of habit and custom as the effective medium of life. Alternatively, there are images – perhaps derived from the civic tradition – of nature as an insidious presence on which order must be artificially imposed.[22] Yet again, there are hints of a Rousseauan *pitié*, of powerfully immediate attachments quite independent of convention.[23] The use of the term is exceedingly complex and follows no single pattern. Given the relativity that Tocqueville sees in pictures of the natural world, however, it is implausible to suppose that what is natural can be put to use as an objective criterion of choice between regimes, or of political commitment.

The point at issue here, however, is that nothing would follow *politically* from Tocqueville's commitment, either way. If he does not tell us, perhaps that is because, in terms of his objectives, it does not matter. What above all distinguishes him from contemporaries such as Proudhon on the one hand and Comte on the other is that he does not attempt to rest his political conclusions on foundations that are undemonstrable by political knowledge itself. They may not be demonstrable by any knowledge at all, as his remarks about the inherent imperfection of the human mind may well suggest. His position does not, however, *rest on* scepticism either, for what is crucial to it is not what can be known but what can be done; we can act and make choices only within the 'circle' marked out for us by providence, and what we succeed in doing within the circle is independent of what (if anything) we succeed in knowing beyond it. That ontological truth may be found, or may not be found, does not govern what can be politically achieved or not achieved; it is here that Tocqueville's human point of view is decisively relevant, in distinguishing between what we can know about the consequences of a belief and what we can or cannot finally know about its truth. And that point of view suggests that for Tocqueville *humanité* is to be sought not in any doctrine about man but in a sense of the spaces that doctrine does not fill.

If aristocratic man lacks above all a sense of resemblance, what democratic man lacks is a sense of structure, which of course the aristocrat abundantly had: unlike the world-view of aristocracy, the 'general ideas' of democratic society do not foster a sense of the relationships between political actors but only a sense of the properties they share. While this makes moral association stronger – or at least broader: 'I do not know,' Tocqueville says, whether it is stronger or not[24] – it does not inherently induce a sense of political association in the manner in which the dependencies of aristocratic society drew its members into an awareness of public questions. Because of their dependence on one another, 'men living in aristocratic ages are ... almost always firmly attached to something placed beyond them.'[25] whereas in democratic ages individuals are juxtaposed rather than associated.[26] To be sure, the numerous small differences among them form the basis of sets, or 'circles,' in which similar distinctive interests are gathered; but these are to be clearly distinguished from the classes of aristocratic society, for they contain nothing to link them concretely with any wider context. Nor does Tocqueville attribute much force to the division of labour as a source of interdependence. From an objective point of view commerce and industry create a high degree of interdependence, as Rousseau had said and as Durkheim above all was to stress; but Tocqueville does not believe that subjective interdependence follows from the specialization of economic functions. Though roles are different, status may become if anything more homogeneous, for almost all are wage earners and see themselves in this light rather than as bearers of distinctive skills or functions. Though differences of role are very marked, rapid mobility renders them virtually invisible; and since contractual relations replace patronage relations, inequalities in the workplace do not spill over into a wider system of class relations.[27] Though there is quite as much inequality of wealth and disparity of responsibility as in aristocratic society, a democracy nevertheless wears the aspect of 'one single mass, composed of elements that are all analogous though not entirely similar.'[28]

In aristocratic society, where rights are unevenly distributed and patronage relations create centres of social and political power, the force of will is evident. Events may be traced to the intentions of this man or that, and in aristocratic ages historians explain the changes that occur as willed and intended achievements; those who can effectively will and intend are, of course, few in number. But when opportunities are more evenly dispersed and social hierarchies levelled, processes of causation become infinitely complex, reflecting a web of initiatives to no one of which can dominance be ascribed. A different kind of history, Tocqueville says, comes to be written. 'When all the citizens are independent of each other and each is weak, no one can be found exercising a very great or, above all, a very lasting influence over the masses. At first sight individuals appear to have no influence at all over them, and society would seem to move on its own by the free and spontaneous interaction of its members.' The historian, 'lost in a labyrinth, unable clearly to see or explain individual influences, ... denies that they exist.'[29] The processes of democratic society are experienced, therefore, not as things in which intelligible purpose is displayed but as quasi-natural occurrences that impose themselves upon social actors. We are not far here from the alienation Proudhon described, men losing the sense of themselves as agents and resigning themselves to the role of historical patients.

On the economic plane there is no invisible hand by which unintended benefits are generated but, on the contrary, a crisis-inducing mechanism. 'The Americans make immense progress in industry because they all devote themselves to it at once, and for this same reason they are exposed to very unexpected and massive crises. As they are all engaged in commerce, commerce is affected by such various and complex factors that it is impossible to foresee what difficulties may arise.'[30] More generally, the same logic induces a gap between the reality and the self-perception of democratic society. While as naturally equal individuals its members may all make equal claims, in the actual interrelation of their efforts their very equality hampers the satisfaction of their desires: 'The same equality that allows every citizen to entertain great ambitions renders all citizens individually weak; it constrains their powers on every side, and simultaneously allows their desires to expand.' For 'when men are almost alike and follow the same path, it is very difficult for any one of them to advance and forge ahead through the uniform crowd that surrounds and presses him.'[31] What Tocqueville detects in democracy is, then, rather than an invisible hand, a fallacy of composition.[32] From the fact that an opportunity is open to anyone it does not follow that it is open to everyone, for everyone's attempting it generates conditions that do not arise when one person, or a minority of people, attempts it. To this logic Tocqueville attributes the danger of an administrative despotism: individuals 'may well admit, as a general principle, that public power should not intervene in private affairs; but, by way of exception, each of them desires its aid in the particular business that engages him, and tries to persuade government to take his part, all the while wishing to curtail it in other cases.' Thus 'the sphere of central power insensibly extends on every side, though each wishes to restrain it.'[33] It is here above all that the root image of resemblance, though morally compelling, may be treacherous and deceptive. Resemblance, as a social principle, does not take account of the interdependence of actions or of the fact that what one person can achieve depends upon what others attempt. This fact was, as we have seen, one that was brought home vividly to the inhabitants of aristocratic society, who were constantly made aware of the interrelation between their success and the interests of others.

It can be brought home to the inhabitants of democratic society, as the Americans have shown, by 'associations,' or by the habit of allying with others to pursue common ends. Tocqueville attaches enormous weight to associations, throughout *Democracy in America* and in its concluding chapter, as the ingredient that makes the difference between a democracy that remains free and a democracy that will become tyrannical. Because associations permit individuals to achieve jointly what one magnate could do single-handed in an aristocracy, he calls them aristocratic, but his calling them this has a further significance, for two reasons. In terms of Tocqueville's conceptual framework, the role played by these associations runs counter to the 'natural' tendencies of democracy as a type but *is* natural to the type of aristocracy. They are aristocratic, as it were, by virtue of their typological place, constituting features essential to the definition of what aristocracy is and definitionally inessential (however functionally vital) to democracy. In terms of Tocqueville's sources, the pluralism of association that he is advocating here is a theme that, in French political thought, is decidedly aristocratic: that there should be political actors with a social existence distinct from that conferred by sovereign will, that these are media through which power should flow, are precisely the components of the *thèse nobiliaire*, and it is just these that Tocqueville resurrects in the face of a new sovereign. Just as democratic majorities acquire 'sovereignty' by a sort of metaphorical displacement – which Tocqueville takes very seriously – so too local associations are the metaphorical aristocracy of the new regime. The new sovereign, like the old, seeks to cultivate a 'courtier spirit,'[34] majorities requiring adulation – claiming 'majesty,' as Proudhon said – no less than kings do; it was, of course, this spirit that had ruined the political independence of the French aristocracy, and it is by means of independent associations that, Tocqueville hopes, the spirit of abject flattery can be avoided in democracy.

It must be stressed that the argument is conducted wholly in terms of what has been called functional equivalence.[35] There is no question of restoring an aristocratic world-view or ontology, for that has vanished through a shift of consciousness that has placed society in 'a new world,' from the interior of which the old one is no longer comprehensible. What is politically crucial in Tocqueville's eyes, however, is not the world-view that is held but the manner in which it is institutionalized: the survival of political life and the cultivation of citizenship flow not from the diffusion of a general idea but from '*the way ... it is established.*'[36] Despite the differences that have rightly been noted between the two volumes of *Democracy in America*, this theme is consistently maintained in the foreword to volume 1 and the conclusion to volume 2: *that* there will be democracy is providentially guaranteed, but *what* democracy will be is a matter of human choice.

How confident he was about good choices being made and about democracy being 'artificially' deflected from bleak passive uniformity is no easy question. Different readers, catching different nuances of Tocqueville's tone, may, of course, reach different conclusions as to his precise degree of optimism. But it might perhaps be noted that this theme is not uniquely tied to the contentious question of his attitude to democracy. Consider, for example, his analysis of the potential linkage between democracy and tyranny, an analysis that hinges on the theme of social atomization: one striking feature of this account is that it is paralleled with some exactness in his description of pre-revolutionary France, where, he maintains, the French too were 'split up ... into small, isolated, mutually indifferent groups.'[37] Here the causal element is not the progress of democracy but a persistent trend of French policy, the endemic centralization that deprives social groups of any political function and thus destroys their life. If in the case of the old regime it is a political element, not a social principle, that he finds to be the social basis of tyranny, then there seems no reason to doubt that Tocqueville believed what he said about democracy: that if it became tyrannical it was because of its institutions, not its principle. And this point is of course quite independent of whether or not he happened to be optimistic about tyranny being avoided, or whether he was optimistic or pessimistic in varying degrees at different times.

A second passage in the *Old Regime* is also revealing here. Tocqueville contrasts the fate of aristocratic societies in England and France: the former, he says, survived, while the latter did not, because it adapted its institutions to changes 'quite unknown to medieval society ... It was precisely these novelties, introduced gradually and artfully into the old order, that gave it a new lease of life and renewed its vigour.'[38] If, then, Tocqueville also imagined that democratic society could retain its political life by adopting (aristocratic) institutions beyond the purview of *its* principles, this would not be in his view a unique or unprecedented occurrence. Indeed, the argument in the *Old Regime*, together with several passages in *Democracy in America*, suggests the view that the normal task of politics is to correct, modify, or compromise social principles, that politics, far from reflecting moral or ontological visions, must resist them.[39] Such a view, as it stands, does not at all imply that the retention of 'life' is inherently improbable; a polity retains life by a method that is indeed contrary to what is natural, but what is natural is defined in terms of the conceptual implications of abstract social constructs such as democracy and is no more probable, as a matter of history, than what is only accidental in the light of the essential logic of such constructs. Such a view would be perfectly consistent with what he says about the inherent partiality of human vision; every regime, its view of reality systematically coloured by its idea or principle, suppresses features of the world with which it cannot easily come to terms, and its survival is at risk for that reason. The risks are different, but there is always, as Proudhon too had come to think, a risk. Such a (Machiavellian) concept of permanent risk is perhaps more precisely appropriate than the model of false consciousness, which, while otherwise illuminating, may blunt the force of Tocqueville's point that there is no *true* consciousness with which the selective social mind can be contrasted – not, at least, of a kind that is available to human knowledge.

In stressing that time brings choices between freedom and corruption and that personal responsibility and self-restraint must be learned, Tocqueville evidently owes much to the civic tradition in political thought; the values taught by associations, and also by local self-government, are plainly the values of citizenship. But as in Proudhon's case, the fit is far from perfect. He sees patronage as a source of politicization rather than corruption, viewing patron-client relations as a spring of public consciousness and treating the independence of citizens from one another as a risk rather than a merit;[40] independence may bring individualism and political isolation. And he does not attribute the maintenance of a political order to its adherence to original principles, as the Machiavellians had done. To enjoy a new lease of life, he held, a polity must, on the contrary, compromise its principles in a sense and adopt institutions that are accidental rather than essential to its type. It is perhaps here that we should look for what is distinctive (though by no means, of course, wholly novel) in his approach, for it is an approach that takes as fundamental the space between principles and action, which is filled, institutionally, in crucially different ways.

It is just for this reason that 'no man on earth can affirm, absolutely and generally, that the new state of societies is better than the old.' What the old was and could have been, what the new is and could be, depend upon the way in which old and new principles come to be 'established.'

What Tocqueville implicitly but fundamentally rejects is a deductive conception of political theory in which all the evaluative decisions are made at the level of ends, and means are treated as of merely instrumental importance, if indeed it is possible, in the context of Tocqueville's approach, to distinguish with any strictness between ends and means in any case. What may cause some discomfort in reading Tocqueville, and may also have led to the posing of inappropriate questions, is a conception of political theory that takes *Leviathan*, by assumption, to be the model for all political argument. There, of course, there is a superbly orderly progression from ontology through psychology and ethics to political obligation, a progression that Tocqueville's manner of arguing does not even faintly resemble. There, too, there is a relative indifference to modes of institutionalization, the manner in which sovereignty is embodied and applied, matters that, while commented upon, scarcely belong to the main architecture of Hobbes's account. Tocqueville's political theory occupies the spaces that Hobbes left vacant; and what it suggests is that an account such as Hobbes's is structurally linked to the rigorously instrumentalist view of reason that *Leviathan* advances. Ends being set, reason suggests means: corresponding to this, at the institutional level, is a formal indifference to the manner of ruling, as opposed to the grounds of legitimation upon which ruling rests. 'Tyranny,' Hobbes says, is merely monarchy 'misliked,' and 'despoticall dominion' is indistinguishable from political sovereignty.[41] The *how* is strictly subordinated to the *what*.

What is stressed in one French tradition, however, and notably by Tocqueville, is the manner. Montesquieu, of course, separated monarchy and despotism as types, while Tocqueville, following classical models still more rigorously, effectively denied despotism the 'honour' of counting as a political type at all.[42] Where both differ radically from the Hobbesian view is in declining to differentiate between regimes in terms of the location of sovereign power and in insisting upon the decisive importance of the mediations between power and obedience. Such mediations, which for Hobbes could only be conditional upon sovereign will and were thus legally dispensable, are the central objects of concern for a tradition that takes the distinction between political and despotic rule to be a qualitative one. In his depiction of monarchy, therefore, Montesquieu imposes conditions upon the administration of justice, conditions that in a Hobbesian model would be outrageous; and Tocqueville depicts a well-institutionalized democratic society as one in which the sovereign people, no less than Montesquieu's monarch, must secure the active concurrence of its subjects in order to exercise its rule. In neither case are distinctions made to hinge upon the location of sovereignty; they hinge upon the mode of its exercise. Nor is this way of thinking confined to theorists who are describable as liberals. Proudhon, in *Principle of Federation*, constructs his theory of political types in terms of the exercise, not the location of power, and this among other things distinguishes his federalism from the theory of sovereignty that we might expect. Georges Sorel, a generation later, was to dissent however unwillingly from Marx in insisting that what matters is not class rule but the manner in which a class institutionalizes itself – that socialism is a meaningless category until its institutional, cultural, moral, and mythic content is supplied. In Sorel's protean politics we may perhaps see an extension, or travesty, of that catholicity of vision that opens theorists such as Montesquieu and Tocqueville to such diverse interpretations. 'Absolute' and 'general' commitments to ends are impossible when the so-called means are decisive, and they may take second place to shifting empirical assessments of institutions and their possibilities.

In Tocqueville's case, this theoretical disposition was strongly reinforced by what he was to make the central theme of *The Old Regime and the French Revolution*: the continuity of administrative styles between the old regime and the new. Viewed from the standpoint of public administration, the upheavals of the Revolution are barely visible; there is a continuous, accelerating trend of centralization, fostered by Capetians, Jacobins, and both Napoleons. The contrast between Tocqueville's view of administration and what he says about the history of moral thinking is striking: in that history there are discontinuities, incommensurabilities, and leaps of imagination – yet these find no parallel in the monotonous history of administration in France, in which local liberties are relentlessly expunged under the most different pretexts but essentially to the same effect. Administrative history is to be taken seriously, quite simply, because institutions are misconceived if taken to be means to ends. It is not just for their policy outcomes that they are significant but, more importantly still, for their reflexive impact upon the society in which they are introduced. It is from the mode of their operation that people learn the most basic attitudes of independence or dependence, responsibility or irresponsibility.

To place American local self-government in the category of 'administration' rather than 'politics,' as Tocqueville does, is not at all, therefore, to demean its importance; even if, on some fairly naïve conception, politics is thought to set ends while administration is thought to set means, that would be no reason to think the former decisively more important than the latter, for in processes of evaluation the two categories, if distinguishable at all, are inseparably linked.[43] It is the latter, moreover, that exercises the more decisively educative force: 'The democratic peoples who have introduced freedom into the political sphere while enlarging despotism in the administrative sphere have been led into the strangest paradoxes. In the conduct of small affairs, where plain common sense is enough, they hold that the citizens are not capable. But they give these citizens immense prerogatives where the government of the whole state is concerned ... It is difficult indeed to imagine how people who have entirely given up managing their own affairs could make a wise choice of those who are to lead them. It is hard to believe that a liberal, energetic, and wise government can ever arise from the votes of a people of servants.'[44] Likewise, when Proudhon says that provinces in a federation should be 'sovereign,' and continues, 'or at least should administer themselves,'[45] no bathos is intended, for Proudhon takes it for granted that self-administration is as crucial as the possession of sovereignty. And when Sorel asks, rhetorically, 'What will happen, then, if after the social revolution industry will have to be managed by groups incapable of running a co-operative today?'[46] we can see how deeply this trend of thinking has penetrated even ideologies in which the political tradition is rejected. It comes to be *socialism* that is presented as a theory of 'local groups ... which one joins in order to achieve something by oneself, to co-operate effectively in projects whose use one can understand'[47] – a description that Tocqueville could have accepted word for word, provided only that the subject were changed. Behind all this we may perhaps see the profound imprint on French political culture of royal politics in the old regime, of policies that, without at all seeking to shift the locus of sovereignty, sought in so predatory a manner to centralize administration that the style of ruling impressed itself as a distinct and crucial issue. The difference between legitimate and illegitimate rule is, as Montesquieu put it, only the difference between the river and the sea; despotism arrives unannounced by any formal transer of powers, and arises from the manner of their employment.

The rival tradition, in which administration is viewed as rigorously subordinate, is perhaps best exemplified by Saint-Simon and Comte and, before them, by the philosophes as Tocqueville describes them in the *Old Regime*. Here the instrumental conception of thinking emerges as the pervasive notion of technique. In one of Saint-Simon's parables a caravan of travellers entrusts itself without reserve to its guides, once its destination has been selected:[48] so too a society must confine itself to the setting of ends and entrust the choice of means to those qualified by knowledge to establish them. Here Hobbes's 'authorization' passes over into a sort of technical commission by which the inexpert empower the expert. That means are separable from ends and also subordinate to them is argued, too, by Comte in an early essay on the separation of desire and opinion. A desire is a wish for some end ('liberty,' 'peace'), while an opinion is a belief that ends can be achieved by 'such and such means.' It is 'reasonable, natural, and necessary' that citizens should have desires but absurd that they should have opinions, for the validity of these depends upon 'a chain of reasoning and reflection' and hence upon 'a special study.'[49] The implications are drawn out by Comte into a scheme of social organization that, if fanciful in some detail, is far from eccentric in depicting a state whose central task is that of economic and social management and whose criteria of achievement are technical in nature.[50] Comte's dream is Tocqueville's nightmare.

The managerial vision had been entertained, too, Tocqueville complained, by the rationalists and reformers of the Enlightenment, who came to see political society as an artefact of power that could be shaped and directed by its rulers and their advisers. What they neglected, above all, was that a polity is not an artefact of one mind but a concurrence[51] of many minds that is shaped by the manner of their relations. The institutions through which relations are established are not mere instruments but serve to define how people see themselves and one another, a point that the old regime neglected to its cost, for its own autocratic style and its contempt for due process gave its subjects a 'revolutionary education.'[52] Its autocracy was often well-intentioned, but how it proceeded was in the long run more decisive to its fate than what it had attempted to do. This contrast between artefact and concurrence, between things *made* by human design and things *composed* by human interaction, is quite fundamental to Tocqueville's view of theory and practice. Theory and practice are different, and theorists are often disastrous practitioners, because an order composed of active agents who respond to one another's acts simply cannot have the order that the mind can impose on things or concepts or words. The logic is different. 'One finds it almost as difficult to be inconsequent in one's speech as one generally finds it to be consistent in action.'[53] And 'What is a merit in the writer may well be a vice in the statesman.'[54] The writer can organize and shape his material at will, but the statesman who tries to do so can produce order only by suppressing citizenship.

Tocqueville is a liberal, though as an aristocrat rather than a bourgeois, a Frenchman rather than an Englishman, his liberalism doubtless has features not to be found in other liberalisms.[55] But because of the structure of his political thinking, we should be cautious about attributing to him a certain familiar kind of liberalism, for to do so would be to miss his point precisely. Liberalism is currently familiar as a doctrine of diversity: in opposition to totalitarianisms of the right or the left and in opposition to the monistic ideologies that underpin or justify them, liberalism is frequently presented as a doctrine to which ethical and cognitive diversity is central. In liberal society, we are told, many ways of life can flourish and many divergent choices can legitimately be made; and what justifies liberalism, we are told, is that philosophy itself cannot decisively privilege one way of life or one moral choice above another. Sometimes the argument is made in terms of the absence of a hierarchy of values, no preference for one ranking over another being rationally demonstrable;[56] sometimes it is made in terms of the corrigibility of thought and the impossibility of final judgment;[57] sometimes it is made in terms of incommensurability, normative and cognitive elements being locked together, it is claimed, in self-enclosed and self-reinforcing sets, no undisputed cognitive ground remaining upon which normative issues can be resolved.[58] For one reason or another the contestation between rival views is *essential* – not, that is, merely a product of ignorance, which is in principle remediable. And because there is legitimate moral disagreement, a legitimate political order must respect it and is called liberal to the extent that it does so.

In a curious way such a picture depends upon the deductivism that is so marked a feature of very illiberal conceptions of politics. It is Comte turned upside-down. In the technocratic vision, ends being given, means are properly authoritarian. In diversitarian liberalism, since ends are contested, institutions must permit freedom. The conclusion is liberal, but the argument has illiberal credentials and authoritarian implications: if we could agree, then freedom would have no place, for political freedom depends for its rationale solely upon the presence of contestation in other realms. From a liberal point of view this ought to be worrying. But whatever general worries may be provoked, in the context of Tocqueville's thinking there are reasons for questioning this proposed definition of liberalism. What concerned Tocqueville was precisely the question of achieving liberty under conditions of agreement, or, to use Comte's terms, 'consensus' – which was precisely what was supposed to render freedom unnecessary. But Tocqueville's argument for a human point of view, a point of view to which complete and perfect knowledge is denied, is easily confused with a diversitarian argument that he was not at all concerned to make.

Every society, according to Tocqueville, is a *closed* one, to employ a later vocabulary; like theorists such as Maistre or Burke, he insists upon the necessity of prejudice, of a substratum of opinion that is not open, normally, to doubt and that makes possible both the stability and the progressiveness of a society. 'It can never be that there are no dogmatic beliefs, that is, opinions that men accept on trust and without discussion ... [F]or a society to exist and, even more, for the society to prosper, it is essential that all the citizens' minds should always be ordered and held together by some leading ideas; and that could never happen unless each of them sometimes came to draw his opinions from the same source and was ready to accept some beliefs ready made.'[59] When he speaks, then, of the sameness of belief as a distinguishing feature of democratic society, it cannot be the holding of the same beliefs that he means, for that is a feature of all societies; it is, rather, belief in sameness, or a condition in which beliefs are not only commonly held but also of such a kind that diversity is only weakly recognized or encouraged. In this he sees certain dangers. But his response is not at all to seek either to weaken or to modify democratic belief. Consider, for example, what he says about America: 'In the moral world, everything is classified, co-ordinated, foreseen, and decided. In the world of politics everything is agitated, contested, and uncertain. In the one case obedience is passive, though voluntary; in the other there is independence, contempt of experience, and jealousy of all authority. Far from harming each other, these two apparently opposed tendencies work together and seem to lend mutual support.'[60]

This passage is extremely revealing of the nature of Tocqueville's political proposals. It shows, first, that he did not at all consider diversity of belief to be necessary to freedom or 'independence' and that, in his view, uniformity of belief 'in the moral world' may perfectly well accompany (non-revolutionary) political conflict. Secondly, it shows that he did not consider belief in diversity to be necessary to freedom either, the Americans as he observed them having achieved a vigorous political life despite the homogeneity of their world-view. Thirdly, it reveals the operation in Tocqueville's thought of independence as something not to be confused with uniqueness or variety; to be independent is not to be different but to act for oneself, and independence is neither more nor less likely to occur in a homogeneous than in a diverse society.

The conditions for independence and for variety are, of course, in part substantially similar, and arguments for the one and for the other may significantly overlap. Tocqueville's account of democracy was to be put to emphatic use in Mill's *On Liberty* in support of a classic diversitarian case. Mill and Tocqueville share a fear of public opinion, the wearing down of the individual by social pressure, and clearly one may entertain this fear whether it is the independence of the individual from others or the difference of the individual from others that one fundamentally values. What we find in Tocqueville, however, is not primarily a valuing of that 'eccentricity' or difference that Mill saw as the motor of progress: what Tocqueville stresses, rather to the contrary, is the necessity of trust or consensus or custom to progress, and if the progress of civilization is endangered, that, he says, is due to democratic man's lack of faith in anything he has not demonstrated for himself. What we do find in Tocqueville is something much more akin to the argument for autonomy that Mill himself presents alongside his plea for diversity.

When Mill says that what matters is that an individual's plan of life should be 'his own,'[61] he is proposing a value that can be defended quite independently of any case for diversity. Indeed, it retains its force in that age of consensual uniformity that, borrowing from Comte, Mill foresees: when truth is settled, it is still essential that each individual's understanding of it should be his own, that it should be present to him not as someone else's fiat but as something whose justification each personally can grasp.[62] It is a sense of oneself as a thinking subject that Mill here regards as crucial and that allies him with Tocqueville even in the more Comtean moments of *On Liberty*; and this sense, while of prime importance politically, has little enough to do with the issues attending the philosophical justification of belief. Whether there is diversity or unity in the standards of justification is one question: another is whether or not institutions and political culture permit individuals to retain a picture of themselves as deliberative, active centres of conscious life, capable of thinking, willing, and planning, whose deliberate actions can make a perceptible difference to the circumstances in which they find themselves. It is to the recovery of this self-image that Mill's argument in part and Tocqueville's in general are directed; and while Mill's risks assimilation to a very different argument about cognitive or ethical diversity, Tocqueville's should not, for, as we have seen, he is convinced of the compatibility of a 'decided' moral world and a political world that is 'contested and uncertain.' They are compatible because and to the extent that appropriate institutions mediate between social beliefs and individual action – and appropriate institutions would solicit co-operation rather than mere obedience, foster a sense of responsibility, and bring home to individuals what they can achieve by collaboration.

The difference between tyranny and political life, then, is established neither by the location of sovereignty nor by the diffusion of one set of social beliefs rather than another, nor indeed by diversity in social belief. Tocqueville shares with Montesquieu the view that sovereignty may be tyrannically or politically mediated in its exercise; in an age of ideology he adds to this the point that social doctrines may likewise be differently mediated and that, from a political point of view, everything hinges on the nature of their mediation. The principles that govern the success or failure of mediating institutions are distinct from the principles governing the justification of the ends that are sought through them. That democratic beliefs are morally true, or that in some way their truth does not exclude the truth of rival social beliefs, or that one cannot properly speak of truth in a realm beyond what is strictly speaking one of knowledge – all are possibilities at which Tocqueville may hint but to which he gives only fragmentary and quite inconclusive attention; for he does not see such questions as politically central. It would be a mistake to suppose that he therefore saw political science as value-free; he plainly did not. But the values that are central for the political scientist are not necessarily the same as the values whose contestation and expression are displayed in a given society. Of this, ironically, Tocqueville's only indifferent success as a political actor supplies compelling evidence.[63]

What Tocqueville calls 'political life' is a morally charged concept. It involves the moral rejection of what we may call political *death*, a condition to which, as we have seen, both old and new regimes may tend, a condition in which the inhabitants of an order become mere recipients of government, losing – sullenly in the old regime, quite cheerfully in the new – the capacity to act for themselves. Political life arises only with the recognition that order is constituted by the interrelation or concurrence of agents who count for something, who can form and execute projects singly or jointly, and who see themselves and others as bearing responsibility. Other images of order, of course, underpin social life and set limits to what can be done politically: the image of a chain of being, from which aristocrats derive notions of hierarchy and honour, or of the pacific flock, from which democrats receive images of universal justice. But these can lend themselves to a *political* order only under particular institutional conditions; and it is these, not the ultimate ends that politics is made to serve, that determine whether or not citizenship is possible. As Proudhon too had come to think, one is a citizen only in confronting a question. He did not insist, though, as Rousseau had done, that it had to be the *right* question, because, seeing the process of self-government as having its own inherent worth, he did not need or wish to represent it as the expression of a moral doctrine.

PART III: CITIZENSHIP DISPLACED

5

Comte and the Withering Away of the State

Decentralist themes have formed a persistent undercurrent to the *étatisme* of modern French political experience, as the examples of Proudhon and Tocqueville clearly show. There is no single decentralist impulse: there is, rather, a series of diverse complaints and proposals elicited by a state that has sought, for one reason or another, to erase local sentiment, to standardize the administration of its regions, and to concentrate political life at a national centre. One kind of objection has been prompted by social or political pluralism; a second kind – perhaps the most familiar – is inspired by ideals of self-government, ideals that would, it was feared, be wholly thwarted in a centralized unitary state; a third kind of objection expresses the conservative anxiety that central power is the instrument wielded by levelling masses. In each case conceptions of decentralization reflect 'a whole philosophy' of society and government, as Stanley Hoffmann has stressed,[1] and the mode of decentralization that is envisaged throws light upon the philosophy that inspired it. It is for this reason that much interest attaches to a case that falls outside the scope of Hoffmann's classic discussion, that of Auguste Comte, who in the *Système de politique positive* called for the dissolution of the nation-state into regional units, sometimes termed 'cités,' sometimes 'républiques,' sometimes 'patries,' sometimes 'sociétés civiles.' For just how this proposal relates to Comte's 'whole philosophy' has never been explored.

Comte's proposal sets something of a puzzle for the historian of ideas. Diverse though the strands of decentralist thinking are, none of them appears to suggest a context for what Comte was to say. He was, obviously, no pluralist, but the founding theorist of consensus. He was no classical republican theorist of self-government and did not for a moment regret the extinction – which he saw as inevitable – of political consciousness by executive power. He was not in any proper sense a conservative, condemning 'la doctrine rétrograde' as acidly as he rejected democracy (and specifically condemning the conservative fondness for local powers).[2] Though a provincial by birth, he was a Parisian by adoption and did not share at all in the hostility to France's capital that so frequently surfaces in modes of decentralist thought. He was not (to employ one obvious contemporary contrast) a Proudhonian who saw decentralism as a weapon against financial power; he proposed to confer absolute power on bankers. Nor was he (to employ the second obvious contrast) a Tocquevillean who valued decentralization as a means of diffusing responsibility; he saw in history a progressive concentration of responsibility and welcomed it. He was an authoritarian, a rationalist, a believer in hierarchy; his essential themes are those against which decentralizers have rebelled.

Comte's decentralism, then, is in some respects peculiar. Moreover, if we turn to the evolution of his own thinking, it is hard to identify even there a context for his proposal, which is scarcely one for which his earlier writings have prepared us. In the *Cours de philosophie positive* the persistence of the nation-state appears to have been assumed. In a still earlier essay Comte had explicitly contended that the expansive power of industrial civilization was such that 'men and nations are continually driven to form wider and wider associations.'[3] Like Saint-Simon, together with whom he is the founding theorist of 'industrial society,' Comte had stressed the ecumenical properties of *industrie*; like Proudhon he had drawn from Saint-Simon a contrast between a belligerent order of nations founded upon war and a pacific universal order founded upon work. But unlike Proudhon he had not previously attributed to pacifism any challenge to the existence of nation-states. Even where the context of his argument naturally invited such a challenge, Comte had contented himself with predicting more 'amicability' among industrial nations,[4] without suggesting at all, as he was later to do, that their very existence would be undermined by the substitution of work for war as the typical mode of human behaviour.

Why, then, did Comte change his mind? The reasons, to be explored below, are complex, and to find them we must pick our way through thoughts that are both intricate and obsessive. But the drift of Comte's thinking is not difficult to see. What it reveals is a series of displacements through which the attributes of citizenship are systematically transferred from the political to other realms, displacements through which the polity is progressively drained of meaning. The beginnings of this process are evident even in Comte's earliest surviving writings, where we can already see the transformation of civic themes into themes of organization. In the *Discourse on the Arts and Sciences*, Rousseau had written: 'We have physicists, geometers, chemists, astronomers, poets, musicians, and painters: we no longer have any citizens'; his point, of course, was to distinguish public spirit from intellectual specialism and to rescue what had been meant by citizenship from that malign sophistication in which Europe had come to place its faith. But compare the equivalent passage in one of Comte's earliest essays: 'Where are the scientific ideas common to our physicists, our geometers, our doctors, our chemists, etc.? It is only too clear that there are none – and they believe themselves to be associated! See what happens at their meetings; take as an example the most enlightened body in Europe, in the whole world, the Academy of Sciences in Paris. When a discussion arises that demands knowledge of chemistry, only the chemists take part, and the same goes for the other sciences. Where, then is the society?'[5] He complains, no less than did Rousseau, of dissociation, but it is to 'general ideas,' or to 'une connaissance plus générale,' not to a general will, that he looks for a solution. The society that he has in mind, moreover, is in the first instance a society of savants who, in reflecting on their own interrelation, are eventually to supply political society with a principle of order. Political society must, Comte stresses, receive this principle willingly and must freely renounce the absurd counter-principles that it has learned from deluded or unscrupulous sophists; but its role – as theocrats such as Maistre had also held – can only be to accept. It is not the citizen who is to practise the art of generalizing: it is the savant, or, later, when even the savants prove disappointing, it is the savant of savants, the sociologist, who in turn passes over into the figure of the secular priest.

As this trend of thinking develops and accelerates in Comte's argument, the idea of *political* society becomes increasingly unintelligible. In fact, as the notion of a general order is identified first with a common philosophy and then with a secular religion, the idea of political society becomes increasingly threatening to Comte. Its claim to enjoy a general authority is perceived as a rival claim, and its proposed dissolution is evidently intended to leave nothing standing between the organs of brute material production and the spiritual authority of the positivist Church. The devolution of powers is not intended, then, as in the later Proudhon and in Tocqueville, to cultivate political citizenship: on the contrary, it is intended to assure that the political locus of civic values should not stand in the way of their metaphorical displacement to the realm of knowledge and spirit.

Comte's proposal for the abolition of the state is developed in general in chapter 5 of the second volume of the *Système* and in detail in chapter 5 of the fourth volume; there is also a useful and often revealing abridgment in the *Catéchisme positiviste*, Comte's didactic manual of the moral and social doctrine. While the proposal as such is new, it is presented as an essential part of a program that he had long advocated: the separation of spiritual and temporal power, in turn a case of the separation of theory from practice. That theme had been emphatically introduced in Comte's seminal 1822 essay, 'Plan des travaux scientifiques nécessaires pour réorganiser la société.' Even-handedly hostile to the popular or 'critical' doctrine and the royalist or 'retrograde' doctrine, Comte ascribes the vices of both these political trends of post-revolutionary France to a common source. Both have failed to separate the theoretical task of constructing 'a system of general ideas' from the practical task of deciding upon 'the mode of distributing power.' Their common failure to arrive at a system of general ideas appropriate to the (industrial) character of modern society renders their mutual squabbles sterile; it also brings to power a class of incompetents, for, in the absence of a co-ordinating theory ('conception'), the 'subordinate' faculty of eloquence ('expression') acquires a wholly false predominance.[6] Comte opposes the just claims of the savants to those of the current political class: 'Since [the] tasks are theoretical, it is clear that the men whose profession is that of forming theoretical combinations in a methodical manner, that is, the savants engaged in the study of empirical science, are the only ones whose mode of capacity and intellectual training satisfies the necessary conditions.' They alone enjoy 'uncontested authority' in the modern world. They are, moreover, men who form a truly international society, 'a real coalition, compact, active, all of whose members understand and communicate with one another easily and continuously.'[7] Even *les industriels*, who also have supra-national interests, fall prey to 'savage patriotism.' Only the savants, therefore, can conduct a movement of European (and eventually global) regeneration: the mission of *les industriels* is to wield temporal power under the spiritual authority of the savants and to 'organize the administrative system.'[8]

Comte's proposed redistribution of authority recalls somewhat two famous political parables: Plato's parable of the ship, and Saint-Simon's *parabole*,[9] a thought-experiment in which Saint-Simon had invited the French nation to compare the consequences of a sudden hypothetical loss of its entire ruling class and a numerically smaller loss of its best scientists, industrialists, and master craftsmen. But it is Comte's differences from both Plato and Saint-Simon that are more revealing. Like Plato, Comte sees current political debate as vacuous bickering among specialists in rhetoric (whom he too calls 'sophistes'), and like Plato he ascribes authority to the man of knowledge; but whereas Plato sought a 'coalescence' of power and philosophy, Comte wishes to maintain the separation of the two, distinguishing strictly between the spiritual dominance of the savants and the temporal dominance of the *industriels*. Like Saint-Simon, whose own parable had implied a transfer of power to the scientific, intellectual, and industrial classes, Comte seeks to demonstrate the lack of functional legitimacy enjoyed by the present political class. But he is equally concerned, as Saint-Simon, in Comte's view, was not, to distinguish the proper role of science on the one hand from that of industry on the other. This was, indeed – as far as one can tell from a tangled story of bruised egoisms – the source of Comte's break with the Saint-Simonians shortly after the 'Plan des travaux ... ' was published.[10] Saint-Simon's failure to distinguish between the theoretical and practical tasks of renovation was the issue that Comte announced as the reason for his break; and it was the Saint-Simonians' confusion of spiritual and temporal functions that was the principal target of Comte's continuing hostility. For all their claims to modernity and their rejection of ancient models, he notes, they present 'as the final stage of social perfection, a sort of revival of Egyptian or Hebrew theocracy, founded upon a veritable fetishism, vainly concealed under the name of pantheism.'[11] In the light of Comte's later enthusiastic view of fetishism as a mode of religious belief well suited to conveying a sense of reverence and devotion, this critique of Saint-Simon's disciples is noteworthy.

The proper division of spiritual and temporal power – 'le grand fait politique' of the Catholic and feudal period – is further explored in another early essay, 'Considérations sur le pouvoir spirituel' (1826). Here the topic of associational scale is given some attention: the separation of spiritual from temporal power permitted a European spiritual community overarching the temporal polities. By uniting 'populations' that were 'too numerous and too varied' to dispense with separate temporal governments, the Catholic church 'was thus able to reconcile, to a degree that was hitherto chimerical, the opposed advantages of political centralization and dispersal.'[12] But political dispersal ('diffusion') here does not refer to the dissolution of the nation-state or, to avoid anachronism, kingdom. The most obvious reading is that the dispersal in question was that from empire to kingdom. True, Comte refers some ten pages later to the possible dissolution of the nation into 'partial communities':[13] but this, he says, was a possibility raised by the erosion of spiritual power, which deprived the kingdoms of the 'lien moral' upon which their unity depended. Disintegration was in the past averted by the 'concentration' or intensification of temporal power; and since what Comte is proposing is the restoration of the *lien moral* by a renewed spiritual power, it would be reasonable to infer that in the future, according to Comte's scheme, the possibility of disintegration will altogether vanish. It is true that spiritual authority is said to be indefinitely extendable in space, while political authority is not, but nothing is said to suggest that there has to be any absolute reduction of the territorial scale of political association; indeed, it is claimed that 'as civilization advances, both kinds of association increase in their extent.'[14]

Comte's critique of the state, then, bears at this stage upon its concentration of power, not its territorial extent. Such concentration is of course directly offensive in that the removal of spiritual support obliges the state to be oppressive with regard to other temporal associations within its boundaries. This theme is continued in the *Cours*, for which the earlier essays were written as prospectuses. Comte offers criticisms of the 'sovereignty' and the 'dictatorship' of temporal power[15] but again with reference only to its improper concentration of functions. He speaks again of 'désagrégation,' but again the reference is most naturally taken to be to the progressive collapse of a system of rule ('theologico-military') rather than to the disintegration of territory.[16] Moreover, the *Cours* adds to this some remarks of a quite strongly centralist tendency. One of the very few merits of the revolutionary school, he says, was that it understood the need for political centralization and rejected the 'retrograde' doctrine of 'the dispersal of political sites' ('foyers').[17] Political centralization makes possible the healthy dominance of capital cities, which are the true sites of progress.[18] The preoccupation with 'small populations' limits the modern relevance of ancient political theory, despite its genius.[19] Patriotism, though (as in the 1822 essay) a 'savage' sentiment, can be moderated and tamed by 'la charité universelle' and thus become a creative force.[20] And most

tellingly of all, Comte declares himself in favour of French centralism –
'essentially normal' – rather than English localism. The forces of
indsutry may ally themselves either with 'pouvoir central' (as in France)
or 'pouvoir local' (as in Engländ); the former alliance is to be preferred,
as it frees industrial forces from 'local pressures.'[21]

Now the *Cours* reserves the detailed discussion of the political forms
of renovation for the later *Système*.[22] We should not, therefore, be
surprised to find in the latter work proposals that are absent from the
expressly general discussion of the former. But it is surely surprising to
find in the *Système* a striking proposal not only unannounced in the
earlier writings but even contra-indicated there. For now the deconcentration of political functions is taken to require territorial disintegration, the direction of industry by *pouvoir local*; this, indeed, is what it
seems principally to require. As Comte enumerates the various modes
and levels of association in the second volume of the *Système*, the state
literally vanishes even as a possible category. There is the family, the
city ('cité'), and humanity; and the 'smallest city already contains all the
elements and tissues required by the existence' of humanity.[23] Any
concept of association intermediate between city and humanity is
merely an arbitrary one; the 'generic term "state"' is 'superfluous'; it is
'an impossibility to distinguish precisely among the various intermediary *states*, under the almost arbitrary names of "province," "nation,"
and so on.'[24] In the completed associational vision, the (positivist)
Church 'freely unites the cities, as each city spontaneously unites the
families within ... It alone can contain universality.'[25]

There is, as we have seen, nothing new in the stress on the difference
in scale between spiritual and temporal orders, nor in the stress upon
the independence of the two, though there is something new, and
perhaps suggestive of a more conflictual view of the relations between
the two orders, in the claim that the independence of the spiritual order
depends upon its larger and more comprehensive scale.[26] But what is
more obviously new is the treatment of the nation-state as a purely
artificial and (as the *Catéchisme* puts it) 'anomalous' thing.[27] Its
'exorbitant' (and, in the *Catéchisme*) 'monstrous' dimensions are the
result of a premature attempt to extend the scale of human association
before the spiritual foundation had been prepared. Any temporal
association larger than the city rests on 'factitious and violent bonds,'
the 'natural limit' of association being fixed by the city and its rural
environs.[28] And 'Instead of becoming larger as human association extends, political domination must, on the contrary, greatly diminish.'[29]

Hence, in the final order the normal size of temporal units will not be greater than that of 'Tuscany, Belgium, Holland, and eventually Sicily, Sardinia, etc.' Population will range between one and three million inhabitants, with a normal density of sixty per square kilometre. 'Before the end of the nineteenth century, France will have been freely decomposed into seventeen independent republics, each made up of five of the present departments.' The other great nations will follow suit; at the beginning of the twentieth century 'Portugal and Ireland, if no division occurs there, will be the largest republics of the West.'[30] In the fourth volume of the *Système* Comte adds to this already sufficiently exact prediction a wealth of detail, including a full geographical definition of the seventeen independent regions into which France, the model for other nations, is to be dissolved, and a program and timetable of devolution by which the present states are to divest themselves, step by step, of their sovereignty.[31]

Proudhon's *Du principe fédératif* – published nine years after the final volume of the *Système* appeared – epitomizes the theme of radical decentralism in nineteenth-century thought; it also draws to the fullest extent possible upon the provincialist and pluralist critique of sovereignty that forms a persistent undercurrent to French political writing. But Proudhon's critique of the 'monstrous' nation-state is anticipated by Comte's in its insistence upon the inherently limited scale of administration, its theme of *libre association*, its critique of theocracy, and even in its proposed regional division, though Comte's mania for precision here is not matched by Proudhon.[32] Comte even anticipates Proudhon's (unpopular) opposition to the unification of Italy. But Comte's proposed decomposition goes beyond what Proudhon was shortly to demand. For Proudhon retained, beyond the 'republics,' a 'state,' which he describes as 'prime mover and general director,' as 'the highest expression of progress,' and as 'the spirit of the community.'[33] The attributes that even Proudhon would be willing to leave to a minimal federal state are stripped away from temporal organization by Comte. The role of 'general director,' the task of ensuring 'progress,' and the symbolic representation of 'community' are precisely the properties that Comte reserves to the spiritual power, or 'sacerdoce.' Only the spiritual power, overarching the cities, has 'généralité,' for 'spécialité' is a feature of the practical men, bankers and entrepreneurs, who rule in the city.[34] Only the spiritual power embodies progress, for the temporal power – as its very name implies, Comte points out – inhabits only the present.[35] And only the spiritual power bears the spirit of community, for 'union will be religious, not political.'[36]

If an explanation for the later Comte's radical critique of the state can be found, it must surely lie in the currents of intellectual transition that led him from the *Cours* to the *Système*. This, unfortunately, is an area in which one can say little with complete confidence, for the relation between the earlier and later Comte is one on which there is no complete agreement. Some, such as F.A. Hayek – disposed to admire neither Comte – see the later writings as a continuous extension of the fallacies of the earlier.[37] Others, such as, notably, J.S. Mill, distinguish between the rigorous and constructive rationalism of the earlier writings and the sad intellectual decline so evident in the later.[38] This is not an issue that can possibly be resolved here. All one can hope to do, in a limited context such as this, is to identify some incontestable general transitions, without passing any judgment as to their weight in Comte's philosophy considered as a whole.

Comte himself admitted no discontinuity between the *Cours* and the *Système*. At the outset of the latter work he claims merely to be addressing a question different from that which had preoccupied his 'ouvrage fondamental': in the *Cours* he had defined the nature of the positivist renovation; now he sets out to discover its conditions. 'Ici le coeur domine,' he writes:[39] the task is to establish the motivations essential to the transition to a positivist order and to its maintenance. We need not, of course, attach any special weight to Comte's obviously self-interested claim, and in at least two (related) respects it is disingenuous, though probably unconsciously so. First, the 'religion of humanity' developed in the *Système* cuts quite across the view, affirmed in the *Cours*, that the morality of positivism 'requires no religious consecration.'[40] The opening pages of the *Système* present the claim that the earlier work had been directed against 'theologism' rather than religion as such, but this claim is not borne out by what Comte had actually said. In the *Système* the forms of primitive and non-theological religion, which are called 'fetishist,' are held up for admiration as precursors of the positivist spirit; in the *Cours*, fetishism, as we have seen, was a term of abuse, employed at the expense of the retrograde tendencies of the Saint-Simonian school.

Second, and notoriously, Comte came to adopt a quite different view of women, albeit one that is no less offensive to modern feminism. In the *Cours* Comte had maintained the traditional and patriarchal view that women, like children, were properly subordinate to the husband and father or were, even, directly assimilated to the category of children.[41] They were unsuited not only to citizenship but even to the government of the household.[42] Such a view is overturned in the *Système* (and *Catéchisme*), in which the view of family life changes significantly. Though they still do not command, women are elevated to a new status as scarcely terrestrial objects of adoration (of a decreasingly physical kind).[43] Intriguingly, Comte's categories, strictly interpreted, rescue women from the permanent childhood decreed by the *Cours* only at the cost of consigning them, in the *Système*, to the realm of the illustrious dead,[44] for, like the dead, they can represent but cannot act.

These two revisions – Comte's new-found admiration for primitive religion and his discovery of ideal womanhood – are linked in the new stress on *le coeur*, love, and sentiment. Primitive religion foreshadowed the organization of emotional life that the positivist age is to perfect; and the women are celebrated as 'le sexe aimant' or 'affectif.' It is hard to avoid the suspicion that Comte's radical critique of the state is in some way related to this movement in his thinking. For the affective superiority of women and the new fetishism of the religion of humanity are the twin supports of the positivist *sacerdoce*; and it is evidently for the sake of enhancing spiritual authority that the state is required to dissolve itself. But the connections are indirect and sometimes intricate, and must be established by reasonable speculation rather than by direct evidence.

To consider, first, the question of religion: Comte seeks to deflect his earlier critique from religion as such to 'theology' and thus distinguishes emphatically in the *Système* between theistic and non-theistic religion. What he now admires in the fetishism that preceded polytheistic and monotheistic religions is its capacity to relate together 'man' and 'the world' and to convince men of their dependence upon and necessary submission to their natural milieu.[45] The theistic religions, in contrast, assigned to man an altogether exaggerated importance, granting him privileges that distinguished him essentially from other orders of life.[46] Now it is just this relation between man and world that provides a point of departure for the doctrine of political organization in the *Système*. Man expresses his relation to the world through the ownership of property; through his possession and use of physical things he comes to terms with his dependence upon his milieu and the necessary predominance of the 'outside' over the 'inside.' Just as 'one cannot conceive of any family that does not have possession of the supplies and instruments required by its daily wants,' so too a *patrie* requires territory, 'general property.' Only 'through the soil' can human powers be related to 'the external order.'[47]

The fetishist-positivist conception of man's place in the world and his necessary accommodation to it carries with it a distinctive view of territory, the 'material foundation' of the *patrie*. Its territory is imagined as productive material, 'le sol,' and not at all as a public space in which actions are performed and observed, experiences shared and compared. The *patrie* or city is brute materiality, a 'nutritive apparatus.'[48] Its meaning comes to light not in its own institutions but in the Church, which explains, guides, and celebrates its tasks; the honour that was once attached to its own public life – 'civic enthusiasm' – is merely a form of 'collective egoism.'[49] This, surely, supplies a primary reason for the elimination of the state as a level of organization beyond the city, and also for Comte's refusal – despite his admiration for Aristotle – to distinguish the city from an economic institution, or from 'une simple ville.'[50] Temporal organization is productive by its very nature, and any further dimension of meaning is inappropriate to it: hence, a state, as a general ordering of productive regional associations, or an Aristotelian city, as something more than a 'village,' is a conceptual impossibility. All public manifestations other than those of the positivist Church are therefore out of place. The theatre is to be 'irrevocably extinguished' as an irrational and immoral rival, not, as in Rousseau's *Lettre à d'Alembert*, to civic institutions but to the festivals of unity organized by the spiritual power.[51] The long-despised 'parleurs,' the specialists in publicity, are finally to be removed from power,[52] and their chief instrument of domination, parliamentary government, is to be among the first institutional victims of the transition to positivism.[53] Moreover, and perhaps most significantly, what is retained from earlier political tradition is not the language of citizenship ('civic enthusiasm') but the language of executive power. In civic thinking – Rousseau again provides the most convenient contrast – the particular loyalties of the executive agent were seen as the most pressing threat to the public loyalties that defined the citizen; but Comte advocates what is, in Rousseau's terms, the total corruption of public life, by seeking to transform all 'citoyens' into 'fonctionnaires.'[54] Duty is exhausted by the fulfilment of an officially sanctioned productive task, to which general reflection (as opposed to general consecration) is inappropriate.

Now, as it happens, all of these themes – the proposed extinction of 'the public professions,'[55] the onslaught upon the *parleurs*, and the transformation of the citizen into the functionary – had been anticipated in Comte's earlier writings. So, of course, had the primary theme of the transformation of temporal association into productive organization, which is the foundation of the whole doctrine in its social aspect. But this theme and its associated aspects are linked now to a rejection of space as the primary medium of association. An essentially spatial society is to give way to an essentially temporal one; for what the religion of humanity takes over from natural religion is above all the worship of ancestors. 'It is not only today that each man, in striving to appreciate what he owes to others, recognizes that the ensemble of his predecessors made a far greater contribution than his contemporaries. Such disproportion was evident, to a lesser degree, in the most distant epochs, as is indicated by the moving tributes always rendered to the dead, as Vico remarks so well.'[56] As humanity progresses, what each generation can contribute becomes smaller in relation to what it has inherited from past generations. Consequently, the sharing of territorial space by contemporaries becomes decreasingly important, proportionately, as a field of moral experience. It is one's existence in time, celebrated in dogma and cult and omnipresent in the structuring of time enforced by the positivist calendar, that supplies one's identity. It is this, above all, that permits Comte to reduce territory to productive material and to draw out from his old hostility to public life so radical a conclusion.

An important index is provided here by Comte's changing use of three associational concepts, 'sympathie,' 'solidarité,' and 'continuité.' In the *Cours*, he had distinguished between the former two.[57] Sympathy is a purely affective element, he maintained, with little if any cognitive significance; it is something spontaneously excited by 'all sorts of representations of human life,' even fictional ones. Solidarity, which is the conception of unity induced by the completed hierarchy of positive knowledge, consists in a 'rational history' or 'real science,' which brings 'the ensemble of human events' into 'co-ordinated series' and thus demonstrates their necessary relations ('enchaînement'). But in the *Système* the two concepts, together with a third, continuity, are demarcated and valued differently.[58] Sympathy is no longer ranked below solidarity, for with Comte's new trend of thinking the ties of sympathy, expressed in the family and celebrated by the Church, are the foundation of social order. What he had previously called solidarity, the conception of humanity's essential unity and integration in time, is now called continuity and is the central principle of spiritual dogma. This leaves solidarity in a curious and difficult position. It is no longer a principle of either affective or intellectual unity; Comte now uses the term to refer to the interdependence of contemporaries, sharing physical space and lacking either the affective unity of the family or the intellectual unity of the Church. But it is just this equivocal mode of association that is assigned to temporal organization: 'the civil power can never be anything but an organ of solidarity.'[59]

What Comte has constructed for himself here, without any apparent borrowing from Hegel or other identifiable sources, is a triad equivalent to that of family, civil society, and state. His occasional use of the term 'société civile'[60] may reflect his sense that the associations of productive life are intermediate between the immediate unity of the family on the one hand and rational universality on the other. Like the civil society of Hegel and his eighteenth-century sources, Comte's *société civile* is a web of merely objective reciprocities and interdependencies not wholly distinguishable from the realm of private egoism. Even in their own sphere, that of production, the directors of practical life lack the requisite sense of general order, which is supplied instead by the spiritual power.[61] Civil society, in short, is inherently incomplete, lacking that sense of itself that the scope of its own relations demands. Even the process of government is brought within this model of imperfect association: the desire to command is a useful egoism, a 'fortunate ambition' that, though private in motivation, is incidentally of public benefit to those who are commanded.[62]

But what is set beyond the civil society is not, as we have seen, a state – a 'superfluous' concept – but spiritual authority itself. Disguised beneath the long-standing theme of the separation of temporal and spiritual power is a transfer of attributes from the former to the latter. Perhaps that is why, as Comte predicts in a sombre passage, the temporal leaders ('patriciat') 'secretly hate' the *sacerdoce*.[63] The theme of separation, as such, is conflict-free, resting on that natural respect of one intelligence for another that the *Cours* had especially stressed: 'spiritual authority ... always rests on the confidence spontaneously accorded to intellectual and moral superiority.'[64] But the hidden theme of transfer brings into play a bitter though unavowable rivalry. The spiritual power is not only the object of the secret hatred of the *patriciat* but is also unable to win more than the 'cold respect' of its adversary, the proletariat.[65] Suspended between the two great temporal forces of wealth and number, the spiritual power maintains only precarious security; it is tolerated by the employing class as a source of legitimacy in the face of proletarian resentment and provisionally welcomed by the employed class as an ally against patrician exploitation. It has, in short, become a strikingly political institution, the heir not only of the conceptual attributes of the state but also of its problems. Comte's vision of a universal order is not, as most are, a vision of essential harmony, and his proposed elimination of the state is not the product of any imagined cessation of essential conflict.

The second tempting line of inquiry concerns the social basis of order and Comte's self-conscious reliance in the *Système* upon traditionally non-political elements. Here the case of women is by far the more important, but his argument bears in part also upon the proletariat. Though proletarians are given to 'brutalités collectives,'[66] from which only their wives can deflect them, and though they are generally incapable of rising from respect to love, their consciousness nevertheless has a certain affinity to 'la pensée féminine.' Like women, though less perfectly, the proletarians bear 'the general traits of humanity,' and they rather than their employers will respond more readily to the influence of renovation.[67] Comte stresses that the traditional exclusion of both women and proletarians has preserved them from the vices of political life, so that 'feminine and proletarian thought' is fitted as the vehicle of reform.[68] Most interestingly, the linked figures of the woman and the proletarian are contrasted primarily with the familiar and malign figure of the *parleur*, Comte's travesty of the Aristotelian citizen. J.G.A. Pocock has remarked that *homo politicus* is allied above all with *homo rhetor* and opposed above all to *homo credens*:[69] and it is certainly *homo rhetor* who is extinguished by Comte as his doctrine of *homo credens*, and more specifically *femina credens*, reaches its culmination.

The expansion of social constituency was, from the eighteenth century to Comte and Saint-Simon and beyond, a well-marked theme of French theories of industrial society: the revaluing of a traditionally suspect activity had necessary consequences for views of civic qualification.[70] But it was no part of Comte's intention to emancipate either women or proletarians politically. Though women are to be esteemed as never before, as models of human affection, they are still to be confined to the privacy of the household: the pre-eminence of feeling 'resides spontaneously in the women. But this superiority, so powerful in the family, cannot provide the city with a sufficiently distinct power.

In fact, it is wholly tied to the purely domestic existence of the loving sex; it cannot then become, in public life, an adequate source of counsel, devotion or discipline ... As soon as the woman leaves her private sanctuary, she necessarily loses her principal value, which relates much more to the heart, properly so called, than to the mind or character.'[71] As for the proletarians, their happiness is to be found in domestic bliss, which their employers and rulers, loaded down with responsibilities, are unable to appreciate to the full.[72] 'Happy insouci- ance' is their reward for their political subordination. Their lack of citizenship is compensated for, as Maistre had said, by the status of 'bon laboureur': Comte adds to this the status of 'bon mari.'

It is Comte's revised estimation of women in the *Système*, combined with his continued refusal to grant them political emancipation, that has direct and profound consequences for his conception of the state, for it challenges the system of correspondences that was essential to his theory of social integration. In the organizational order outlined in the *Cours*, the household – in a manner reminiscent of Bodin and many others – was a microcosm of political rule. In the patriarchal household the rational man rules the emotional woman, just as broader social and political relations are arranged in tiers of ascending rationality. A consistent principle of subordination is essential: 'In such a hierarchy, each class can deny the superior dignity of higher classes only by abandoning at the same time its own essential title in relation to lower ones, given the constant uniformity of the co-ordinating principle; even the most inferior classes cannot forget that this principle coincides with that which, in a broader application, legitimates the superiority of man to other animals.'[73] If the boss is hard on you, in other words, you can always go home and kick the dog. But Comte's revised view in the *Système* wholly subverts this hierarchy, for the 'co-ordinating principle' of the *Cours* is supplemented by another. Though excluded from the practical world of doing, women are supreme in the world of being, and it is to being that the household is consecrated. It is plain, then, that the domestic elevation of feminine authority must damage the 'constant uniformity' of the ordering principle, and equally plain, given the essentially private nature of feminine virtue, that the incoherence cannot be repaired by giving women a corresponding political role.

This difficulty is resolved, somewhat circuitously, by what amounts to a further displacement of the attributes of the state. As a realm now of 'sentiment,' the family cannot microcosmically represent the city, whose realm is 'activity'; but it can find a macrocosm in the Church, whose realm is 'intelligence,' for now new parallels are struck.[74] The women, bearers of sentiment, and the priests, bearers of intelligence, both decline to command, for the role of both is to civilize, moderate, and direct, at different levels of organization, the bearers of 'la force pratique.'[75] Both likewise must divest themselves of personal property, for their lives are in both cases lives of altruism and service, for reasons of sentiment on the one hand and of science on the other.[76] It is only between them, among the various classes and divisions of positivist society, that 'profound sympathies' can arise.[77] Thus it is to family and Church and not, as before, to family and state that the theme of correspondences applies its integrating power. In the *Cours* the state, as a macrocosm of the household, enjoyed a certain transcendence in repeating the structure of its components at a more general level of power; but the city of the *Système*, though necessary as an intermediary between family and Church, is an organ of *spécialité* and does not share in the *généralité* that is rationally constructed by the spiritual power and intuitively grasped by its auxiliaries – the women, the fifth column of the *sacerdoce*, dispersed throughout the constituent domestic units of temporal organization, and taming their husbands and sons.

Comte's denial of any general character to temporal organization is perhaps the most revealing element of his discussion. It is, it seems, because of its special or local nature that government must also be local in the territorial sense; it must embrace nothing but the 'natural' economic community of the region, extension in space and generality of meaning being equated. From the very beginning Comte had stressed an analogy between corresponding degrees of generality in cognitive matters on the one hand and questions of organization on the other,[78] and in the 'Age of Generality' – an alternative name for the positivist era itself[79] – the maximum possible degree of generality is to be achieved in both realms, particulars of both cognitive and social kinds being set firmly in their places. It is in his shifting conceptions of what is general, a topic essentially bound up with his evolving social, organizational, and sexual categories, that the fullest implications of his view of the state are brought out.

Throughout, as in Rousseau – whom, however, Comte despised as vehemently as Maistre and the counter-revolutionaries had done – the legitimacy of an order is identified with its generalizing capacity: it is legitimate only to the extent that the general rules the particular, or the more general the less general. But in the *Cours* his discussion of this topic had been riven with a profound ambiguity. A central project there is the demonstration that social and organizational hierarchy reflects and is reinforced by the structure of human knowledge itself. In the fifty-seventh lesson this parallel is elaborately pursued: in the right ordering of society, in which savant is set above artist, banker above entrepreneur, man above woman, we are to perceive the ordering of disciplined cognition, that is, the natural inclusion of the particular in the general. Comte refers his readers back to the second lesson for a preliminary statement of this theme; but what we actually find there is something quite different. The social hierarchy of the fifty-seventh lesson concerns what may be called the span of understanding and responsibility, generality thus increasing with level of organization. The encyclopaedic hierarchy outlined in the second lesson and subsequently pursued with such impressive energy concerns what may be called the diffusion of attributes, the generality of a science thus *decreasing* with its complexity: as we ascend the ladder of the sciences, physics is less independent of particularity than mathematics, biology more general in scope than sociology, each science dealing successively with phenomena of a more restricted range and a greater degree of complexity. It is this that explains Comte's grand scheme of the history of science, in which different sciences attain a positive character at different rates of progress. But on that model the proposed social hierarchy ought to be precisely inverted, for as we proceed from the labourer to the savant we depart further with each step from what is generic. Now what has happened in the intervening argument, and especially in the forty-ninth lesson, is that the meaning of generality has simply changed. It is now claimed that generality *increases* as the encyclopaedic ladder is ascended, the more complex sciences, despite the increasingly restricted range of phenomena with which they deal, being more synthetic. The most synthetic science, sociology, plays an integrating and directing role with regard to the less synthetic, thus saving them from the pedantic specialism to which they are otherwise prone. This 'reaction of the ensemble upon the parts' provides an appropriate analogy for the view of government offered in the *Cours*, in which a reorganized state is to exercise a general control over its components.

This difficulty was to elicit from Comte, in the *Système*, a rare admission of 'confusion': his error, he says, threatens to render his entire philosophy 'equivocal' in its application.[80] In the later work he seeks to distinguish between two kinds of generality, objective and subjective; the term refers 'sometimes to phenomena and entities, sometimes to human thoughts.' The two vary inversely: human thoughts become more general in the subjective sense (more synthetic) as they concern objects that are less general in the objective sense (less generic). Formally, this meets the difficulty posed by Comte's earlier argument in the *Cours*. But Comte is here doing far more than simply resolving a difficulty in his exposition. His new formulation – developed in the context of his social and moral discussion – is related intimately to questions of political organization.

The doctrine of organization in the *Cours* had been inflexibly hostile to the merely generic. The very concept of organization implies difference and subordination, the separation and ranking of tasks; the concept of generic equality, such as is exemplified for Comte by the idea of rights, is thus wholly out of place, for organization is founded upon the complementarity of differences, not the identity of properties.[81] What establishes the dignity of the person is not a shared human status but the performance of a distinct task. The *Système*, however, while still rejecting any notion of rights, emphatically reasserts the value of the generic. In addition to *acting for* humanity, in taking up a role in a system of divided labour, one may also *represent* humanity, in the sense of bearing fundamental human properties. It is the women who, as affectionate beings, do this most perfectly.[82] In this revised picture, therefore, two chains of generality extend through the positivist order, one culminating in the synthetic capacity of the *sacerdoce*, the other in the generic attributes of women:[83] or – Comte permits himself a dry pun – in their 'generosity.'[84] In the 'secret alliance' between the priests and the women, celebrated especially in the dialogue of the *Catéchisme*, the two chains converge.

The formal statement of this secret alliance is provided in an extension of the encyclopaedic ladder. In the *Cours* there were six sciences, the last of which, sociology, was declared to be 'truly definitive.'[85] But now a seventh, 'la morale,' is added, and it transcends sociology just as sociology had transcended the disciplinary rungs below it.[86] It does so because it brings to light the affective meaning of the sciences that had prepared its emergence, and guides their application to human use. For *la morale* is also an art; at the new summit of the encyclopaedic ladder, theory rejoins the everyday world of practice. It is thus doubly general, for it is at once the most inclusive science and the most diffusely applicable art. 'Whether one ascends or descends, the encyclopaedic program always reveals morality to be the science par excellence because it is at once the most useful and the most complete.' What permits this uniting of theory and practice is the spontaneous convergence of feminine inductions and priestly deductions: what the priests determine by science, the women discern by feeling.[87] What is cognitively transcendent is also what is most socially diffuse, for *la morale* bears upon the whole range of social activity.

In the light of all this the subversion of political organization in the *Système* becomes understandable, even necessary. Whichever *généralité* one considers, the generic representation of human properties or the synthetic capacity of human thought, temporal power is evidently defective; from one point of view it is inferior to the household, while from the other it is inferior to spiritual authority. By distinguishing between the two notions, Comte effectively removes from temporal power that relative generality that it had enjoyed in the *Cours*. In merging the two, not in public institutions but in an informal alliance of domestic and spiritual authority, Comte also removes from temporal power the task of uniting theory and practice, a task for which, in the *Cours*, it had been responsible.[88] That, one must judge, is why 'le chef pratique' is ousted by the priest on the one hand and the woman on the other, and why he is now held capable of providing no more than 'a *sort of* general government.'[89]

Comte's treatment of the decentralization of power thus is very different from the nearly contemporaneous treatments offered by Proudhon and Tocqueville. For both of the latter theorists the pluralist strand of French political thought, especially its finest expression in Montesquieu, was an important source. In their different ways both Proudhon and Tocqueville sought to re-establish *corps intermédiaires* between individual and state, valuing regional association in this light; and though their ends were significantly different, they both sought in decentralization a means of restoring the citizen to his place. But Comte, though admiring Montesquieu as a precursor of sociology, does not draw on his pluralism at all. He does not seek to establish intermediaries between family and political power but to transform political power itself into an intermediary; he does not seek, as did Proudhon and Tocqueville, two tiers of political power but insists that there should be one alone, for, it was suggested above, a second tier (the state) would contain elements of transcendence that the later Comte was determined to remove from the temporal order.

It is not in a political tradition that the roots of Comte's program are to be sought, for what he envisaged was the displacement of politics by means of an elaborately extended metaphor. It is not to pluralism that one should look but to a diffuse Augustinianism and the transformation of the political city into the *civitas Dei*, a transformation in which

Comtean secular religion faithfully follows a theistic model. The *Civitas Dei* is a required text in the positivist library, and Augustine is the principal saint of the first week of the sixth month (Saint Paul) of the positivist calendar.[90] The *Summa*, one notes, is not listed in the positivist curriculum, and Aquinas is celebrated only as a philosopher in the month of Descartes. For Aquinas had seen in political citizenship a value that, if subordinate, was real, divine grace perfecting rather than cancelling man's naturally civil condition. If Comte prefers Augustine, surely that is because he wanted to drain the political city of any immanent value and to make the City, as Augustine had done, merely the ground of a normative metaphor. Comte claimed, with suprising obstinacy, to be a republican:[91] but his proposed order is republican only in the transfigured sense in which the *civitas Dei* is a *civitas*.

It is not hard to discern in Comte's treatment of the state an Augustinian theme, fantastically reconstructed. The vision of a universal order that 'freely unites the cities, as each city spontaneously combines the families within it,' does not appear in any of the political theorists to whom Comte admits a debt: Aristotle, Hobbes, Montesquieu, Condorcet, De Maistre. It does appear, however, almost word for word, in the *City of God*.[92] Moreover, in both Augustine and Comte the possibility of such an order rests on the same logical basis: the existence of a good that can be shared without being diminished. 'For industrial activity, as opposed to military activity, has the admirable characteristic that its free and full development in one individual or people does not result necessarily in its suppression in others.'[93] This is Augustine's argument, taken up again by Pascal, for the infinite abundance of divine goods and for the attribution of conflict to the pursuit of temporal goods whose supply is scarce. Like Augustine, Comte contrasts a pacific and universal society, devoted to the love of an infinite good, with military societies whose relations are necessarily conflictual. He sees, too, as did Augustine, that the pursuit of exclusive ends by military means may bring into play a semblance of virtue, 'la morale antique'; it is in fact no more than a disguised egoism or will to command but nevertheless supplies an example of 'admirable devotion.'[94] This is precisely Augustine's view of Rome: a society built upon the value of domination, on Cain's sin, yet nevertheless representing the highest point that virtue could reach before the truth of history was revealed, and valuable, though to a limited extent, as a moral example.

The later Comte's city or *patrie*, the miniature unit that is to succeed the state, is placed emphatically in the *civitas terrena*. It arises, after all, from man's necessary connection to *la terre*. It is a medium only of 'objective life,' or biological existence; one's membership in it is wholly transcended by one's 'subjective life,' as a participant in a non-temporal association in which true virtue, as opposed to earthly success, is faithfully recorded and rewarded.[95] One belongs to temporal association, in short, only temporarily, as a sojourner whose final identity is established elsewhere; only in death is it revealed. The positivist Church gives Abel his posthumous reward: a Stakhanovite Abel, whose virtue is measured by his devotion to the progress of industrial society. But in temporal organization Cain holds sway, for to pursue command is to pursue a scarce and non-universalizable good; the desire to command is a 'cerebral imperfection,' a sin original to human physiology, which 'torments many more families than can be satisfied.'[96] But it is, for all that, useful, and has a necessary place in a providential economy of sin, for it provides an order to which the positivist Church can apply its teaching: 'We must then give due scope to the vulgar satisfactions of pride and vanity, which alone are normally capable of sufficiently provoking the zeal required by command and counsel.'[97]

Augustine's *civitas dei* was composed of both men and angels who loved an infinite good and were careless of scarce goods. So is Comte's universal order. Its angels are, expressly, its women; and it is hard to escape the conclusion that Comte's discovery of 'la femme-ange,' in the person of Clotilde de Vaux, carried with it a reminiscence of an older vision in which what is angelic and what is best in man conspire together against the official organization of temporal relations.[98] Here, for once, psychohistory could play a highly constructive role: Mme Comte, rescued from prostitution, was plainly a fallen angel, while Clotilde de Vaux, with whom Comte spent a year in unconsummated love, was an angel who declined to fall. Comte's biography provides rich materials for an account of two symbolic cities in which men are united with either fallen or upright angels and thus are divided between temporal and spiritual loves. But such an inquiry goes far beyond what a discussion such as this can attempt. All we need note for the present purpose is that the dualistic vision that Comte appears to have made his own is one in which the state, with its characteristic admixture of materiality and idealism, enjoys a conceptually insecure place. It is to wither away because it is outdone in materiality by the city and in spirituality by the Church. Comte's proposed elimination of the state thus rests upon rather the same grounds as his hope that in positivist society human reproduction will be accomplished parthenogenetically:[99] the gross and the ideal will at last be consigned to their separate realms.

6

Citizenship in Industry: Georges Sorel

This is, according to Sheldon Wolin's wide-ranging and influential discussion, an 'age of organization.'[1] The individual's attachments and concerns have been deflected from the traditional sites of citizenship to the enclosed and particular sites of corporate life, which, Wolin suggests, have thus arrogated to themselves themes once reserved to the polity. In this process of sublimation, however, the idea of citizenship has necessarily lost a crucial part of its meaning: particular associations cannot offer what the polity, as it was once understood, ideally supplied. Wolin writes: 'To contend that individual participation can be satisfied in a political way within the confines of non-political groups is to deprive citizenship of its meaning and to render political loyalty impossible. When used in a political sense, citizenship and loyalty have meaning only in reference to a general order.'[2]

In such an account of the modern history of ideas Comte evidently deserves an altogether central place: his partitioning of life into functions and his substitution of functionary for citizen, his collapsing together of public and private realms and his fusion of corporate and political power, are intended precisely to sublimate the notion of a general order and to substitute administration for politics. Durkheim, too, is stressed in Wolin's discussion, though for his sociology of belonging rather than for the civic theory that he also attempted to construct. Georges Sorel, however, seems at first sight to be in rebellion against the pacified administrative order of which other theorists have dreamed. He appears fleetingly in Wolin's account, in company with Kierkegaard and Nietzsche, who mounted 'last-ditch efforts to secure some place for unorganized individual action' or represented the 'last gasps of a romanticism doomed to expire before the age of streamlined organizations.'[3] His work has such a character, it is claimed, by virtue of that 'heroic impulse' that he perceived in the myth of the general strike, through which the industrial proletariat was to achieve a spontaneous and *un*organized unity. Now such a view of Sorel as essentially a romantic outsider is not uncommon: but whatever there is to be said for it, it neglects the crucial respects in which his colourful rebelliousness masked a belief in organization as profound as, though quite different from, that of Comte. Far from exemplifying the last gasp of a romanticism doomed to failure by organization, Sorel's case is among the most striking and interestingly complex examples of the sublimation of politics. We may interpret his complicated, diverse, and often wayward writings in terms of the gradual absorption of a classical picture of citizenship by an ideal of industrial organization. If there is a single developmental point in modern political thinking at which the idea of citizenship lost its traditional moorings in the polity, it is in Sorel that we are likely to find it.

The sublimation thesis confronts another well-developed and forceful recent theme, one that is directly contrary in its logic. According to Wolin the migration of citizenship from polity to enterprise necessarily represents a loss; for other theorists of democracy, from G.D.H. Cole to the present, it represents a clear gain in reality, since, they maintain, a citizenship reserved to the polity can be no more than a fiction. Cole wrote: 'the Guild Socialist conception of democracy, which it assumes to be good, involves an active and not merely a passive citizenship on the part of the members. Moreover, and this is perhaps the most vital and significant assumption of all, it regards this democratic principle as applying, not only or mainly to some special sphere of social action known as 'politics,' but to any and every form of social action, and, in especial, to industrial and economic fully as much as to political affairs.'[4] Later writings in this vein have often been severely critical of those who, like Wolin, have argued for an essential difference between general and particular contexts of action; in ascribing reality to an illusory general order standing over and above the concrete and specific relations of productive life, Wolin, it is contended, is guilty of 'reification.'[5] In all of this there are hints, of course, of Marx, whose essay 'On the Jewish Question' is sometimes invoked; but Sorel, none of whose writings are ever invoked by theorists of citizenship in industry, anticipated some themes of that school with rather more precision, in seeking to transpose the realm of citizenship rather than (as in Marx) to obliterate or transcend the category. Indeed, if the term had not been put to other uses and made to stand – misleadingly – for a voluntarist and romantic mood, one might well describe as Sorelian all those trends of recent thinking in which citizenship has been located in the industrial realm. In examining the paths of thinking that led Sorel himself to such a vision, we may arrive at some general suggestions about the coherence of the vision itself.

How, though, does the idea of citizenship enter into Sorel's central concerns? Paradoxically, perhaps, it does so by way of a conception that, on the face of it, eliminates citizenship altogether: that of an industrial society. What Sorel (and his disciple and editor, Edouard Berth) understood by 'la société industrielle' was an order following the organizational contours of industry itself, in which no political structure mediated the relations between one productive grouping and another, professional ties replacing civil ones as objects of loyalty. The use that Sorel and Berth made of this conception lent it a quite new edge and brought into play a most interesting and unexpected convergence of disparate themes. While Saint-Simon had contrasted a society organized on industrial principles with an aristocratic or ascriptive society, Sorel and Berth contrasted it, rather, with a commercial society, 'la société marchande.'[6] In offering this contrast, they implicitly link hands with an older tradition that likewise had often seen commerce as a menace to virtue: the tradition of citizenship itself.[7]

Montesquieu, Hume, and Tocqueville, among many others, had noted the contradiction between the classical ideal of the self-repression and self-forgetfulness of the citizen and a social order in which the predominant motive was profit seeking.[8] While some – including all three of those named – had resolved or eased this contradiction to their own satisfaction, offering grounds for supposing that citizenship could indeed be preserved and fostered in a society of merchants, they had in so doing perpetuated the long-standing distinction between a life of business and civic life; in particular, they and others had done so in contrasting the essentially military virtues of the classical citizen with the pacific values of 'le doux commerce.' And here one can hardly fail to be struck by the continuity of Sorel's argument with that of these earlier theorists. For, in the first place, Sorel expressly (and unfavourably) contrasted the commercial bourgeoisie of his day with the citizen class of Athens: 'The ancient Athenians were much superior to our envious, ignorant, and greedy bourgeoisie ... The citizens were not merchants, demanding guarantees for their transactions and protection for their industry, or seeking favours from government. They were soldiers whose very life was linked to the greatness of the city. The slightest weakness placed the state in danger.'[9] Secondly, as this quotation itself indicates, the idea of loyalty and devotion, conceived of upon an essentially military pattern, was quite fundamental to Sorel's conception of order; and in proposing to replace the 'envious, ignorant and greedy bourgeoisie' with a society of industrial producers, Sorel also assimilated the latter to a soldierly image – 'Socialism returns to ancient thinking: but the warrior of the city has become the worker of advanced industry; weapons have been replaced by machines.'[10] It was, of course, the supposed warrior-like character of the syndicalist worker that Sorel was to take as his starting-point in his notorious defence of violence and of 'class *war*' – an expression that, as the text of *Reflections on Violence* makes very clear, is no mere synonym for generic conflict or struggle but is to be taken quite literally.[11] The syndicalist worker represented the citizen in Sorel's mind, while the bourgeois represented the citizen's negation. Austerity and self-abnegation are contrasted with frivolity, luxury, and dependence; and it is this essentially moral contrast, so characteristic of a long-standing tradition of civic thinking, that figures in Sorel's picturing of the relations between worker and bourgeois, rather than any Marxian thesis of exploitation, in which Sorel displays little if any interest. Sorel claimed, not without justification, that his refusal to discuss the nature of the achieved order of socialist justice was Marxian, for Marx too had been wary of utopianizing; but one may also judge that Sorel was less interested in the definition of socialism than in the warrior-like manner in which the struggle for it was conducted and in the austerely virtuous commitment that the struggle demanded. He was not, as is sometimes thought, uninterested in outcomes: but given his view of historical development, he believed that the ends achieved are narrowly governed by the means that are used to achieve them.

The essential connection between war and citizenship is evident as early as 1889 in Sorel's remarkable book *The Trial of Socrates*, in which Socratic philosophy is condemned, as it had been by Socrates' prosecutors, for its damaging effects upon tradition and convention, by which alone the intense solidarity of the city-state could have been maintained. Convention unites; philosophy divides, for dialectical skills are very unequally distributed and thus separate the philosophical few from the unphilosophical many.[12] That, in essence, is Sorel's radical critique of Socrates, who, he contends, had cast potentially ruinous doubt on the unquestioning loyalties and faithfulness to routine upon which classical citizenship depended: 'Socrates strove mightily to break the chains that bound the citizen to the ancient city. These chains were those of military discipline. The citizen was a soldier, closely confined and watched; he was obliged to submit himself to a system of education designed to integrate him and to prepare him well for war.'[13] This education was provided above all by a civic poetry and drama; and it is interesting to note that exactly these vehicles of civic education were to reappear, transformed, in Sorel's socialist phase, as the 'social poetry' of Marx[14] and as the 'drama'[15] of the general strike, the *educative* force of both of which is stressed especially. Moreover, even in *The Trial of Socrates*, which displays little interest in, let alone any inclination towards, the socialist position, Sorel was already disposed to efface any clear distinction between the realms of war and of work, noting approvingly the military analogies for production in Xenophon's *Oeconomicus*,[16] a theme that was later to be very amply developed. Of course, such a theme cuts sharply across the view, offered by earlier theorists of *industrie*, that war and work are profoundly antithetical things, marking two distinct epochs of social development.

When we turn to Sorel's conception of contemporary citizenship, we find that here, too, essentially military themes are stressed. In 1889 he had written: 'It is impossible to understand the ancient constitutions without relating them to military institutions.'[17] Likewise, he later insists that the political spirit of republican France draws what force it has from 'military institutions': with the rediscovery of the citizen army by the French revolutionaries 'a quite new notion of the City was born, with strong analogies to that of antiquity, and patriotism became a force of hitherto unsuspected importance. Democracy still lives off this tradition.'[18] And as before, this living citizenship, military and patriotic as was that of antiquity, is sharply contrasted with a vacuous and rationalistic understanding of the city. What the revolutionaries *did* gave birth to a new order; what their theorists *said* displayed no understanding whatsoever of the nature of order. 'Once the *believer* of the Church, then the *subject* of the king, man was to feel his strength and become a *citizen*; but what is to be understood by this term? Theorists asked what would be left in man after the ties subjecting him to Church and king had been dissolved; this residue was natural man, an abstraction formed out of the virtues and faults of eighteenth-century educated man.' This abstraction could be made real only by the application of political power: 'discussion was continued in the manner of the old political theorists; the doctrine that summed up the fundamental principles of government was taken to be of prime importance.'[19] The French republican tradition rested, therefore, upon a wholly deluded self-understanding in which the real sources of civic attachment were overlooked in favour of 'abstraction' and political 'doctrine,' abstractions and doctrines no less dry, corrosive, and uncreative than those for which Athens, and Sorel, had condemned Socrates. The point is quintessentially Sorelian. *What* was sought was one thing – it was too abstract, too doctrinal; *how* it was sought was something else – the recourses forced upon the Revolution determined its real significance. In fact, Sorel complained (and this is one of the most striking Sorelian paradoxes), the (futile) intentions of the revolutionaries came close to sabotaging the (productive) unintended consequences of their movement.[20]

It is with the true source of citizenship, the military and patriotic consciousness of the citizen army, that Sorel later expressly links the syndicalist movement. It is the revolutionary syndicalists, he maintains, 'who represent at the present time the spirit of the revolutionary warriors who, against all the rules of war, so thoroughly thrashed the fine armies' of France's enemies.[21] Nothing could make it plainer that the substance of the city, in Sorel's view, has been wholly severed from the political realm and that the concrete experience of citizen-like devotion and solidarity is no longer to be found in the official manifestations of *civisme* but in the industrially based institutions that stand in opposition to them. By this device Sorel transforms the theme of civic solidarity into a thesis of class war. Where theorists of civic virtue had seen integrity in the transcendence or forgetfulness of particularity and in the recognition of an interest of a general kind,[22] Sorel locates integrity in the class identification displayed in and reinforced by an internal war. Interclass solidarity, as he came to say, was 'hypocritical,'[23] resting as it did, he believed, upon self-interested collusions and not upon any vivid communal or co-operative experience capable of bringing into being a passionate and unreflective loyalty.

But Sorel's historical imagery may seem very imperfectly lucid, for in his description of the revolutionary syndicalist movement he also employs an apparently contradictory analogy. He provocatively describes syndicalist militancy as 'barbarous' and thus appears to invite us to imagine the revolutionary movement not in the light of the ancient city but in that of the barbarian invaders who destroyed it. This provocation has not been lost on his interpreters, among whom Wolin himself is impressed by it;[24] and certainly, on the surface, it lends plausibility to the reading of Sorel as a theorist of sheer élan. But it should not be overlooked that in the civic tradition the distance between ancient citizen and barbarian invader was much closer than mere historical fact would suggest. As Pocock has reminded us, theorists of civic virtue had appealed at once to Spartan, Roman, *and* Gothic images.[25] Sorel's Goths, too, are essentially orderly beings, more civic in fact than the citizens themselves; they brought new forms of juridical and social order to a world that had forgot what virtue was. It is no surprise that Sorel should have found Macaulay's notion of revolutionary 'paganism' appealing,[26] for 'pagan' embraces Roman and Gothic in an ideologically convenient fashion. The barbarians did not destroy the city, for, as Sorel explains at length in *The Fall of the Ancient World*, there was no city left to destroy, its spirit having been ruined by processes of internal corruption. Likewise the syndicalists, as heirs to the barbarians, bring to the world a new source of 'droit,' which is to be found in the practical co-operation and solidarity of the factory and not in the patched-up compromises of interclass relations upon which the present city expends its declining energies.[27] If, then, Sorel regards the syndicalist movement as a movement of barbarians rather than of citizens, he does so just to the extent that his picture of the barbarians contains in advance that theme of the civic spirit's migration to a new bearer, a theme to which his syndicalist writings were to give a new application and a fuller development.

One problem that Sorel confronted, therefore, was that of distinguishing the true *civisme* of a movement that he admired from the sham citizenship of an order that enjoyed the symbolism and formal trappings of a city. The problem was not new: one might compare Cicero's remark, quoted by Augustine, that we retain 'only the name of a commonwealth, but we have lost the reality long ago.'[28] Sorel likewise contrasted the vices of the city-in-name, especially the 'voracious appetite'[29] or political passions and ambitions of its inhabitants, with the self-repression and devotion to common ends that the idea of citizenship demanded. A second problem, to which we must now turn, required a more novel adaptation of tradition. In seeking to locate citizenship within the realm of industrial life, Sorel was attempting to put that idea to a historically incongruous use. While his dislike of commercial society was wholly traditional, his admiration for industrial society was not; and in seeking to enforce a radical distinction between production and trade,[30] investing the former with virtue, the latter with its corruption, Sorel was doing something almost wholly unprepared for in the civic tradition, whose exponents – from Aristotle on – had been no more inclined to value the producer than the merchant. *Homo faber*, it has been noted, is a version of man that the theorists of *homo politicus* had largely ignored.[31] Here Sorel's thinking brings into play a quite different train of antecedents, many of whose themes had been in some respects profoundly opposed to those of the classical doctrines of citizenship.

As one illuminating study has shown,[32] the immediate roots of the notion of *industrie* are to be found in eighteenth-century political economists such as Pierre-Louis Roederer and Jean-Baptiste Say, who sought to establish the managerial, productive, and inventive skills of the *industrieux* as a factor of production distinct from capital, labour, and land. If their principal target was the Physiocratic doctrine that land was the primary source of wealth, they were as well led to dispute the doctrine that it was the capital of the entrepreneur that constituted his productive function, and also the labour theory of John Locke, for it was not only the *peine* (labour) that one suffered in acquisition but the *adresse* (skill) that one exerted that constituted a property title. *Industrie* no less than land or capital was something in which one could have *propriété*, and the *propriétaires d'industrie* therefore rightfully deserved the citizenship traditionally attached to property and should be admitted to political participation. It was in this way that the notion of *industrie* acquired its ideological edge: it issued in a demand for the extension of the franchise to the *industrieux*, by establishing *industrie* as a property.

Industrie therefore emerged initially as a criterion of *civisme* or of inclusion in the civic body, a criterion that fundamentally challenged the Aristotelian view[33] that the direction of labour enjoyed no higher a status than labour itself. But it is the further extension of this argument that has a particular relevance here. Initially conceived of in terms of the Aristotelian model of inclusion – Who should participate? – the idea of *industrie* was quite soon to figure as an answer to the Platonic (and exclusive) question – Who should rule? From correcting Aristotle, in short, the idea of *industrie* passed over to revising Plato, in proposing *les industriels* as the exclusive legitimate bearers of authority by virtue of the crucial importance and privileged character of their special knowledge and skill. It is in Saint-Simon's celebrated parable that this transition is most clearly revealed. At first a liberal who sought to modify the criteria of citizenship and to include *les industriels* within the polity, Saint-Simon eventually moved to a radical demand – 'socialist,' or 'managerialist,' or somewhere in between the two – that industrial, technological, and creative competence should supersede all other criteria of membership. In the later Saint-Simon, as also in Comte (who added to the doctrine some features peculiarly his own), what began as a project of political reform ends up as the far-reaching enterprise of founding a new social order upon the basis of a newly recognized principle of capacity. Saint-Simon's parable is designed to show the uselessness of ascribed status: the passage is striking, however, not only because it is (as one commentator has put it) a 'concise and vivid expression of the theme of an industrial society'[34] but also because it expresses so clearly the transition from the notion of *estate* (defined by the nature *of* what one does) to the modern notion of *élite* (defined by capacity *in* what one does); for the qualities of *industrie* are, it seems, concentrated disproportionately in the hands and minds of a few thousands of *industriels*. Increasingly, in both Saint-Simon and Comte, the idea of the *industriel* comes to be separated from that of the *prolétaire*. It is not merely that the priority of the industrial realm over others is stressed but that within that realm a new social principle generates a new social hierarchy of merit.

'Industrial capacity, that of the arts and professions, is what must be substituted for feudal or military power,' Comte wrote.[35] This theme, common to both Saint-Simon and Comte, is explained by Comte as follows: 'There are only two ends that may be sought by a society, however large, just as there are for a single indivudual. These are violent action directed against the rest of mankind, or conquest, and action upon nature in order to modify it to human advantage, or production. Any society that is not clearly organized for one or other end will be nothing but a hybrid and characterless association. The military end was that of the old system; the industrial end is that of the new.' The pregnancy of this remark is evident, for the military organization of the city had been essentially tied, in a long tradition of political thinking, to the very notion of citizenship; bearing arms for the city was conceived both as an expression of and a prerequisite to full membership in it, as a city necessarily confronts other cities, and the valuing of its identity implies the readiness to defend it. It is no surprise to find, then, that in the industrial and pacific vision, as it reaches its epitome in Comte, the city is inexorably displaced on the one hand by *la simple ville* and on the other by a spiritual order that arrogates to itself the general meaning that political organization had once enjoyed. *Les simples villes* are essentially productive communities, linked in the temporal mode by ties of economic interdependence; in the spiritual mode they are linked by their acceptance of the authority of an élite, whose universal theory is a necessary foundation for the local practices of productive life.

Now Sorel despised Comte and his disciples with real vehemence. What provoked him was in part the positivist view of history as the march of enlightenment, for Sorel was a shrewd methodologist and hence a sharp critic of notions of inexorable historical progress. That we can extrapolate from what has happened to what will happen was a belief for which he castigated both Saint-Simon and Comte, and even Proudhon, whom he was greatly disposed to admire. Sorel distinguished fundamentally between what has happened and what will happen, between 'un tout-fait,' or a completed sequence that opens itself to inspection, and 'un se-faisant,' a process in mid-course whose ends are essentially indeterminate. Here he owed much to Bergson, or at least shared much with Bergson, in distinguishing between the necessity that retrospection may reveal and the freedom that prospection must recognize. Given that certain ends are adopted, Sorel believed, social science ('if there is such a thing')[36] may estimate their chances of success; but it cannot predict what ends will be adopted any more than natural science can penetrate into the causes of things. Natural science can examine relations and predict consequences: social science likewise can hope only to predict the consequences of what is done and cannot hope to predict what social actors will do. Ideas of inevitable progress, moreover, are morally pernicious: they teach people to be indifferent and frivolous, to relax the tensions that only 'pessimism' can induce and that alone can generate moral strength.[37] Like Tocqueville, Sorel thought that a society that believed that history made itself would soon abandon any interest in acting.

What also provoked him was Comte's view that practice was the child of theory, that technology depends essentially upon a chain of abstract sciences that are the province of the *savant* and that find their ultimate expression in a set of rationally connected and stable theoretical doctrines. In truth, Sorel believed, science is the child of technology, and the theoretical tenets of science are no more than abstractions performed upon the concrete operations of the factory. 'If one wished to establish a history of the human mind, one should not divide up the process as A. Comte did on the basis of the dominance of theological, metaphysical, and positive concepts but according to the nature of industrial workplaces.'[38] It is therefore no accident that Comte should have called for the harmony of 'hands' and 'heads'[39] while Sorel called for a 'philosophy of the hands' that would exclude a 'philosophy of the head.'[40] But Sorel's evident rejection of the Comtean tradition, as of the Saint-Simonians – whom he called 'bookworms' – should not blind us to the fact that what he was offering was not at all a rejection of the idea of *industrie* but an internal modification of it. Saint-Simon may or may not have been a socialist – Comte was not; but when Sorel insists that a socialist order is one that is organized according to the requirements of production, he is clearly echoing the theorists of *industrie* in constructing his picture of socialism. Sorel's socialism no less than Comte's technocracy was motivated by a dislike for the political class in general and for lawyers in particular – for abstract and manipulative skills that do nothing, as Sorel put it, to keep the factories running;[41] and the ties binding one *polytechnicien* to another, one suspects, go deeper than mere ideology.

What made Sorel's picture socialist was precisely that he differed from Saint-Simon and Comte with respect to the identity of the *propriétaires d'industrie*; in Sorel's view, which is certainly eccentric[42] and which may very well be plain wrong, the conditions of advanced technology call for a wider and wider diffusion of skill and technical knowledge, so that in effect the criterion of *industrie* tends to become increasingly inclusive, embracing those whom earlier theorists had called *prolétaires*. Nor can there be much doubt, despite the fact that Sorel described himself with perhaps surprising persistence as a Marxist, that it is this French tradition rather than a Marxian one that lends intelligibility to what he wrote. For whereas Marx primarily stressed the dispossession of the proletariat, its reduction to bare labouring humanity ('peine'), Sorel stressed above all its acquisition of technical capacity ('adresse'), hence not its dispossession but its proprietorship of productive skills. In fact, in a most intriguing passage Sorel suggests that property itself is valuable only as a medium for the development of skill;[43] and he thus shifts the focus of concern from the Marxian question of ownership to the question of the opportunities presented by the work process.

Sorel's belief that modern industry enhanced the skills and technical capacity of the workers is so odd a view and cuts so sharply across a powerful and familiar trend of social criticism that we may well speculate about the reasons for it. Here Comte's blunt distinction between what he called theory and practice, between the hierarchy of abstract sciences and the loyal but merely laborious application of the worker, may provide a valuable clue. Such a distinction, which Sorel found so offensive,[44] recalls the central theme of his early book on Socrates, who, Sorel maintained, had ruined the ancient city by separating the able and knowledgeable thinker from the simple and unreflective doer. By separating thinking from doing, he had destroyed the civic unity founded upon the shared central symbols expressed in poetry and drama; the city's judgment against Socrates (technicalities apart) was in the last resort correct, for Socratic philosophy was indeed destructive of the city. It is surely not fanciful to suggest that Sorel's critique of Comte should be read in the light of his earlier critique of Socrates. The technocratic division of industrial society into scientists and managers on the one hand and labourers on the other echoes the Socratic division of the city into philosophers on the one hand and warriors and artisans on the other. 'As soon as a society is divided into classes that are distinguished in terms of their knowledge, oligarchy is not far behind.'[45] In criticizing Saint-Simon and Comte, Sorel was recalling implicitly an archaic vision of the city, with an undivided life and a common end; and we may speculate that his astonishing picture of the industrial workplace expressed his need to find a contemporary bearer for this long-standing image.

Comte, moreover, had contrasted 'conquest,' the 'violent action' of a city 'directed against the rest of mankind,' with 'production,' or 'action upon nature in order to modify it to human advantage.' It is of the greatest possible significance that where Comte spoke of action upon nature in contradistinction to conquest, Sorel spoke, rather, of the conquest of nature,[46] bringing to the technological exploitation of nature a language strongly infused with military images. Sorel imagined men and nature as an antithetic couple, men's efforts being constantly thwarted and obstructed by the resistance of the natural world. The producers' virtues are citizen-like, too, not only in their belligerence but in that they display that 'excellence in the mass' of which Aristotle had spoken; they require heroic solidarity, not heroic personality, and learned practical competence, not esoteric knowledge. It was in part the reminiscence of this image that led Sorel to depart so sharply from the Saint-Simonian or Comtean picture of science and society, just as it intensified his distaste – itself inherited from such as Saint-Simon and Comte – for the elite of orators and intriguers who were ruining France just as they had once ruined Athens. And with Sorel's adaptation of the notion of *industrie* that notion undergoes a further transformation: at first a criterion for citizenship (in Roederer and Say) and then a substitute for citizenship (in Saint-Simon and Comte), it eventually becomes a new model of citizenship, the industrial world bearing all the idealized properties of the city itself.

These idealized properties are, as a necessary corollary, drained out of the *political* city, which comes to bear all the antitheses of order. It is evident that this logic points strongly towards the images of war that were to figure so prominently in *Reflections on Violence*, for it tended increasingly to assimilate the relations between classes to the relations between hostile cities. Revolution becomes internal war. It is no longer a transition of the kind imagined by earlier theorists of *industrie* such as Comte, a developmental process undergone by a whole society, in the course of which all the parts of an order are operated upon by factors that eventualy culminate in a new and total way of life and thought; it cannot have this character, for a city, unlike a historical tendency, requires acknowledgment and loyalty and cannot be the cumulative product of successive unwitting contributions. Nor, on the other hand, is revolution a catastrophe, an extraordinary and destructive event *after* which the form of a new order of things will eventually come to light; it cannot have this character either, for a war presupposes an already existing recognition of solidarity and identity.[47] In opposition to both of these broad conceptions of transition Sorel insists that a revolution is the displacement of one order by another that has already developed its institutions and loyalties, and that the *civisme* of the new order should have emerged in advance among the members of the insurgent movement.

That a revolution should be war-like, a confrontation between two organized societies, follows from Sorel's deepest assumptions about morality. Morality exists only in organization. It does not reside in formulas or doctrines, which are mere shadows of moral experience and live only in the books of moral philosophers. Morality rests on, or perhaps simply *is*, the lived solidarity of a society or class or movement, sustained by common memories and collective hopes. Such a thing cannot be produced to order. It is self-deceiving to suppose that a morality will spring up merely because it is needed by an abstractly viewed scheme of social relations: if socialism is to have a morality, it must derive it from the movement that will have created it. 'Experience shows that a new culture becomes effective only with the help of a very long process of preparation; it is therefore now, within capitalist society, that the means of realizing a new juridical system must be prepared. *The only manner in which we may cultivate a sentiment is by exercising it whenever an opportunity presents itself.*'[48] A revolutionary movement, then, defines itself through its actions as a bearer of distinctive moral conceptions, or as a new society struggling to separate itself from the old. What is put to novel use here is the moral psychology of Pascal, whom Sorel greatly admired (as a fellow 'pessimist'):[49] it is not reason that leads us to virtue but what Pascal called 'la machine' – a term that has intriguing though irrelevant felicity in this case – or a process of habituation and practice that silences doubt and erodes self-centredness. Much of that view had also entered into Rousseau's account of the generation of civic consciousness, a process to which, likewise, experience rather than reason is crucial: what Rousseau had said about the creation of political order is said again by Sorel about its revolutionary overthrow.

The centrepiece of Sorel's revolutionary-syndicalist thinking is, of course, the 'myth of the general strike': and the analysis sketched above should help to shed light upon the political meaning of this construct, which may indeed be seen as the culmination of Sorel's effort to transpose the values of *civisme* to the world of *industrie*. Much attention has been given by Sorel's commentators to its mythic character; much less attention has been given to its equally significant general character. But in both respects its features evidently derive from what we may call the civic dimension of Sorel's thinking. The idea of myth has an altogether incongruous place among the highly rationalized conceptions of *industrie*, which, according to Sorel, brings about the progressive extension of what is made at the expense of what is given and thus inexorably reduces the realm of mystery. In this respect it belongs to Vico's third age of men and not to the mythic ages of gods or even of heroes.[50] Sorel's civic theme, however, allows an ample and quite fundamental role to myth, for, he writes, 'it is impossible to express ideas about the *patrie* except in a mythical form.'[51] Generality belongs likewise – as Wolin stresses – to the civic ideal; and we may suggest tentatively that its application to the claims and imagery of the socialist movement forms an essential part of Sorel's effort to understand an industrial organization as a city.

During the 1890s Sorel had espoused a highly individual but not wholly unorthodox social-democratic position that allowed a significant place for political reform and for the political institutions permitting reform to be pursued. After the turn of the century, as is well known, he abandoned this position for a version of socialism in which all political instrumentalities were condemned root and branch, and everything made to hinge upon the autonomous or even perhaps antinomian development of a revolutionary movement. This transition is most economically viewed in terms of the shifting relations that Sorel perceived between the two cities with which he was preoccupied. The Augustinian echoes of this expression are not out of place; for, like Augustine, Sorel stressed the fact that the two cities, the true and the false, were 'mixed' together,[52] their members – though destined for different ends – spatially interspersed and highly interdependent: Indeed, it is only by a 'mental effort'[53] or by a process of abstraction that Sorel calls *diremption*[54] that the lines of demarcation between the combatants can be clearly grasped, so manifold and concrete are the ties between one and the other. Though Sorel's cities, like Augustine's, have different 'times,' different ideal schemes of beginning and destination, the industrial city being defined by its 'socialist future,'[55] the two share for the time being a common 'history.' What is still more to the point is that Sorel admits, as Augustine did, that the false city may offer a field of experience in which the loyalties of the true city are tested, and also an analogy or model through which the virtues of the true city may be taught. In the writings of his social-democratic phase Sorel did not claim anything more than that for political participation in Third Republic France. When, in the course of the Dreyfus affair especially, he had advocated political involvement on the part of the socialist movement, he had done so on the grounds that such involvement would stimulate and render habitual a sense of justice of crucial long-term importance to the movement itself: 'Since we propose the effacement of classes, we must exercise the sentiments of justice, especially in circumstances in which they conflict with class divisions. In fact, we cannot be sure that we are pursuing justice unless we are quite certain that we are disinterested.'[56]

What justifies political action by the socialist movement, therefore, is the resemblance between the struggles internal to the political city and those to be waged against it, a resemblance that is sufficiently strong that participation in the one reinforces commitment to the other. At this stage, indeed, Sorel is prepared to see both as involving the cause of a universal principle of 'justice,' a notion that here makes one of its rather rare incursions into his argument. Ten years later all such appeals to principles or ideals supposedly transcending class boundaries are roundly condemned and commitment to the struggle against the Third Republic is held to exclude all participation in the struggles internal to it. But there is no fundamental change in the structure of Sorel's thinking here, for it is the *resemblance* of one city to the other that now displays a second facet of its ambiguous potential. Resemblance may supply an argument for continuity, the experience of action within the political city coinciding with and reinforcing the ideals that are eventually to lead to its destruction: or it may supply an argument for displacement, the two cities posing a choice precisely because of their resemblance as rival orders with sovereign claims, which would exclude all accommodation between the two. As this second version of the argument evolves in Sorel's thinking, we find the language of civic loyalty penetrating his discussion still more deeply. The working class becomes 'a people';[57] the institutions of the Third Republic become 'foreign' to it;[58] and most notably, it is now that the notion of war against another class is added to the metaphorical war against nature in which the industrial city is said to be engaged.

This new people is no longer to form and model itself by participation *in* the institutions of the city that confronts it but by participation in an act of revolutionary opposition *to* them. Nevertheless, it is still in the city-like activity of war that the movement is to define itself, and to that extent Sorel's new strategy still insists upon the need for the city of industry to draw upon the logic of the political city in order to disentangle itself from it – just as, in the manner of other sovereign entities, it must define and found itself by myth, a conception that, in the history of political thought, bears an especially close relation to the question of beginning or founding.[59] The loyalties upon which an established city depends are secured by the force of convention or tradition transmitted over time; but a process of transmission requires a beginning, and here myth seems a necessary complement to tradition, for there must have been a time when the loyalties later to be sustained by convention and habit required to be sustained by vivid prospective anticipations and by epic events that were to reveal their full meaning only with the passage of time.[60] Sorel's myth is above all a foundation myth, describing events in the light of which an order is to understand its identity and from which later generations will draw their traditions of understanding and behaviour.[61] As in his social-democratic phase Sorel's central concern is still with 'the genesis of morality,' with providing the institutional and psychological conditions for that spirit of devoted self-sacrifice upon which the new order eventually will rely.

What is meant by the 'irrationality' of Sorel's myth, therefore, may need to be revised. The myth does not represent a cult of spontaneity but, on the contrary, a painfully intense effort to conserve and foster a distinctive and organized moral order. Its irrationality is not, as some have supposed, that of a romantic gesture, an attempt to keep the flame of commitment burning without regard to the consequences of doing so: Sorel's approach is thoroughly (and ambitiously) consequentialist in its assessment of the manner in which institutions and practices exercise their long-term impact upon belief and action. Its irrationality would appear to be, rather, that residual irrationality of the city itself, a feature that has migrated to industrial organization along with the other features of *civisme*. Simply because it is a bounded and exclusive entity, a city draws limits to the scope of reason: it accepts an intensity of violence in its external relations that it cannot tolerate internally; and it must take as given the accidents, the force, and the sentiments, prejudices, or legends that make it one city, for its boundaries are not determined by anything more than that. ('Why are you killing me?' ... 'You live on the other side of the water.') The apparent romanticism of Sorel's argument, one suspects, springs wholly from the fact that it transfers claims from a context in which we are accustomed to see them to a context in which we do not expect them to appear. His warrior-like syndicalists, unified by a colourful epic of struggle and triumph, parody the idea of the city; but like all parodies, Sorel's picture retains some significant faithfulness to the original.

As for the generality of the mythic strike, may we not suspect here, too, a parody? The general strike displaces, yet also imitates, the general will of citizenship. Like Rousseau, who saw in the art of generalizing the ability to link particular with civil ends, so too Sorel values the general strike as the means of overcoming local particularity of interest. The workers' movement, as he insists, rests upon essentially local organizations, upon the networks of personal and professional ties among the inhabitants of provincial towns;[62] and the function of the idea of the general strike is precisely to link such complexes of local interest and attachment to a nation-wide movement. 'Strikes would be no more than simply economic events of negligible social significance,' he wrote, 'if the revolutionaries did not intervene, changing their character and making them episodes in the social struggle. Each strike, however local, is a skirmish in the great battle known as the general strike. The association of ideas here is so simple that one has only to point it out to striking workers in order to make them socialists.'[63] By virtue of this association of ideas, 'each,' in Rousseau's words, is to include himself in the 'all,' so that the ends of all are motivated by the interests of each. For Sorel, no less than Rousseau, was worried by the menace of particularity, and also by that of the 'will of all,' which substitutes a self-interested coalition of forces for the expression of the general ends of the movement.[64] Even more like Rousseau, Sorel insists that the solution to this problem lies in the effective organization of communal will, not in subordination to government; just as an effective general will is to render government a mere instrument of a community made one by its own consciousness, so too the general strike is intended above all as an alternative to the imposed and artificial unity of bureaucratic organization: syndicalism is to reduce 'central committees' to mere 'administrative offices.'[65]

But the critique of bureaucratic organization does not imply a critique of organization as such. On the contrary, what is eventually to substitute itself for the artificial organization of government – or for that of political socialism – is the organization of industrial production itself. The Rousseauan general will of citizenship collapses into the 'generality' of production, which is, Sorel says, 'générale, anonyme, inconsciente.'[66] It is general in that each producer figures only as a small part of an immense and interdependent order, whose time is constituted by the patient, methodical, and cumulative progress of achievement, the scale of which altogether exceeds individual control. It is anonymous in that the producers – like Rousseau's citizens, who recognize that any law bears equally upon themselves and others – are interchangeable, each filling a role that another might fill equally well. Since it is also unconscious, it requires for the time being an organization of consciousness that draws directly upon the model of the city, a class war that transposes to the workers' movement the themes and images of the political city itself: the myth of the citizen-army, of the revolutionary *levée en masse*, is to be detached from the Jacobin tradition and attached to the socialist movement. But after victory, as class war in turn fades into memory and legend, it is the endless struggle against nature that is to supply the new order with its organizational principles, and the generality of productive organization that is to displace the generality of will.

Sorel is often viewed as a romantic opponent of the organization that has displaced the city. It has been suggested here that, on the contrary, Sorel romantically reduced the city to an organization. Any notion that he revered the unorganized should be rapidly dispelled by his account of what he took the perfected industrial order to be like: 'It must be understood that the socialist factory will be a grouping of producers who will always be on the alert in criticizing received practices, who will be guided by supervisors comparable to the demonstrators employed by professors of chemistry, and at the head of whom will be engineers who will speak to their men as a master speaks to his students.'[67] Whatever this is, it is not a cult of spontaneity. On the contrary, it is connected with a long-standing view of Sorel's that the strictest control of the individual by order does nothing to diminish his freedom.[68] As Sorel continued to make clear even in his last writings,[69] in his interpretation of classical and civic themes it is the citizen's devoted self-abnegation that is especially stressed. I have tried to show above that in the general logic of his thinking his admiration of industrial organization sprang principally from a highly selective picture of the nature of citizenship: what he regarded as its fundamentally military character came to be connected in his mind with an equally selective picture of the nature of industrial work, and as these themes progressively fused, the political city came increasingly to be dispensable, no longer of value even as an exemplification or reinforcement of moral experience. It is in terms of this fusion of themes, it was argued above, that Sorel's relation to both the civic tradition and Saint-Simonian industrial society should be understood; and it is in terms of this fusion, too, that the central concepts of his syndicalist writings acquire a degree of coherence and that the nature of its irrationalism may be defined.

As noted above, however, the themes touched upon here may offer more than a revised interpretation of Sorel. What has been at the centre of this discussion is Sorel's *pars pro toto* argument, and this is an argument that, as Wolin stresses, interestingly underpins so much of modern social and political thought. In particular it is one that later theorists of participation and self-management have emphatically reinforced in taking the industrial enterprise to be an analogue of the polity itself. To be sure, a discussion of Sorel's position can shed light only indirectly upon that of later theorists who have not shared in many of Sorel's central assumptions. But the general theme that Sorel played a part in introducing has very far-reaching implications.

Sorel, as we have seen, drew attention to certain resemblances between the (industrial) part and the (civic) whole. Here he has been followed by later theorists[70] to the extent that they too have denied that any qualitative gulf exists between the values attached to the citizenship available at the level of political institutions and the values that may be taught and learned at the level of the industrial enterprise. In several respects, it may be noted, Sorel has not been followed. First of all, Sorel spoke the classical language of self-repression or self-discipline, while the later writers have employed the more modern and appealing language of self-development and self-realization. Secondly, Sorel distinguished between the civic and the political, regarding the former with favour, the latter with contempt; later theorists, however, have entirely abandoned this distinction, investing the industrial enterprise with political no less than with civic properties. Thirdly, the later writers have connected citizenship essentially with democracy, while Sorel – as his view of the socialist factory makes quite clear – did not. We shall consider shortly how much difference this makes to the theme at issue.

In Sorel's notion of the equivalence of industrial and civic identifications we have observed a series of conflations or elisions. What has in particular been elided is the distinction between the features of a thing and the definition of it. Participation in *industrie*, initially proposed as a criterion of membership in civil association, comes to define the nature of the city itself, and what began as an idea of qualification *for* citizenship comes to determine what citizenship *is*; what originated as a test becomes an analogy. Likewise, military capacity had once been viewed as a qualification for citizenship, serving either as a test or as a preparation for the enjoyment of political rights – those who fought *for* the city were entitled to be members *of* it. But Sorel's war against nature is not a preparatory but a definitive value, and it defines what the industrial city is in a manner in which war did not define what the political city was, however essential it may have been to it. In this respect, we may note, Sorel's proposed analogy between warrior-citizen and producer-citizen breaks down entirely, for the former is a citizen by virtue of being a warrior, the two statuses being distinguishable if inseparable, while the latter is citizen-like in being a producer, the two terms being merely interchangeable descriptions. Finally, we have seen that Sorel sought to make a transition from political to pre-political analogies: initially valuing the socialist movement for its capacity to participate in political struggles over issues of concern to a whole society, he quite rapidly transferred his allegiance to a movement that rested upon an exclusive myth. Political struggles, as he contended, require 'disinterestedness,' the setting aside of exclusively sectional attachment; myth, on the other hand, requires the identification of sectional and general ends, the setting aside of particularity and the recognition of a common attachment now being accomplished within and not beyond the socialist movement. And the movement now retains its equivalence with the civic, not by virtue of expressing a comparable mode of action but by virtue of resembling the city in its extra-political aspects, that is, in relying likewise upon violence and myth.

The consequences are revealed in Sorel's sketch of the factory of the future. The engineers are to 'speak of their men as a master speaks to his students': the factory has become a school. It is not, however, a school of citizenship in the sense that what it teaches is preparatory to some further activity; it is not a school *of* anything. Here it contrasts with those other educational devices that Sorel so admired in the ancient city – poetry, drama, myth, and war – whose function was, after all, to equip the citizen for something else. Sorel has abstracted the experience of civic education from the ends that made it civic and is thus led to his disturbing picture of a lifelong and intense preparation that is not, however, a preparation for anything. Now if all that concerns us here is the transmission of experiences of a certain kind, then indeed the relation between part and whole ceases to pose any problems at all. We can readily imagine that an experience of collective attachment could occur no less easily at one level than at the other, that such a value is wholly mobile between city and enterprise, and that differences among levels are, as it were, merely quantitative. But we may wonder if the notion of citizenship, thus understood, has any specific meaning left to it at all and whether what is being discussed might not better be placed under the heading of moral education or personal development.

It is here that what needs to be said about Sorel also may need to be said in the context of later thinking. There can be no doubt that various attributes of the polity are also to be found elsewhere, whether we choose to stress (with Cole) a sense of responsibility, or (with Pateman) a sense of personal efficacy in the making of decisions that affect one, or (with Bachrach) the existence of power and authority relations, or the making of societally relevant decisions. But in these cases no less than in Sorel's one may wonder if the nature of a polity is altogether exhausted by analogical arguments; for analogy by its very nature is selective, and the resemblance of one institution to another – even in important respects – cannot establish their mutual substitutability. In those cases in which the analogy drawn bears upon the occurrence of some experience, the acquisition of some skill, or the learning of some attitude, we may indeed, as in Sorel's case, take this experience or skill or attitude to define what citizenship is; but then, as also in Sorel's case, we may wonder whether citizenship could not be exchanged for some other and more precisely descriptive term.

Unlike Sorel, later theorists speak of self-development and also of democracy as values. The idea of self-development may carry with it the implication that the attitudes or skills acquired in the context of the enterprise can then be applied by the individual elsewhere.[71] Similarly, to speak of *democratic* citizenship is to introduce an appeal to a set of values that can and presumably should be brought to bear in any relevant context, and thus again to suggest that the principles learned in the enterprise may form the basis of action within, or reform of, a larger context of institutions. Unlike the various analogies offered above, such suggestions provide causal assertions that are open to empirical test, and do not simply assert a more or less plausible resemblance; the claim that what is learned or acquired in one context is subsequently transferred to another is, on the face of it at least, a convincing one, and one that has important implications for democratic theory. But this version or aspect of the participatory argument seems curiously at odds with the analogies that are held to support it. For if indeed an enterprise is an arena of citizenship, or a polity, why should it be so important that the experiences gained within it should be capable of transfer beyond? It is important that such a transfer should take place only to the extent that the further context of action is seen to be *un*like the context of original acquisition; for if the two were not in some respect different, the original experience would be complete (as Sorel, apparently, actually came to believe).

This conceptual difficulty is compounded by the transposition not only of citizenship but of politics itself from whole to part. Here later theorists have departed drastically from Sorel, who had no wish at all to claim the mantle of politics for the renewed citizenship of *industrie*. He evidently did not feel that the restriction of politics to the institutions of the state hampered in any way the cultivation of civic properties in the enterprise. The later theorists, however, dissent sharply, and take the view that their case for enhanced participation at the level of the enterprise hinges fundamentally upon the recognition of its political status. But this seems doubly unfortunate. If citizenship is to become a category of moral experience, then we clearly need another term for the category of relations among those institutions within which that experience occurs; and if politics follows citizenship along the Sorelian path of transposition, it is hard to see what term is left. If, by contrast the political character of the enterprise is taken to refer directly to its structural position – for example, to its impact upon general questions of distribution[72] – then once again the argument from analogy loses its point, for the internal similarity of enterprise and polity becomes irrelevant to the argument.[73]

Sorel's contribution to modern political theory is usually taken to have been malign. I have tried to show above that it is often condemned (or dismissed) for the wrong reasons and that his central contribution bears a closer relation to some important current views and assumptions than is usually thought. He is the nearest and clearest ancestor of a transposition of language and image that since his time has become increasingly pervasive. Perhaps, thanks to our emotional distance from Sorel, his writings offer an opportunity to assess not only the political but also the conceptual costs of his revised conception of what it means to be a citizen.

PART IV: CITIZENSHIP AND CIVIC RELIGION

7

Durkheim and the Secular Polity

When Sorel lamented the decadence of the Third Republic, he singled out its educational reforms for special concern, criticizing them from varied standpoints as his thinking evolved but always finding them objectionable. These reforms, the subject of a long struggle between radical and conservative opinion, stripped the Church of any role in public education and forbade religious instruction in state schools, replacing it with moral instruction in the principles of republican *civisme*. It is hard to imagine anything more profoundly offensive to Sorel's deepest convictions: progressivism, vapid bourgeois patriotism, shallow anticlericalism, relentless centralism, and, above all, a naïve faith in the power of abstract doctrine were all to his eyes combined here in a manner horrific to the moralist. That the reforms sprang, ideologically, from an odd mixture of Comtism and the principles of 1789 – a mixture achieved, *pace* Comte, by Emile Littré and Jules Ferry – must have compounded Sorel's fears: a false view of science was allied to a false view of politics. But for Durkheim – who was not wholly unsympathetic to Comte and was wholly sympathetic to democratic republicanism – civic education was an essential component of the secular polity. Secular order requires the teacher, just as traditional order had required the priest; 'he is the interpreter of the great moral ideas of his time and country.'[1] Durkheim lavished much time and effort on the task of conveying a sense of this mission to teachers and also to giving orderly formulation to the 'moral ideas' that had to be instilled if democratic citizenship was to be possible. These ideas were to be 'purely secular' ('laïque') and rational in their justification, for Durkheim did not at all share the view, held by Sorel and Bergson among others, that moral belief inherently has an 'obscure' and perhaps mystical core. Morality can become rational, as he claimed in an almost purely Comtean passage, just as other areas of knowledge have freed themselves of 'mysterious principles'; morality may have proved more obdurate than physics, chemistry, biology, and psychology, but 'there is no reason to suppose that this last barrier, which some still try to oppose to the progress of reason, is more insurmountable than the others.'[2] Durkheim, like Comte, attempted to surmount it: the difference is that while Comte, in doing so, transformed the citizen into the sociologist, Durkheim's ambition was to transform the sociologist into a citizen.

Secularism and democratic citizenship were thought to be linked for two related reasons. First, in the protracted conflicts over the army's conspiracy against Dreyfus, the long-standing conflict that Tocqueville had so regretted – between secularist left and Catholic right – was brought to a head. Expanding far beyond a question of the propriety of a judicial decision, the issue became a test of loyalties, exposing the fractures of French political culture. As opinion on the question came to be identified with broader polarities, to support Dreyfus's cause was to ally oneself with democratic republicanism, while to uphold his sentence was to defend 'national institutions' such as army and Church. A prominent member of *dreyfusard* and republican associations, Durkheim, in an essay entitled 'Individualism and the Intellectuals,' was to situate the issue in terms of a philosophy of history. The 'intellectuals' – a new term – who came to Dreyfus's aid were accused by F. Brunetière, from the standpoint of a Catholicism that allied itself with political reaction, of neglecting the conditions of political order and of preaching anarchy. In his reply to this solemn critique – Maistre, but with all the wit removed – Durkheim most interestingly tries to show that the defence of rights and the preservation of order are in fact, or have in fact become, one and the same. To uphold an individual's right to justice is not, he argues, to imperil national identity or national institutions but, on the contrary, to foster national identity by preserving the very institution upon which it has come to depend: for the cohesion of a modern nation can rest only on the cultivation of those beliefs which, in a modern society, can be shared. The defender of rights 'renders his country the same service that the ancient Roman rendered his city when he defended traditional rites against reckless innovators.'[3]

Second, it is well known that Durkheim's commitment was far from being of a value-free kind. Indeed, it has been said that he 'made his greatest contribution to sociology ... while pursuing quite another objective,'[4] that is, an ethical theory. This is true, though it is also true that the very concept of sociology carried with it an ethical program. As Comte had conceived of it, its ends were at once cognitive and pragmatic (though he was later to transfer its pragmatic elements to 'la morale') and its development was essentially bound up with the fate of religious belief. The positive understanding of man by sociology, which was to complete the 'encyclopaedia' of knowledge, would bring about the maturing of the human mind and the triumph of reason (again a view that was later to be modified); in doing so it would demystify both theology and metaphysics. Such a project evidently owes more to the philosophes than Comte's bilious view of their century would suggest. He was to reject, of course, their anticlericalism (for they had not grasped that man, like God, would need priests), and also their appeal to 'nature' (for they had not seen that such an appeal is merely transitional, God having been lost and man not yet found). But he is entirely faithful to the Enlightenment in his belief in inexorable progress, in his talismanic use of the word 'humanité,' and above all in believing that *humanité* itself, the structure of human relationships, could supply an immanent source of order that would render divine order dispensable as a criterion of value. His encyclopedia owes much to the spirit of an earlier one.

Now Durkheim did not swallow Comte whole by any means, but he too believed in the inherently educative objectives of sociology. In making these objectives his own, Durkheim also made his own the enlightened project of displaying the immanent moral order in human association and of substituting – in terms of an older language – *droit humain* for *droit divin*: obedience once sustained by God can be sustained by man alone. The conclusions of sociology emerge, in their pragmatic mode, as an official ideology of citizenship, which derives from the conditions of human association both obligations and rights. Since Durkheim (like the later Comte) viewed religion in a purely sociological way – it is, simply, 'a system of collective beliefs and practices that have a special authority'[5] – this ideology may also be called a civic religion. But it is important that such a thing should be distinguished from what Rousseau had called 'la religion civile,' for that had been a religion of transcendence, civil only in the sense that its profession was required and that it taught a civil obligation; whatever we may make of the view that civil obligations themselves, in Rousseau's hands, take on what some regard as a 'religious' quality,[6] it is surely noteworthy that Rousseau believed that the polity required the support of something that transcended it. Durkheim, however, did not. In the civil religion that he describes, political society is itself the object of worship; transcendence is demystified, and citizenship depends inherently upon 'l'esprit laïque.'

In the history of political thought in France there are important connections between ideas of citizenship and its possibility (or impossibility) and views of the bearing of religion (or irreligion, or transformed religion) upon civil life. But what *laïcité* or secularization means or should mean is as vexed a question in the French context as elsewhere. In none of the theorists discussed above – even in theocrats such as Maistre – is there a harmony of religious and political objectives such as Bodin had supposed; political obligations are not nested within a divinely ordained cosmic order. But what the alternative to such harmony may be, quite evidently, is disputed. One approach, exemplified by Comte (among many others), is distinctive in stressing the theme of *transference*, which Durkheim too was eventually to adopt. Religious belief is neither to be separated from civil life nor rejected; its essential features are to become features of secular organization, which is secular not in the sense that it has detached itself from religion nor in the sense that it has denied the truth of religion but in the sense that it has itself absorbed what is true, though misunderstood, in religious belief. But that sense is extraordinarily complex, as well as unsatisfyingly so. Comte leaves us in no doubt that, in his view, historical development inherently displaces religious beliefs to human sites; what was given to God is to be given to man, and what was celebrated as God's work is to be celebrated as human creation; but what 'development' is and what kind of displacement is entailed remain very unclear. Several kinds of reading of Comte's view – as, we shall see, of Durkheim's – are possible.

Referring to the celebrated remark in the preface to Pascal's *Treatise on Vacuum*, Comte agrees that 'the same thing happens in the succession of men as in the different ages of single individuals' and that the history of human society is therefore like the biography of 'one single man.'[7] We may discover the essential pattern of historical change by introspective personal memory; we recognize in ourselves three successive 'states,' or modes of cognition, for which the course of history also provides 'evidence.'[8] Indeed, the course of history is more complex, the three states succeeding one another at different rates in different realms of life (a fact that did not, however, prevent Comte from speaking of 'three natural ages of humanity');[9] but all the same, to speak of history as one source of evidence is to imply that the law of development contains a necessity that is achieved *through* history, as it were, rather than *by* it. It is inherently necessary, and the states of cognition contain an inherently necessary relation to one another; contingencies may delay or accelerate the process, but that is all. On such a reading we would most naturally view the religious manner of seeing the world as having a temporary and determinate place, which is transcended as more 'developed' states of cognition render it unnecessary. What is transferred elsewhere is the task of religion.

But Comte sometimes suggests that we should view history in a different way: not as a medium through which a necessary pattern is unfolded but as a process of accumulation and transmission that makes the present the *result* of the past.[10] Here Pascal's image is read differently; there is an analogy between individual life and history only because individuals have been made what they are by history; the test of introspective memory works only for the individual 'up to the level of [this] century,' who has, that is, absorbed into himself the achievements of the past. In this view there is clearly some scope for contingency, and in the case of the history of religion there are at least two important examples of it: the separation of spiritual and temporal powers[11] and the invention of Catholic liturgy[12] exercise a crucial long-term impact even in the positive age itself. Such a view makes it possible to speak of indebtedness to the past in a sense not permitted by the first view; the men of the past are not (only) to be seen as instruments of inherent developmental tendencies but as having created, by non-necessary actions and thought, the social world that we now inhabit. Thus Comte can speak of morality as 'a precious patrimony transmitted by our ancestors' and of Catholic liturgical practice as a creation that may – but should not – be 'lost.'[13] Religion is thus treated as a possession or inheritance and not (simply) as a phase. It is something that we 'borrow' from the past, despite the fact that, perhaps incongruously, the past is viewed only as a 'prelude.'

A third view preserves more exactly the original meaning of Pascal's image, that is, the notion of continuous expansion over time. Here Comte relies upon concepts such as extension and perfection. Change is presented as the progressive, continuous elaboration of a number of distinct principles or capacities through a variety of environing cicumstances rather than as a succession of qualitatively different states or a contingent sequence of effects. History is to be seen as a series of

176 Citizenship and Civic Religion

anticipations of its end rather than as a series of steps *towards* it. The elements of the final regime have been 'slowly developed in silence.' There is a 'slow accumulation, gradual but continuous.' Positive styles of thought have *always* been present in human life, at least in 'germ,' and the positive stage represents their full development. The realm of reason has been progressively extended even within the irrational stages of history, and 'trials' ('tentatives') of the rational regime have sometimes been prematurely made.[14] The successive limited forms of social organization – family, city, state – are 'cores' ('noyaux') of a universal human society, anticipating the positive society of man by closer and closer approximations.[15] The positive age, therefore, will reveal our 'true nature,' the forms of which earlier ages have only 'sketched' as accurately as the constraints of their circumstances have allowed.[16] Here we would wish to imagine religious belief less as a historical moment or a constitutive cause of development than as a temporary container for a secular process that progressively asserts its independence. Religion is, as it were, a provisional shell, and what it encloses comes eventually to explain itself on its own terms.

There are, then, different kinds of implied transference: there is the transference of items of religious life to a secularized society; of attention from other-worldly to worldly aspirations; of aspirations once termed 'religious' to secular realms of thought and action; of the meaning of the word *religious* itself. In inheriting the transference thesis, along with sociology, from Comte, Durkheim inherited an exceedingly complex set of ideas. He was indeed to put these to a different political use, for while Comte's 'religion of humanity' was to expunge citizenship by creating new authorities, Durkheim's was to require citizenship to be operative in the processes by which authority was to be generated. But despite political differences of a very marked kind, some of the same conceptual tensions were to emerge.

What is the 'human association' that in the past has supplied us (obscurely) with norms and now (overtly) is to provide the ground for a moral and civic education? Durkheim rejects the view that it is association in the sense of reciprocity that counts. We cannot generate morality out of the relations among individuals, for in moral experience there is always the sense of something beyond the individual that is obligatory or compelling or both. This, he maintains, is society in the sense of an organized entity (rather than in the sense of sociability); it is our society that speaks to us in our consciences, however much we may wish to represent its voice in 'metaphor.' Durkheim distinguishes two importantly different kinds of society, identified, in the context of political theory, with Rousseau and Montesquieu respectively. 'The unity Rousseau attributes to the sovereign power,' he says, 'is not organic. This power is constituted, not by a system of diverse, interdependent forces, but by a homogeneous force, and its unity results from this homogeneity ... He did not conceive of [society] as a whole made up of distinct parts, which work together precisely because they are distinct. His view is rather that it is or should be animated by a single, indivisible soul which moves all the parts in the same direction by depriving them, to the same degree, of all independent movement.'[17] Of Montesquieu's conception of monarchy, however, he says that 'Montesquieu had come to conceive of a society whose unity not only did not exclude the particularism of individual interests, but presupposed it and followed from it. In his view, social harmony resulted from the division of functions and from mutual service. There were direct ties between individuals, and the cohesion of the whole was only a resultant of all the individual affinities.'[18] Durkheim's preference is clearly for the latter, and his conception of the democratic republic owes something to the pluralist tradition. He constructs a philosophy of history that guarantees the triumph of the second kind of society, which he calls 'organic,' over the first, which he calls 'mechanical.'

It is the social division of labour that accomplishes this historical transition. In the society of mechanical solidarity the principle of association is likeness, and it is served only by the cultural and political enforcement of a single type of personality and behaviour. It cannot permit diversity, for difference threatens its integrity, and deviations are visited with savage punishments as threats to society's central norms. As the division of labour advances, however, individuals come to be related to one another by their complementarity; association becomes organic, and the specialization of roles makes diversity not only permissible but necessary. Freedom is achieved, for the cultural and legal pressures of consensus are relaxed, individual differences no longer placing the society's central norms at risk. In *The Division of Labour* this distinction between two kinds of association is very rigorously pursued, association by resemblance being viewed as inherently repressive, association by complementarity as liberating. If 'affinity' is valued at all, that is only because it supplies a primitive social order on which diversity can exercise its liberating work; wherever resemblance is mentioned, it is connected with prejudice, exclusiveness, loss of identity, or the 'agglutination' of the individual.[19] Every remaining source of resemblance, such as consanguinity and locality, is destined to occupy an increasingly marginal place in modern society, the family giving way to the workplace as the focus of attachment and the division of society into local 'segments' being replaced by a principle of functional division.[20] Consistent with this view is the model of democracy that Durkheim advocates, in which functional constituencies ('corporations') would eventually replace territorial constituencies; freedom and reason are to be found in the realm of difference, not in the realm of affinity, and the persistence of territorial identifications inherently expresses a residue of mechanical solidarity.

In Durkheim's thought at this stage, the 'so-called human' (as he disparagingly puts it)[21] is not valued. For the approximate sources of his social vision are Montesquieu's idealized picture of medieval France, as well as a reminiscence of the system of producers' guilds ('corporations'), a system that indeed he calls 'normal.' The good society is imagined as a plenitude of differences and not, as in the Stoic and natural-law style of the eighteenth century, as an assemblage of people sharing fundamental common properties. To imagine society in the latter way is quite simply to deny sociology. It is to imagine that there is a realm called 'human' that is somehow exempt from social determination, a notion that has retarded the emergence of social science, deflecting even Montesquieu from the truth. Typically, it led social theorists to the (literally) preposterous device of a social contract, which ignores all social determination by presenting society as a human construct. 'For such a contract to be possible, at a given moment all individual wills must direct themselves towards the common bases of social organization, each particular mind thus posing the political problem for itself in all its generality. But that would make it necessary for each individual to leave his special sphere ... '[22] And to detach individuals from their special spheres is to detach them, fictitiously, from precisely those concrete interdependencies through which social order constructs itself over time. The argument is parallel to Rousseau's and, like so much post-revolutionary argument, turns Rousseau the sociologist against Rousseau the jurist.

Now it is well known that there was a transition in Durkheim's thinking after *The Division of Labour* and that he adopted a position that, if quite intelligibly related to what he had said before, is nevertheless in some respects surprising. The values of what he had called 'organic' society remain consistent throughout, and the division of labour retains ultimate primacy as a factor of social causation; but what it brings about is very differently explained. Still drawing upon the division of labour, he contends, in 'Individualism and the Intellectuals,' that diversity has so far extended that 'we are proceeding towards a state of affairs in which the members of a single social group will no longer have anything in common other than their humanity, that is, the characteristics which constitute the human person in general.'[23] Similarily, in *Lectures on Sociology* he writes of 'that set of causes that, by differentiating the members of societies, have left them with no essential characteristics in common except those they get from their human quality.'[24] Thus it is no longer that social diversity as such makes us free; it is rather that diversity, extended to its limit, produces something socially undetermined – a human status. By an implicit and almost dialectical self-transformation, sociology annuls itself and issues in a sort of Stoicism.[25] Sociology can understand only what is common; when no social properties are common, only generic humanity – 'the individual *in genere*' – remains. It is from this socially empty being that new forms of obligation are constructed: to arrive at obligation we *must*, after all, detach the individual from any special sphere, but we do not have to do it fictitiously, for social evolution does it for us. Social change enables us to see that there are 'obligations laid upon us that arise solely from our intrinsic human nature, or from the intrinsic human nature of those with whom we find ourselves in relation'; Durkheim identifies, alongside civic duties, 'morals that govern the relations of men as human beings,' and 'beyond' the state 'something more universal and more enduring';[26] he hints at the ultimate possibility of a human society in the most literal sense, that is, a cosmopolitan order, and though he sees this hope as only a distant one, he maintains that civic duties can correspond to, 'carry into effect,' the ethics of cosmopolis.[27] Of course, the generic individual who makes all this possible is socially empty only because he has been *socially* emptied, by processes of diversification which remain the province of social science; but that only serves to reinforce Durkheim's Stoic vision by stripping away any pessimism or resignation, presenting moral order as the outcome of advancing civilization itself and not as a feature of a lost golden age. It is, as it were, a somewhat Romanized Stoicism, in which the duties of man merge with the obligations of civil life.

What is new here is not that the status and dignity of individuals are recognized – Durkheim had done so no less in *The Division of Labour* –

but that they have, in forming the core of a new set of collective beliefs, apparently become the sole source of cohesion. That is how Durkheim turned the tables so ingeniously on the anti-*dreyfusards*: since national cohesion depends upon shared values, which are now individualist, the defence of the individual is demanded by national loyalty and is as civic as it is moral. In *The Division of Labour* too he had said that social change would generate a new set of collective beliefs, but he had also argued that this transformed 'conscience collective' would diminish greatly in the 'intensity,' the 'determinateness,' and (probably) the 'volume' of its demands:[28] he could accept this, obviously, only because he no longer thought that solidarity hinged upon consensus but that it derived from multiple reciprocities. His new stress upon moral consensus, of a new kind, does not at all require the abandonment of the thesis of organism in social and economic relations, but it does bring into question the thesis of organic *solidarity*; for in organic or modern society, no less than in mechanical or tradional society, it is necessary that members 'fix their eyes on the same end and come together in a single faith.'[29] The mode of association that he now envisages, therefore, resembles the mode that he had identified with Rousseau, in contrast to Montesquieu: it is 'constituted' by a 'homogeneous force,' although he has ceased to believe that homogeneity as such necessarily deprives a society's members of 'independent movement.' It is not the existence or the saliency of a *conscience collective* that is decisive for the question of freedom, but, simply, what its content is; in the new *conscience*, individuals themselves enjoy the 'sacredness' that once, when views of a different kind held sway, reduced the individual to nothing.

Religion is, plainly, conceived of differently as Durkheim's thinking thus evolves. In *The Division of Labour* he had written: 'If there is one truth that history teaches us beyond doubt, it is that religion tends to embrace a smaller and smaller portion of human life.'[30] In *The Elementary Forms of Religious Life*, however, as well as in the later political and ethical writings, Durkheim offers a view of religion as an essential constituent of all societies; the view is, according to one commentator, 'effectively a reworked theory of mechanical solidarity,'[31] religion being identified simply with common beliefs of a kind to which special importance attaches. Since such beliefs are indispensable, we need not even ask whether religion must exist, only 'what the religion of today should be.' There is a risk, Durkheim admits, that this new religion of individual rights and civic duty may be a little colourless and thus lacking in educative force, but this is no insuperable obstacle: 'To ward off this danger ... we must seek, in the very heart of religious conceptions, these moral realities that are *lost and dissimulated* in it. We must disengage them, find out what they consist of, and express them in rational language. In a word, we must discover the rational *substitutes* for those religious notions that for a long time have served as *the vehicle* for the most essential moral ideas.' He continues: 'It is not enough to cut out: we must replace. We must discover those moral forces that men, down to the present time, have represented only under the form of religious *allegories*.' Unless we can discover these forces and construct from them a new moral ideal, we shall have no 'contribution to bring to the *moral patrimony* of mankind.'[32] The profusion of images here is striking. Dissimulation, vehicle, and allegory are very different things, but they all imply that 'moral reality' could be *better* conveyed if unadorned by religion; yet it is in 'the very heart of religious conceptions' that moral reality has to be discovered, and when discovered it will be a 'substitute' for 'religious notions.' Moreover, while the models of vehicle, allegory, and so on imply that moral reality is always accessible, made obscure only in its expression, it is nevertheless said to constitute a patrimony – that is, something that would *not* be available to us if someone else had not passed it on. There are here several distinct implied conceptions of the relation of past and present, and, very much as in Comte's argument, we are left in some doubt as to whether religion is a mere prelude to secular morality or whether secular morality must borrow from religious experience; or, if both, why?

But the case of religion supplies only one of the transitions, though perhaps the most striking, in Durkheim's thinking: another, of equal importance to the meaning of secularization in its political sense, is that of the state, which likewise is reconceptualized, and in a somewhat parallel way. In the pluralistic conception with which Durkheim had begun, the whole stress falls on the horizontal relations of civil society, the reinforcement of which by the division of labour tends to displace the vertical relations of political command. Because he stressed 'mutual service' expressed in 'direct ties between individuals,' he envisaged the whole as 'only a resultant' – a view obviously similar to the social vision of political economists, though Durkheim, as we have seen, prefers to identify it with Montesquieu's political thought. The state, then, diminishes in saliency as society comes to be diversified. It is certainly a mistake to suppose, in the manner of some political economists, that regulation diminishes, for, if in some respects public regulation of life does decline or even vanish, in others it actually extends; but its character changes, and regulation assumes the function of preserving the conditions of co-operation among individuals rather than, as before, 'repressing' deviations from a rigorously imposed social type. While it is true that Durkheim abandoned his distinction between two kinds of law as indexes of social change – conceivably because he came to recognize political as well as purely social reasons for legal variation[33] – he certainly retained the view of the modern state as more tempered and benign than the states of mechanical society. In the *Lectures* he writes: 'There is no doubt about the real nature of the ends pursued ... by the state: to increase its power, and render its name more glorious, was the unique or principal end of public life. The interests and needs of individuals counted for nothing. The religious character imprinted on society's politics displays the state's indifference to the individual's concerns.'[34] The modern state, however, is not shrouded in sacredness and set apart from profane or ordinary life; it is touchable and accessible, and its essential function, no less than in *The Division of Labour*, is to provide the conditions for individuality and sociability.

In part but only in part, Durkheim's political thought retains its links with the pluralist traditions recalled by his critique of mechanical despotism. He speaks the language of conflict and balance, finding security for liberty in the setting of power against power and advocating a separation of powers between state and professional group. Both state and group are potentially oppressive. The state is because even the demystified and tempered state must retain a residue of the coercive power whose employment had been the central function of the pre-modern state. The group is also potentially oppressive, and for a most interesting reason. Durkheim now stresses a factor that *The Division of Labour* had mutely glided over, the obvious enough fact that specialization creates some resemblances just as it removes others. 'When in a political society there are a number of individuals who share the same ideas and interests, sentiments and occupations, in which the rest of the population do not share, it is inevitable that these individuals be swept along by the current of similarities: they feel drawn to one another; they seek one another out; they enter into relations with one another and so gradually become a limited group with recognizable features within the general society.'[35] There is, then, a mechanical solidarity within the group that would thwart individual freedom if groups were not contained and restrained by a wider system of authority. Durkheim, we may speculate, notices the fact of professional resemblance because, having come to see human resemblance as the basis of political society itself, he finds restricted professional affinities to be potentially threatening. He thus comes to speak of secondary associations in a way that is, as one commentator has pointed out, more Rousseauan than pluralist: 'There must be no forming of any secondary groups that enjoy enough autonomy to allow of each becoming in a way a small society within the greater.'[36] Durkheim's ancient Roman triumphs over the Goth, partial associations being valued only to the extent that they share directly in the purposes of the state.

The overt solution is found, as noted above, in a theory of mutually countervailing forces. But alongside this reworking of the doctrine of the separation of powers, another way of speaking of the state asserts itself. While it is the conflict between state and group to which freedom is attributed – 'out of this conflict of social forces ... individual liberties are born' – a relationship of an essential kind is asserted between liberty and the state. Durkheim's new conception of the state as an agent of liberty does not belong at all to the constitutionalist paradigm of machine-like checks and balances but depends upon a different language. Durkheim speaks of 'duty,' 'function,' 'purpose,' 'aim,' 'fundamental duty,' and 'responsibility'; conceptualized in this way the state is no longer merely a material force to be held in check by other such forces. It acquires a quite special character. It is linked internally, in its 'concept' or 'nature,' as he says, with the creation and promotion of individuality and individual rights. The social groups figure only as 'conditions'[37] under which the state can fulfil its task. Perhaps it is significant that in connection with the mechanical ideas of conflict and balance Durkheim refers, in the traditional constitutionalist manner, to 'liberties,' whereas the other conception of the state on which he relies points strongly towards a notion of 'liberty,' as rational self-determination, a notion more characteristic of Rousseau and of idealist thinking, the growth of the state and of individual freedom being complementary.

Identifying the state with freedom in this way, Durkheim associates a certain kind of consciousness with it. It is a medium through which rationality and lucid self-consciousness are most fully revealed. Political or civic consciousness is not to be confused with the *conscience collective*, those 'vaguely diffused sentiments that float about the whole expanse of society,' sentiments that stay 'in the half-light of the subconscious.' Civic consciousness is characterized by deliberation and reflection. It corresponds to the 'central and relatively clear consciousness' in each individual, which emerges from and stands above 'the nameless and indistinct representations that form the substratum of the mind.' Democratic political forms receive their justification from the fact that they reflect the essential character of the state most fully, bringing 'deliberation and reflection and a critical spirit' to bear in public affairs, relieving societies of 'lack of consciousness, uncharted customs, the obscure sentiments and prejudices that evade investigation.'[38] Although the processes of modernization contribute indispensably to making such rationality possible, in tending to free individual thought from a sacred, all-enveloping consensus, one is dealing here not with something that is causally produced by modern societies but with something that such societies 'need.' If, therefore, as far as social and economic structure is concerned, 'everything takes place mechancially,'[39] in the context of political structure we switch from sociological determinism to a rational response to objective conditions.

Civic rationality is, in turn, strongly associated with the transcendence of particular or local ways of thinking, which are culturally determined and limited. Here the *Lectures on Sociology* display a most interesting and unacknowledged transition, or confusion. Initially the state, no less than the local or professional group, is identified with an essentially limited and partial understanding. Expanding upon the doctrine that morals are diverse, that what is appropriate to a citizen in a democracy, for example, is not what is appropriate under other constitutions, Durkheim places civic morals in the class of particular morals, along with the morals of the family and the profession. But he at once recognizes that there are degrees of particularity and arranges the partial morals of various associations on a bell-shaped curve of 'moral particularism' that 'makes its appearance in the domestic morals of the family, goes on to reach its climax in professional ethics, to decline with civic morals, and to pass away once more with the morals that govern the relations of men as human beings.'[40] Civic morals, then, approach the universal more nearly than those of the profession. Clearly, this cannot be traced simply to the scale of the association, for otherwise the family would be more particularistic than the professional group, whereas according to Durkheim it really is less so. The argument is cast, rather, in terms of what is typical in associations; families of different kinds and states of different kinds have more in common, more 'similarity in their basic features' than professions do, the ethic of the soldier, for example, differing utterly from the ethic of the scientist. But this is only one line of approach to the question. Typicality, or range of diffusion, is one thing; generality of *object* is something else, and it is to this that Durkheim turns later in his discussion.

Durkheim assigns value to moral sentiments in terms of the scale of their respective attachments or of their objects. 'There is no doubt that those aims that are the most general and the most unchanging are also the most elevated. As we advance in evolution, we see the ideals that men pursue breaking free of the local or ethnic conditions obtaining in a certain part of the world, or a certain human group, and rising above all that is particular and so approaching the universal.'[41] Durkheim does not distinguish this quite different argument from his earlier discussion of typicality. He goes on: 'We might say that the moral forces come to have a hierarchic order according to their degree of generality,' but clearly this last word is ambiguous in the context. The extent to which moral feelings are 'diffused' has nothing to do with their generality or 'elevation.' In his passage Durkheim is dealing with the 'breaking free' from limited associations and local conditions, and obviously one would not have to break free from them to attain moral generality if this quality consisted merely in typicality or sameness. The diffusion of sentiments and attachments, unlike their generality of *reference*, is not at all a criterion by which a hierarchy of value is to be constructed but simply an *effect* of the 'advance in evolution' that Durkheim sees. The moral conception of generality is thus conflated with a sociological fact in a way that brings out the quite basic ambiguities in Durkheim's concept of the 'normal.'[42] Norms are at once measurable social regularities *and* moral imperatives; given that Durkheim is a sociologist of morality, he can scarcely be expected to separate the two. But he sanctions the norms that he values by equating what is normal in one sense with what is normative in another.

In his slightly later lectures on *Moral Education* Durkheim wrote: 'Those moral objectives that are most abstract and impersonal, those that are furthest removed from all conditions of time, place, and race are also those that emerge as pre-eminent.'[43] He repeats his argument that throughout historical evolution morality has become 'larger' in its object, that this evolution displays a constantly developing transcendence of what is local and partial and now arranges groups into a hierarchy of moral value that is unequivocally a hierarchy of scale. The echoes of Rousseau are clear indeed: 'The will that is most general is also the most just.' But what is especially Rousseauan is that Durkheim, having constructed a moral argument that logically implies the absorption of the state within some larger order, deflects these implications quite consciously by presenting the state as the largest *effective* association and as a vehicle for the morals of *humanité*. Rousseau had rejected the notion of a universal society because morality, even if its internal logic is universal, can exist operatively only where there is a *lien social* among men, and since such *liens* exist only at the level of particular societies, the moral life must be confined within their borders. Durkheim likewise and in the same words contends that since there is no 'constituted society' of man,[44] the state, as the largest association and hence the closest approach to a universal order, effectively marks the limits of moral obligation. For, he contends, as Rousseau had, the expansive tendencies of morality are contradicted by an opposing psychological trend – 'the more the society extends beyond the individual, the less can the individual sense within himself the social needs.'[45]

But, again like Rousseau, Durkheim wishes to regard this merely empirical limitation as no more than quantitative, as it were, a limitation that does not change the quality or essential content of the obligation. It is by virtue of becoming citizens that we become men, according to Rousseau; or, according to Durkheim, the purpose of the state is that of 'making men of its citizens.' 'All contradiction between cosmopolitanism and patriotism' disappears if the political association is fulfilling this task.[46] If in *The Division of Labour* Durkheim had found the notion of *humanité* excessively abstract, he now sees its abstractness as a positive merit; it is, he says, a sort of general model from which different nations draw different but complementary sketches, embodying these 'perspectives' in diverse but non-exclusive cultures.[47] Durkheim differs significantly from Rousseau only in carrying this argument enthusiastically to the point of promising not merely a revolution in the domestic arrangements of states but also an end to war among them. For if national attachments are stubborn, despite their clear moral inferiority, national feeling can, perhaps, be deflected from the pursuit of aggressive and competitive ends to the pursuit of pacific ones. Two sets of rules emerge from the same 'source,' society; nevertheless, they amount to 'two diverging currents flowing through our moral life,'[48] the irrational and retrograde closure of the exclusive group and the belief in the rights and dignity of man as man. It is to this latter set of rules that Durkheim appeals exclusively in his arguments about the justification and the legitimate forms of political order, and it is these he expects to triumph over the residue of the former.

Durkheim's thinking about both religion and the state thus follows complex and shifting paths. Consequently, the implied pictures of the secular polity that we are offered are varied and sometimes contrasting. We know that we are to suppose divinity to have receded and to recede further, and that human association is to find sources of value in itself and not in fictions; we know that 'le croyant' is to give way to 'le citoyen' and that repressive hierarchy is to be replaced by co-operation and personal responsibility. But when we try to specify the meaning of these very general and somewhat polemical themes, any single answer eludes us. There are several different models, in Durkheim's argument or behind it, of what a secular order is.

On one model, there is in human thinking increasing universality and rationality (Durkheim links the two) because of the erosion of the force of local prejudices. Such prejudices assume a religious form, *are*, in fact, religion, for a religion, according to Durkheim, is nothing more than a set of collective sentiments and practices of more than usual intensity. Consequently, as thought disengages itself from the taboos and dogmatic prescriptions of the group, seeking universal standards of right, religion implicitly declines. We cannot speak of its elimination, for since every society rests upon some collective sentiments, every society must have a religion. But the place of religion becomes progressively more modest. Alongside its religion society constructs new structures of thinking that are distanced from dogma and ritual.

Or we may stress, rather than the increase of rational and abstract modes of thought, the pragmatic element that Durkheim also connects with modernization. There is a shift in the relative volumes of sacred and profane things. The category of things that are sacred or set apart from human interference shrinks in scope; the category of profane or modifiable things expands accordingly. When social activities are all approximately similar, they are absorbed within the image of a single type of behaviour heavily invested with a sacrosanct aura. But when functions are differentiated from one another and dispersed widely among increasingly autonomous groups, the degree of variability and of individual initiative increases enormously. There is (in functional, not territorial terms) a 'localization' of effort in which immediate situations become progressively remote from authoritative dictation and in which, therefore, activities become increasingly subject to criteria of pragmatic need. God 'withdraws' from the world.[49]

Or we may think instead in terms of the changing content of the religious and the sacred, not in terms of a change in their saliency or social place. It is not that religious belief declines in any sense; it is that the object of reverence changes. It is no longer society as a whole, in divine disguise, that is revered; it is the individual. More precisely, perhaps, since Durkheim also says that the object of all religions is society, we should say that the object changes from a society conceived of as a whole to a society conceived of as composed of individuals. Likewise, the sacred objects are less and less the symbols of collective life; the individual and his rights are imagined to be inviolable. There is a 'cult of the individual.'

Or perhaps we should see the process involved as an *inversion* of the sacred and the profane rather than a proportionate shift of volume from one to the other. For what was sacred comes to be described in profane language, and what was profane acquires the character of sacredness. The collective symbols of rational life, once a crucial component of a society's religion, are described and accounted for by Durkheim in relentlessly positivistic terms, demystified and relegated to the pre-rational level of mere prejudice. but the democratic state, rendered profane by its disengagement from collective myth, is described in teleological language as the bearer of 'sublime' proposes and duties. And it is, therefore, the state that figures as the instrument of a sacred history or meaningful design, whereas the shreds of once-sacred social myth become merely an empirical accompaniment to the progressive revelation of meaning.

Or, finally, it may be wrong to speak of the decline or diminution, or specialization or transformation of religion in anything more than a loose, conventional sense. For what declines or diminishes or is otherwise modified is not what is essentially religious at all. It is merely its dispensable apparatus. Religious notions have served as vehicles for human and moral ideas, ideas 'lost and dissimulated' in its dogmas. A secular society, in educating its citizens, 'must discover those moral forces that men, down to the present time, have conceived of only under the form of moral allegories.'[50] Here Durkheim is at his most Comtean. The 'religion of humanity' (as he too calls the new creed) is, it appears, the truth of religion, the hidden essence disguised under provisional forms, and a secular society, in which the disguise is thrown off, is that in which the truth of religion is finally revealed.

There are, at best, only 'familial' correspondences among these alleged or hinted-at conditions of a secular order. The incongruencies are at least as striking and bring into question the unity and consistency of the process of evolution that Durkheim outlines. For example, there is a certain lack of accord between the notion that modern cultures are progressively distanced and *separated* from religion and the attempt to reduce religion to culture and hence to identify the two. Similarly, there is an incongruity in combining the claim that modern societies display an increasing preoccupation with the profane, with the claim that they rest on and promote 'civic morals' that are closely linked to, if not identified with, a revised conception of the sacred. What is human is linked sometimes with what is approachable, touchable, the ordinary or the profane, and sometimes with a new, essentially religious (though non-divine) order. There is no reason why we should not regard these two processes as two aspects or dimensions of social and ideational change that may occur together. Both the saliency *and* the content of religious belief may change.[51] But there is a conceptual difficulty here, for what is essential on one definition becomes only accidental on the other. Certainly we may speak of the specialization or decline in comprehensiveness of religion if we define it conventionally, and we may explore the place of religious institutions, in the ordinary sense, in modern societies in contrast to pre-modern ones. But on the special or functional definition of religion as a matter of strongly held collective beliefs, this is to adopt an irrelevant criterion, for 'symbols and rites,' 'temples and priest' constitute only the 'external apparatus' or 'superficial aspect' of religion.[52] This difficulty is compounded by the fact that the new and rising religion (in the special sense) apparently also has many of the subsidiary features of religions in the ordinary sense: 'This cult of man has for its first dogma the autonomy of reason and for its first rite freedom of thought.'[53] If such things as dogma and rite belong only irrelevantly to religion, properly defined, how are we to explain their reappearance? Perhaps sensing this oddity, Durkheim goes on to refer in passing to the beliefs and practices of the old religion as 'symbols and rites in the full sense,' and so we are implicitly invited to suppose that the symbols and rites that are declining are in some sense more *fully* religious than those that are rising. But the difficulty here is that the co-presence of sociological and liturgical criteria has made it impossible to see what this full sense could be.

It is in part because this uncertainty is part of Durkheim's legacy to it that modern social science deals so ambiguously with questions of secularization. Precisely the same uncertainty has been detected in Talcott Parsons, for whose sociology of religion Durkheim's writings, along with Weber's, were a principal source.[54] On the one hand religion is defined as the 'highest' level of a culture, so that the religion of a society *means* that set of ultimate values from which (allegedly) its other beliefs and practices radiate. This of course rules out the notion of a secular or non-religious culture, for its religion could only assume new forms, its existence being stipulatively guaranteed. But in considering the place of *religions* in society, it would appear, Parsons switches to conventional usage in which religion is identified, roughly speaking, with churches and the belief in transcendence. Exactly the same could have been said of Durkheim. Similarly, among theorists who draw upon Durkheim or Parsons or both, we find entirely disparate pictures of the relationship between religious experience and secular life, both sustained, correctly but selectively, with appeals to Durkheim's authority.[55]

Whether religion is to be identified from the social actor's point of view or from that of the social observer is evidently a crucial interpretative question and one that leads to familiar confusions.[56] Among religions, as defined by the self-interpretation of believers, various kinds of experience are taken to be central, and there are correspondingly varied attitudes to the secular world, ranging from ascetic withdrawal through civic obligation to theocracy. The political meanings of religion are diverse, and the political means of secularization are also necessarily diverse, not only because there are different kinds of separation, elimination, or transference that can be assumed to occur but also because different kinds of religion can be imagined as the base point. Now it is important to Durkheim's method that different kinds of self-understanding should not stand in the way of theoretical models: no less than other sciences, social science must posit concepts of its own, and definitions of religion or suicide or any other social fact must be stipulated in a way that permits the greatest possible clarity and explanatory range. How good an approach this is to social science is much disputed. But it was not merely for methodological reasons that Durkheim viewed religion in a stipulative way. He had to do so in order to sustain a political thesis and to *écraser l'infâme*; he had to define religion in such a way that empirical differences would be rendered insignificant and all religions could be shown to be continuous with religions of group loyalty and social discipline. Where the facts stood in the way of this project, Durkheim's response betrays obvious but quite possibly unconscious embarrassment, as in the case of his treatment of Christianity. His whole sweeping construct of progressive liberation and individualization had been anticipated and even influenced by the account given by Fustel de Coulanges of the decline of the ancient city. In pagan society, Fustel had written, 'religion, law, and government were confounded,'[57] a single constellation of symbols submerging the individual beneath the weight of collective life; it was Christianity that rescued collective life from divine symbolization and made possible the recognition of individual personality. Not only does Durkheim accept this account in its original context; he also transfers the model of change to the modern epoch, substituting religion for paganism, individualism for Christianity: clearly, this leaves Christianity in a conceptually uncomfortable position, as a source at once of liberation and of repression. Durkheim's solution is to describe Christianity as 'an essentially human religion,' but this is to fall dramatically between two stools.[58] For if a dichotomy is made between the religious and the human, something that is essentially human is not a religion, and to call it a religion is to revert to a different kind of definition.

Such problems may evoke some sympathy for what Tocqueville had called 'a human point of view' – not for agnosticism as such but for a *political* agnosticism that does not make political and theological truths hinge upon one another. But that point of view is allied not only with a view of secularization that Durkheim did not accept but also with a view of politics he did not share either. His politics tends to the linear and goal-oriented kind that Tocqueville had disliked; Durkheim's state is inherently charged with the pursuit of ends and with tasks that he revealingly describes in the language of *making*. It is because it has to 'make men of its citizens' that the state must undertake to enlighten them and to instil in them, by means of a rigorously uniform system of education, a rational morality. With this, Tocqueville's view of political education may usefully be compared. For in his view political education is accomplished by demonstration rather than instruction, not by civic texts but by what might well be called the sub-text of institutional life. What it accomplishes, moreover, is not the diffusion of a set of moral doctrines but a sense of the complexities of action, which is to moderate the force of 'general ideas.' Durkheim's politics, like Tocqueville's, may be called 'liberal,'[59] but that simply shows that liberalism can embrace very different and contrasting views of the relations between principle and action and between the moral and political worlds.

Durkheim was in revolt not only against what was later to be called the 'closed society' but also against what had already been called the 'closed religion,' in which he was brought up and which he did not abandon until he entered the Ecole normale supérieure. His abandonment of

Judaism, it is thought, may have owed something to the influence of Bergson himself.[60] Bergson called Christianity (to which, eventually, he was to convert) an 'open' religion: Durkheim, drawing different lines of opposition, called it a 'human' one. His object, after all, was not to discriminate between kinds of religion but to oppose the (conventionally) religious and the secular; and confronting a religion that departed from his closed model, he could make sense of it only by viewing it as something not quite fully religious, a step on the way to a human or secular faith or an episode in the protracted revolution by which morality is severed from rites. He wrote in *Moral Education*: 'Although there are religious duties – rites addressed only to divinity – the place they occupy and the importance attributed to them continue to diminish.'[61]

This view of Christianity is a somewhat rationalistic one: Christianity is regarded as primarily a set of human duties that merges imperceptibly with a moral philosophy. It is tempting to suppose that Durkheim here traces, in reverse, a path that Bergson was to sketch in *The Two Sources*. Compare, he says, 'the doctrine of the Stoics with Christian morality. The Stoics proclaimed themselves citizens of the world, and added that all men were brothers, having come from the same God. The words were almost the same; but they did not find the same echo because they were not spoken with the same accent. The Stoics provided some very fine examples. If they did not succeed in drawing humanity after them, it is because Stoicism is essentially a philosophy ... It is a far cry from that to the enthusiasm that spreads from soul to soul ... Such an emotion may indeed develop into ideas that make up a doctrine ... but it precedes the idea instead of following it.'[62] Durkheim reproduces this problem; demystifying Christianity, he arrives at something much like a Stoic law of nature, the duty of man *in genere*, which he then transposes as the content of a purely secular faith. And the problem set in *Moral Education* is exactly the predicament of Stoicism as Bergson describes it: the idea comes before the experience and must search for didactic experiences in order to convey itself.

Durkheim removes from this natural-law-like construct, of course, any explanatory claim in political theory. He remains unswervingly faithful to his view, stated in the thesis on Montesquieu and *The Division of Labour*, that we cannot explain a political society as something created out of naturally independent individuals. Moral beliefs such as belief in 'rights' are ultimately effects, not causes of society, and the individual *in genere* is produced, as we have seen, only by a long process of sociological elimination. But while this view radically undercuts the explanatory claims of natural-law theories, it gives their moral claims the sanction of a historical guarantee. No longer set at odds with the corrupt artificiality of civilization, they are features of civilization itself, products not only of speculative reason but of objective social change.[63] Consequently, what Durkheim also removes from natural law is any acute sense of distance between the ideal and the actual. The resignation with which Stoic man agreed to be a citizen is no longer in evidence as the state takes on the role of 'making men of citizens' and the gap between exclusive and universal orders approaches its vanishing point. The sense, common to theorists of natural law, that the natural and the civil are in a certain tension, is not shared by Durkheim; he does not recognize, as, for example, Grotius did, that political action is related to its moral basis only in an 'extended' way, precisely because he does not see its moral basis as something pre-social or supra-social that can be realized only with emendations or additions. He identifies the moral ideal, rather, with a certain state of social organization with a characteristic political and legal structure; for, after all, morality does not arise – or arises only mediately – from 'essential traits implanted in man' but from essential traits of social behaviour.

It has been remarked that in some modes of secularism we may see a 'Judaeo-Christianity from which crucial reservations have been removed.'[64] Of Durkheim we may perhaps say that his secularism represents a version of Stoic natural law stripped of its necessary qualifications. And Sociology, which at first glance appears to erect formidable obstacles to Stoicism, turns out in this case to have removed them or, rather, concealed them from view. After Rousseau – but with his reservations, too, smoothed away – Durkheim's doctrine of citizenship represents one of the boldest and most persistent attempts to recover for the democratic state the secure legitimacy that had eluded it. His doctrine did so by seeking to reproduce for the state, in secular terms, a moral order that would give universal sanctions to particular ends. But its persuasive intentions altogether outrun anything that Durkheim's argument can actually prove, and lead the argument itself into several incoherencies.

8

Henri Bergson's Two Cities

A certain tentativeness is called for in discussing Bergson in a political context, for it may perhaps be thought that he does not belong there at all. The major part of his thinking was innocent of any political interest and even uncongenial to one; the themes for which he is especially remembered – the radical interiority of freedom and of the creative impulse – lack any secure place in a realm of institutions, of objective consequences, and of shared or rival meanings. His is a subjectivism that, while unlike Montaigne's, likewise 'refers everything to the self,' reducing order to a feature of personal interest or expectation and in that sense detaching it from the public realm. His last book, *The Two Sources*, marks, of course, a departure, especially in introducing political categories that were later to be put to celebrated use in liberal political theory; but even *The Two Sources*, one brief and rather stern commentary has complained,[1] is fundamentally inadequate to political realities, employing centrally as it does the theme of love and thus ignoring the colder reciprocities of consent.

Now it must be admitted at once that, from the point of view of certain legitimate expectations, the political content of *The Two Sources* is quite thin. What, in terms of commitments and programs, does it offer? A warm if very unspecific reminiscence of the great declarations of the American and French revolutions; an endorsement of parliamentary rule and the alternation of parties in government and opposition; guarded optimism about the League of Nations; and finally, an anticipation of something that can only be called the greening of Europe, a revolution of consciousness, aided by dietary changes and the liberation of women, by which societies would come to accept a simpler and less frenetic way of life. This is not a set of themes calculated to move the more hard-boiled of the political theorists. But beneath what some may see as a rather suspect mellowness – exaggerated a little in the English translation available – there is an unexpected critical edge. This has not always been seen, in part because of the difficulty of finding a context for Bergson's book; it is a peculiarly lonely work, belonging to no school or movement nor founding one, and lacking a clear place even in the lines of evolution of Bergson's own thinking. Is it a late, essentially personal and occasional work by a remarkable philosopher of science, a work interesting because – like the political writings of the still more remarkable Russell or Einstein – its author excelled at something else? Or is it, in offering its dualism of 'open' and 'closed' societies, a precursor of Popperism? Or is its use of dualism only a belated and rather tired flowering of the habits of nineteenth-century sociology, with its 'status and contract,' 'community and society,' 'mechanical and organic solidarity'?[2] Perhaps it is at least worth entertaining the possibility that *The Two Sources* is a work of French political thought: when we do so, a line of thinking is revealed that, while offering very little by way of a political program, nevertheless bears acutely upon long-standing political themes.

The central political doctrine of *The Two Sources* is the distinction between open and closed societies, which originates with Bergson though it may owe something to a distinction previously made in the philosophy of religion.[3] The two societies, as Bergson thinks of them, are not social types in the usual sense: closed societies do not confront open ones, as in later uses of the terms by liberal political theorists. All societies contain elements of closure simply by virtue of having boundaries and needing to maintain them. Some societies, probably all modern ones, also participate in the open society, but this is not (or not yet) a society in the same sense, that is, a constituted and organized one; the word 'society' is in this case used rather as St Augustine used the word 'city,' *mystice* or symbolically – perhaps there is an echo of this in Bergson's description of the open society as a 'mystic' one.[4] The open society is the order implied by moral imagination (either philosophical or religious), which reveals ends other than those of political order. Bergson marks the difference by way of the notions of *obligation* and *appeal*.

The closed society depends upon obligation, as does the beehive or anthill. The human case is significantly different: the bee or ant is driven directly and by implanted instinct to the performance of specific social tasks, whereas members of human societies have a more mediated relation to instinct. The specific obligations that they have are variable, a matter of local human contrivance, but in the disposition to obey them there is, Bergson maintains, the sense of an absolute imperative as implacable as that of the social insects. Obligations may be questioned, for man is an intelligent as well as a social being; but the questions are always answered in advance. Ultimately, *you must because you must.*[5] Intelligence is placated by a closed religion, which clothes obligations with the satisfying imagery of myth; the function of religious myth is to protect the society and the individual from the potentially dissolving power of reflection. The force of obligation, the 'pull' or 'tug' that brings us back to our station and duties when they are momentarily brought into doubt, also makes itself felt in the most highly intellectualized regions of human life: even moral philosophy – Bergson singles out utilitarianism – is at bottom nothing but a further demonstration of the *must*, supplying reasons for what is motivated already.[6]

The open ideals exercise, on the other hand, not an obligatory pressure but a moral appeal. They do not lay down prescriptions and prohibitions; through the figures of the moral 'heroes' who bear them, they present pictures that exercise a radically moving appeal. Thus, 'the generality of the one consists in the universal acceptance of a law, that of the other in the common imitation of a model.'[7] The individual who accepts this appeal or model strives to imitate or to follow, not to obey; whatever prescriptions or prohibitions he is led to are only derivations from this effort of love and not themselves constitutive of goodness. Nor are they essentially connected with order in its social or political sense. Their object is not to submerge individuals beneath their roles, or to secure their submission to authority, or to reinforce the bonds of group loyalty; the society that they point to is that of humanity itself, and the open religion, unlike the closed, is universal or it is nothing.[8]

The Two Sources repeatedly draws attention to the imagery of concentric circles of association, by which, Bergson claims, the purely rationalist mind overcomes dichotomies and renders experience superficially consistent.[9] We observe that we belong to groups or categories of different sizes – family, nation, humanity itself. We imagine that they differ only in scale, that a single associational impulse broadens out progressively to embrace larger and larger objects. But this is not so. The first step, from family to nation, happens to fit the facts: the second does not, for the step here is from an essentially exclusive loyalty to an essentially inclusive one. In a phrase rather reminiscent of Rousseau, Bergson says: 'It is primarily as against all other men that we love the men with whom we live.'[10] An inclusive loyalty or love, which is careless of all divisions, is achieved by means that are quite distinct, structurally and psychologically, from the experience of social solidarity, of shared political identity, or of patriotic sentiment.

Strongly parallel to this, in the dimension of time rather than space, is an insistent stress on the discontinuities in the history of moral thought: neither historically nor geographically can we subsume all differences under a thesis of continuous expansion. In part, of course, history is an elaboration, an unfolding of what is implicit, and the extension of what is known to new objects, just as some moral experiences are enlargements, in a spatial sense, of others. But there are also, simply, new moral ideas, the work of inspired innovators, who induce qualitative changes in the way of seeing the human world. Perhaps the best example of what Bergson means is supplied by a dense and brilliant passage on the idea of justice.[11] From the beginning there are notions of equality, proportion, compensation, of restoring an order that has been upset. These notions are refined, extended, set in new contexts: but no series of adjustments, however ingenious, can bring us to the explosive conception of absolute personal value, a conception that removes justice from the interior of social life to 'soar above it ... categorical and transcendent.' Its essential objective is not to restore order: it demands adherence even at the cost of the destruction of all order. And while the mind is tempted, in looking back, to see in history the progressive emergence of such a conception, in doing so it masks the new creations and leaps of imagination that were necessary.

Bergson's distinction between the order-sustaining obligations and the order-creating appeals recalls the moral philosophers' distinction between the *right* and the *good*, between the morality of rules and the morality (or ethic) of ends. Like other moral philosophers of the earlier twentieth century, he is concerned to show that the conflation of the two leads to misunderstandings, although, speaking as a social theorist rather than a moral philosopher, he believes that conflation to be necessary. The two moralities interpenetrate, laws lending to ends the sense of compulsion and ends lending to laws the notion of attraction. This poses insoluble problems to philosophy, which is unable to explain why it is good to do what one ought or why one ought to do what is good:[12] but this happy confusion may be socially necessary, for to distinguish quite clearly between the right and the good is to risk undermining the force of both. Laws must be thought good if they are to be obeyed, and the good must be thought lawful if it is to be followed.

With this we may usefully compare Durkheim's treatment of the same topic: 'Institutions may impose themselves upon us, but we cling to them; they compel us, and we love them; they constrain us, and we find our welfare in our adherence to them and in this very constraint. The moralists have often pointed out the same antithesis between the concepts of "the good" and of "duty," which present two different and equally real aspects of the moral life. There is perhaps no collective behaviour which does not exercise this double action upon us, *and it is contradictory in appearance only.*'[13] That Bergson sees difference where Durkheim sees unity is of great importance for understanding their respective social and political theories: for we may see in Durkheim's civic ideology precisely those identifications that Bergson saw as confused and set out to disentangle.

Bergson agrees that in (much of) collective behaviour there is a double action, the closed morality of rules and the open morality of ends overlapping extensively – 'in practice they may be indistinguishable.'[14] The taking of innocent life, for example, offends both public order and humanity. But that is not to say that the prohibition of killing can be derived *indifferently* from either source, for the source of the prohibition also establishes the conditions under which it can be set aside. And prohibitions whose conditions of applicability differ, Bergson in effect insists, are not the same prohibitions. Between the conditional prohibition of murder laid down by political societies and the unconditional prohibition that love for humanity dictates, there must therefore be a difference that is one of kind, not simply of degree.

If in domestic political relations this difference is hard to see, the duties of man and citizen intermingling so thoroughly, in international relations it becomes plain. For in endowing us with our first morality, the morality of rules, nature had in mind only groups of a restricted scale, already strained or perhaps exceeded by the scale of the modern nation-state.[15] Even an association of the size of the nation-state survives only by borrowing and enlarging sentiments of loyalty from the intermediate groups within it. Up to a point, then, we may speak of concentric circles of obligation and imagine that duties differ only in their range. But when we reach the borders of the state, we encounter abruptly the inherent limits of natural morality. Nature 'has interposed between foreigners and ourselves a cunningly woven veil of ignorance, preconceptions, and prejudices.' And 'The two opposing maxims, *Homo homini deus* and *Homo homini lupus*, are easily reconcilable. When we formulate the first, we are thinking of some fellow countrymen. The other applies to foreigners.'[16] It is of course in the case of war that the double action of moralities is transformed into a choice between moralities and the apparent fusion of man and citizen comes apart. 'Murder, pillage, perfidy, fraud, and lying become not only lawful; they are actually praiseworthy ... Would this be possible, would the transformation take place so easily, generally and instantaneously, if it were really a certain attitude of man towards man that society had been recommending to us until then?'[17] In showing us where our obligations do *not* extend, war also shows us what they are where they *do*.

But intelligence is infinitely resourceful and rallies to society's defence, even in this last extremity, with a plausible-looking distinction between principle and practice. 'Oh, I know what society says ... It says that the duties it defines are indeed, in principle, duties towards humanity, but that under exceptional circumstances, regrettably unavoidable, their exercise is for the time being curtailed.'[18] Now, what society says is precisely what Durkheim had said on its behalf in his lectures on civic morals and on education. In a distant future, universal ends may be universally applicable: but they require a 'constituted society' if they are to be effective, and 'at the present day, the state is the highest form of organized society that exists.' By this means Durkheim deflects the conclusion that Bergson was to draw from the fact of war, and maintains that the external exclusiveness of states does not impugn the moral universality of their domestic political life. He thus expresses exactly that doctrine that Bergson saw as so central to the fallacies of the too purely rational mind: 'Family, nation, and humanity represent different phases of our social and moral evolution, stages that prepare for one another, and thus these groups may be superimposed without excluding one another.'[19]

In stressing the significance of war Bergson was moved above all by the indelible horrors of 1914–18, which had also had so devastating a personal effect on Durkheim. In what Bergson now says about it, there may well be a hint of self-criticism, for, no less good a citizen than Durkheim, he had lent his support vigorously to the Allies' cause. In an intensely patriotic lecture entitled 'La Signification de la guerre' (1915), Bergson represented the war as a struggle between civilization and a barbarism with the technology of civilization at its disposal. English imperialism, he goes so far as to say, has 'moral force,' while that of

Germany is merely brutal, unrestrained by any notion of a 'higher ideal' than power. As for France, in its devoted spirit of self-sacrifice the ideal and the real 'coincide': '*her cause is that of humanity itself.*'[20] In all this, what he was later to call the open and the closed effectively comprise rival social types, as they were later to do in Popper's politics, rather than occupying a vertical dimension internal to organized society, as in *The Two Sources*. Whether Bergson was aware of the fact or not, his own views in 1915 exemplify that tendency that *The Two Sources* was to expose: the tendency among peoples engaged in war to equate national and universal ends, and warlike pagan deities with the pacific God whom they worship in name.

But even in 'La Signification de la guerre,' where, for perfectly obvious reasons, reservations about the morality of *civisme* are downplayed or extinguished, a theme appears that also establishes Bergson's distinctness. He challenges the view, for which he cites Herbert Spencer but that dates to Comte and Saint-Simon at least, that the progress of industrialization inherently undermines the military disposition, that (in Comte's words) 'industrial capacity' is substituted for 'feudal or military power,' 'action upon nature' for action 'against the rest of mankind.' In fact, Bergson says, industrialization removes all limits to the spirit of conquest, the expansive power of industry being such that its demands for resources are inexhaustible.[21] That theme, unlike the theme of equation between national and universal ends, was to be retained in *The Two Sources*, and it emphatically distinguishes Bergson's views from any thesis of immanent progress. Progress in general, in social visions dating beyond Saint-Simon to the Enlightenment, is often identified with the progress of technique: but technical capacity, as Bergson views it, entails no necessary departure from the closed society that nature has prescribed. Indeed, it was precisely as a tool-making capacity that intelligence was given to us, other creatures having their means of production rigidly and 'instinctively' prescribed, the human race being endowed with a more powerful 'intelligent' capacity to adapt to changing productive needs. That intelligence goes beyond its naturally assigned tool-making role and generates pictures that are subversive of the given order is a consequence that nature did not intend: it is not *useful* to the social order for which nature has equipped us. But in making tools, the intelligence does no more than conform to its prescribed role, devising solutions to problems that other creatures solve by instinct, and it is vain to expect from its productive work any qualitative transformation in human life. That at least one nation was morally barbarous though technically civilized should occasion no surprise.

That Bergson's dualism of open and closed may owe something to earlier dualism is beyond dispute: Bergson himself noted the similarity between his closed society and Durkheim's mechanical solidarity, though he did not accept any equation between his open society and Durkheim's organic alternative.[22] We need not pursue detailed comparisons: the *point* is different. Durkheim pursued a notion of temporal succession, Bergson a theme of essential tension. There is, as Bergson repeatedly stressed, no hereditary transmission of acquired characteristics; consequently there is no decisive relinquishing of the nature with which we began – 'the original state of mind remains, hidden away.' And everything that we may wish to add to or amend in this original state of mind is subject to its consent and its modification. Closure is not, as Durkheim thought mechanism was, a vanishing residue but a permanent 'fond'[23] of social life, and what is displayed in history is not the triumph of the rational over the archaic but a constant interplay between the two.

Rousseau, Durkheim says, 'remains the theorist of our democracy,'[24] and the doctrine presented in the lectures on civic morals is offered as a solution to a central Rousseauan paradox: that the state is something that at once expresses our will and also stands above it.[25] The solution, though quite different on the institutional plane from that of the *Social Contract*, likewise involves presenting the republic as a moral community: it rules us to the extent that a moral will rules over empirical will, and expresses us to the extent that our will is moral. Durkheim sought to achieve this through rather than against 'secondary associations,' and he identifies, rather than contrasts, professional and civil attachments; the professional groups are themselves bearers of the general will of the community, just as in the community as a whole 'the feeling of humanity,' as Rousseau (sometimes) put it, 'concentrated among fellow-citizens, gains new force.'[26]

It is, then, the line of thinking that extends from *Social Contract* to the *Lectures on Sociology* that we may take as the essential target of Bergson's critique, a critique that stresses the illusoriness of moral homogeneity and the ultimately unclosable gap between citizen and man. But intriguingly, Rousseau also stands behind much of the argument of *The Two Sources* itself – not so much the Rousseau of the *Social Contract* but the more haunted and querulous Rousseau whom Durkheim left out.

Durkheim adopts and amends Rousseau's answers, while Bergson raises again his questions. The issue of war makes this strikingly clear. Bergson asks whether belligerence would arise so 'easily' if it was indeed 'a certain attitude of man towards man' that society required of us in civil life; the question is precisely Rousseau's, in his work on Saint-Pierre – if social order indeed were the work of reason alone, would it not be obvious to us that 'in joining a particular group of men, we have really made ourselves the enemies of the whole race?'[27] Where Bergson follows Rousseau is in stressing what it is that states – even partially rationalized states – do not owe to reason alone.

If what Bergson does can be called a sort of conjectural history, then its clear if approximate antecedent is the most accomplished example of that genre, Rousseau's *Discourse on Inequality*. In order to distinguish what is natural from what is acquired, Bergson says, echoing the *Discourse* quite precisely, 'we have to advance tentatively, following simultaneously several methods, each of which will lead only to possibilities or probabilities';[28] we may find clues in the remnants of 'primitive' societies – to be used with caution, for they too have their history – in animal behaviour, and in introspective memory. We must proceed in this way, moreover, for what is essentially Rousseau's reason: origins are opaque to us because there is heterogeneity between the causes of things and their effects, whereas the tendency of the mind is to assume continuity – to foreshorten the past and to explain the origins of things in terms of the ends for which we value them. This is perhaps the most central of the themes of Bergson's work as a whole; the distinction between the prospective and the retrospective is the key to his conception of freedom and, in his biological theory, is especially well developed in his critique of Spencer's evolutionism. Transferred now to the context of social and political thought, it coincides with a critical theme traceable to Hume and Montesquieu but expressed most emphatically by Rousseau. 'The philosophers,' he complains, confuse effect and cause; because principles of rational obligation have become intelligible to them, they assume them to have been intelligible to men from the beginning. They thus 'make man a philosopher before making him a man.' In fact, the art of generalizing and of reaching moral conclusions is not only 'difficult' but also 'belated' and is the product, not, as the philosophers believe, the origin of social experience.

Now Bergson clearly takes Rousseau's side in this dispute with the philosophers, though the context now is the critique of utilitarianism rather than of natural law. He too imagines a hypothetical 'independent man': 'Endowed with intelligence, roused to thought, he will turn to himself and think only of having a good time. Formal reasoning would doubtless show him that it is in his interests to promote the happiness of others; but it takes centuries of culture to produce a utilitarian like Stuart Mill, and Stuart Mill has not convinced all philosophers, let alone the mass of mankind. The truth is that intelligence would counsel egoism first.'[29] Again, therefore, the critique concerns the confusion of end and beginning, effect and cause, and ignorance of 'the time that must elapse.' Moreover – but with a crucial difference to which we shall turn immediately – the critique again concerns the confusion of local or national and 'cosmopolitan' feeling. The sense of mutual obligation, Rousseau insisted, is developed first only in the interior of a society: the notion of a human community comes later, if at all. There are indeed 'a few great cosmopolitan souls who escape the imaginary barriers between peoples, and who, following the example of their sovereign creator, embrace the whole human race in their goodwill,'[30] but they are not the founders of society. The parallel with Bergson is almost perfect: the open society comes long after the closed and is the work of 'heroes of the moral life,' to whom Rousseau's description of the cosmopolitans applies precisely. But these heroes carry out their mission only against the background of an order founded upon passions quite different from their own, and the ends that they envision cannot be employed teleologically as explanations of society's beginnings.

It is true that, as noted above, there is an outstanding difference between the Rousseauan and Bergsonian conceptions of that order: for Rousseau, it has no foundation in human nature, requires, in fact, the 'denaturing' of men; while for Bergson it is rooted in an obligation whose force is physiologically implanted in their 'original nature' and that drives men directly to create a closed morality or religion in which their collective ties are celebrated and reinforced. It is this naturally grounded solidarity, which some have called 'tribal,' that would be the principal feature of later uses of Bergson's picture of the closed society. But Rousseau does not attempt to transform *natural* man into a citizen; his object is to transform *social* man, a being who, by means of a 'slow succession of things,' has at one point been compacted together with others into exclusive but not yet civic groups. This significantly weakens the contrast, especially as Bergson's closed society has certain features in common with Rousseau's account of the social condition. Bergson sees it as a sort of vast theatre in which members of the audience collude in convincing one another of the truth of what they see:[31] 'each is the dupe of all.'[32] 'All are saturated with vanity, and vanity above all means sociability.'[33] 'Deference for others,' Bergson stresses, enters into the very self-definition of social men, and whatever he does is coloured by the processes of opinion. There is, to be sure, as in Rousseau, another self, which Bergson calls 'original,' but we can find this only sporadically and with difficulty, and for the most part we inhabit a 'special ego' that submits itself unquestioningly to social expectations.[34]

Moreover, while Rousseau most certainly does not posit a closed religion of obligation as the starting-point of human social evolution, the theme of closed religion is of course familiar and important to him, figuring in the last and very provocative chapter of *Social Contract* as well as in the chapter on the Lawgiver. And what he says about it again finds echoes in Bergson. The open religion, Bergson says, can exercise enduring social and political influence only by adapting itself to the familiar habits of mind of social man; new moral aspirations 'take shape only by borrowing from the closed society its natural form, which is obligation.'[35] Just as obligations could appear too narrowly oppressive unless clothed in the language of the ideal, so too the ideal would, in its social diffusion, assume too optional a character unless it took on the force of the obligatory. Here it is no difficult task to notice the parallel with Rousseau's treatment of *la religion civile*. One kind of religion, that of the citizen, is socially powerful but essentially brutal; like Prussianism as Bergson describes it, it is unrestrained by any sense that there is something transcending political ends. It is a merely military religion. However, the religion of the man, Christianity, transcends civic obligations too purely; it 'adds nothing' to their force and risks reducing them to mere empirical facts. Between the two Rousseau places a civil religion that, without denying transcendence or trivializing the city, 'sanctifies' law while insisting that there is something beyond it. It is just this comfortable middle ground, where 'all social ends interpenetrate one another,'[36] that, Bergson believes, the social mind must normally inhabit; clear distinctions disconcert it. The history of moral philosophy is the history of vain efforts to discover consistency in something that is essentially a compromise, efforts that make sense only because the empirical dictates of society are tacitly assumed.

Theorists of the 'right' attribute duty to the imperative of self-consistency, neglecting the fact that bare logical consistency would be no imperative at all if it did not (sometimes) coincide with the 'conventions' of a 'human group.' Theorists of the 'good' would be reduced to simple vacuousness if it were not that different expressions of goodness had already been 'graduated' for them by social opinion.[37] Each of the varied tendencies of moral philosophy 'is laden with all that social morality has deposited in it; and we should have to unload it first, at the risk of reducing it to very little indeed, if we wished to avoid begging the question in using it to explain morality. The ease with which theories of this kind are built up should make us suspicious: if the most varied aims can thus be transmuted by philosophers into moral aims, we may surmise, seeing that they have not yet found the philosopher's stone, that they had started by putting gold in the bottom of their crucible.'[38] If Bergson's radically sceptical account of moral philosophy were true, it would enable us to explain the evident opacity of Rousseau's doctrine, to which Kantian, utilitarian, and civic interpretations seem to be almost indifferently relevant: 'all social ends interpenetrate.' For when the city's moral justification is brought into question – just as when its physical survival is brought into risk – logical scruples are exposed to the fiercely centripetal force of a natural imperative, which jealously draws together the threads of argument that a dispassionate mind wishes to keep apart. It must do so because, as Rousseau too had seen in despairing of reason as a motive, to *assent* is one thing, to be *converted* another.[39]

With that point we may feel driven to take yet a further step in this search for filiations – to Pascal, whom Bergson describes as 'the greatest of our moralists.'[40] Durkheim's Rousseauanism is Stoic: universal obligations are found to have political application, the man recognizing civic obligation as inherent in his situation or, if he cannot recognize it, being powerfully encouraged to do so. *Polis* merges effectively with *cosmopolis*, patriotism becoming a 'fragment' of 'cosmopolitanism.'[41] The Rousseau implied behind Bergson's account, however, is Pascalian in discovering that reason cannot impel the will. For both Rousseau and Bergson there is, as well as the first society of vanity, a social and political order that reason would assent to and that, given the constraints of human life, may be thought of as ideal, an order that, while unable to escape all closure, has nevertheless been opened to a morality that is something more than a military ethic. But they both borrow from Pascal's account of spiritual commitment the belief that to *will* such an order goes beyond reason, that the self as a whole must be 'made docile.'

Bergson's three-fold distinction among instinct, intelligence, and intuition, familiar from his earlier writings in philosophy and biology, merges in *The Two Sources* with a three-fold distinction among instinct, reason, and *la charité*.[42] Not only does this resemble closely the three orders distinguished by Pascal, but its function is strikingly similar; the point, above all, is to portray reason as suspended between two other forces, its conclusions determined by one or other or both.[43] Left to itself, Bergson and Pascal agree, reason cannot be relied upon to determine anything, for whatever it concludes can always be argued with – it can only 'adduce reasons, which we are perfectly free to combat with other reasons.'[44] In particular, as Bergson also agrees with Pascal, it is not brought to any resolve by generating a 'metaphysics' of nature, for metaphysical views are connected to action only to the extent that they give intellectual form to what is already a disposition to act. Two things only can bring about a resolve: 'habit' and 'love.'[45] Habit, while its content is obviously conventional and social, is physiologically rooted, the disposition to form and follow habits being part of man's original nature; it is thus inscribed in what Pascal had called 'la chair,' and the interconnected tissue of habits forms a 'second' nature as solid and regular as the first. Pascal wrote: 'Continually repeated exercises are necessary, like those whose automatism ends by instilling into the body of the soldier the moral assurance he will need.'[46] Love, by contrast, accomplishes things that reason cannot, just as intuition can understand things that intelligence cannot. It dispenses with problems where reason poses endless difficulties. It transforms words from doctrines to symbols (as Christianity transformed the 'brotherhood' of Stoicism). *The Two Sources* describes on the collective plane a sequence quite comparable to that of individual conversion in the *Pensées*: reason may point to 'charity' but can achieve it only when a 'first religion' has exercised its discipline. And the alternatives are much as Pascal defined them in his account of 'man without God': 'diversion' and 'depression' are the only two states that reason will achieve unaided.[47]

It is especially important to note that neither in Bergson's case nor in Pascal's is this sequence one of simple continuity whose stages are homogeneous with one another. The first two orders, which govern the life of social man, are separated from the third by 'infinity,' and the gap is not to be crossed by any mere process of generalization or deduction or expansion.[48] We may imagine analogies between the human and the divine cities, but these analogies are merely among those comforting deceptions that preserve us from disconcerting truths. Civil life is ruled by imagination, 'the dominant faculty in man, master of error and falsehood, all the more deceptive for not being invariably so; for it would be an infallible criterion of truth if it were infallibly that of lies. Since, however, it is usually false, it gives no indication of its quality, setting the same mark on true and false alike.'[49] For Bergson, too, imagination is above all the means by which nature imposes its intentions on man; since intelligence can work only on 'representations,' imaginary representations, or 'myths,' are conjured up for it in order to keep it in its place.[50] Like Pascal, Bergson recognizes that this mythic social consciousness is not always false and may overlap in substance with the imperatives of charity. But imagination attaches obligation to the true and the false indifferently. Moreover, where these socially generated myths do coincide with the requirements of an open order, the requirements are expressed as commands or rules and thus are different in character from an appeal inviting a freely given response. Even if there are, then – as Pascal had denied – some things that are praised and blamed by all mankind,[51] it is not from a human consensus that universals can be derived. Generality of *reference* is to be distinguished clearly from generality of diffusion.

In the light of such considerations, one view of Bergson – offered by a well-qualified commentator – seems to misplace the proper emphasis decisively. Jacques Maritain's view deserves the greatest respect, for, knowing Bergson at first hand as a peculiarly brilliant teacher, he was in a position to weigh what may have been implied but not said, felt but not expressed. But to claim *The Two Sources* for the natural-law tradition in Catholic political theory seems at least questionable. Maritain himself noted that such a reading was at odds with some of the 'facts' about what Bergson said, but was nevertheless convinced that in Bergson's thinking he could discern an 'intention' that, if it became fully 'actual,' would 'release and order its potencies in the great wisdom of Thomas Aquinas.'[52] And *The Two Sources* came even closer to actualizing this intention than the earlier writings, as Maritain claimed in a welcoming essay.[53] But surely there are strong grounds for believing that *The Two Sources* is related, through Pascal, to an Augustinian rather than a Thomist tradition. Maritain had little sympathy for Pascal, who represented a strain of thinking, tragic and conflictual, that does not sit well with the harmonic and profoundly synthetic vision that he made his own.[54] For Pascal, Maritain complains, human life is composed of diverse and inconsequential 'fantasies and caprices' that pale into nullity when exposed to truth. In

Maritain's richer and more accommodating conception of truth, diversity is an expression of adaptive power and not an occasion for satirizing human folly. For Maritain as for St Thomas there may be a distinction but there is no discontinuity between good man and good citizen. Although politics is not simply ethical, or ethical *simpliciter*, it is none the less a branch of ethics: the good citizen considers particular goods in the light of universal ones; the good man considers universal goods in the light of particular situations.[55] The good citizen must obey the laws of his state, but these laws, though variable in space and time, are not merely conventional, for they are directed to ends essential to the created nature of man; they are, though incomplete and partial, local 'specifications' of a universal law, and that law is discernible by an innate human faculty. Thus the concrete and the particular, though variable, actualize a universal that is said to 'flower' within them, or 'unfold.' The modes of law, from divine through natural and the *jus gentium* to positive, differ not in object or content but only in their level of specificity. To condemn or despise political society out of moral rectitude is mistaken and pharisaical; political society is, indeed, incomplete, but it is ordered towards an end, or 'implies' a good, in which completeness is realized.[56]

Can we identify such a view, even in 'intention,' in *The Two Sources*, which, as its title indicates, would seem more concerned with stressing dualism than unity? The first ground for doubt concerns the traditional notion of the common good. For Maritain the common good of a particular constituted society participates in a larger good, and the citizen who seeks the common good of his community is thus seeking, though still incompletely, a human good: 'it would seem appropriate to consider the common good of a state or nation as merely an area, among many similar areas, in which the common good of the whole civilized society achieves greater density.'[57] That this good achieves greater density in the common life of constituted societies is a condition of its effective pursuit: the fusion of universal ends with the civic identifications of national life lends them a 'vital and unconscious strength.'[58] But what Bergson has to say about this is more reminiscent of St Augustine's treatment of Rome than of St Thomas's treatment of Aristotle. For he stresses overwhelmingly the military and aggressive elements of civic identification, which he clearly connects with the worship of pagan gods. This pagan worship is, indeed, systematically confused with Christian worship, nations taking the name of God for the exclusive and violent deities that they serve: stressing as he does the war-like potential of the city, Bergson sees no continuity between the ancient notions of civic devotion and the teachings of an open religion. He too thus fully admits the 'vital and unconscious strength' of civic association but sees it as working as much to the detriment as to the reinforcement of a universal end. Here, as we also have seen, he is led to views diametrically opposed to those of Maritain in the passage quoted above, denying that civic ends may be regarded as local applications of human or universal ones; in a somewhat Augustinian manner he sees political associations as imitations or parodies of the divine city and not as participating in it.[59] Although there is an analogy between the two cities, it persuades only the good citizen, not the good man.

The second ground for doubt arises from the absence from *The Two Sources* of a teleology of the relevant kind. From one point of view, of course, Bergson's whole argument has a teleological foundation: he speaks of an 'intention of nature' and claims that it is as valid to do so as for an anatomist to speak of the 'function' of an organ, there being in neither case design or foresight 'strictly speaking.'[60] But what nature can be said to have intended by equipping man with appropriate capacities and dispositions is only the *closed* society. Intelligence was provided as a mere tool-making faculty, nature intending man to be different only in having the capacity to alter his means of production. Intelligence, however, 'developed unexpectedly,' 'outwitting nature' in pointing to an open society in which the limitations prescribed by nature would be overcome. To the extent, then, that there is a teleology in *The Two Sources*, it is one that is not accomplished, but denied, in human history. This point could, however, be contested or at least qualified in the following way. Nature may be understood in one sense as the array of materials and species that compose the world, and in that sense it is obviously true that man, like every individuated thing, has essential limits. But nature may also be understood in another sense, as the force or élan that produced these materials and species by a process of individuation. In recovering or in some sense identifying with this *élan vital*, in freeing itself from created arrests, the vision of the open society may be said to realize the intention of nature in a deeper way. So it may be said that ultimately there is but *one* source, which is drawn upon in two ways, mediate and immediate.[61] This may be true: but it is also true that Bergson makes no *political* use of this argument, for the state is not the essential bearer of this process but is, rather, recalcitrant to it.

By thinking of the state in a different way, no doubt Bergson could have evolved a synthetic vision interestingly parallel to the vision that Maritain admired. But he did not think of the state in a different way, and politically speaking he was a theorist of duality rather than of harmony. Of course, he may still be thought of as a Thomist *manqué* from the standpoint of a theology in which Augustinianism itself is only a Thomism *manqué*, but that takes us far beyond anything that a political discussion can examine. We may say that, on the political plane, *The Two Sources* offers less a theory of the state than a theory of moral tension that the state in part expresses. If, despite the rather troubling vagueness of Bergson's political proposals, we insist on making specific comparisons, it is surely not with the Thomist revival that we should make them; at least as good a case can be made, perhaps a better one, for comparing it with a different contemporary trend of Catholic political thought – with the 'personalism' of Emmanuel Mounier and others, which likewise insists that 'values are not assignable to reality as if they were constituent parts of it,'[62] a view that Bergson (and, later, the existentialists) could accept. For here at least we find a rejection of political teleology and a stress upon the tensions inherent in change; in acting we must grasp 'the two ends of a chain which one cannot rivet ... the two levers of a machine whose action we cannot harmonize,' the constraints of the (socially) real and the impulses of the (spiritually) ideal.[63] But this may be to go too far, and *The Two Sources* is not a book that requires us to make such judgments. It does seem important, however, not to overlook a certain bleakness in Bergson's argument, which relates him more to the specific tensions of twentieth-century political thought than to any recovery of tradition.

That *The Two Sources* is too mystical and generous a book to hold political interest is, the above account has suggested, a misplaced fear. There may be, if anything, a legitimate fear that it leans rather far in the opposite direction. Political society becomes brute materiality, awaiting reform by moral irruptions from outside. Apart from whatever traces these irruptions have left, its institutions only mediate physiological demands, filling in with intelligible content a bare compulsion of nature: *you must because you must*. We may, like Bergson, refuse to see the state as the essential vehicle of something beyond it, or a link in a rational series, or an embodiment of inherent value; but the very proper attempt to make this refusal need not pass over into the claim that the state embodies only material force, or a blind obligation. Even if we grant Bergson's view that the civic mind moves in a circle, simply endorsing pre-reflective demands at increasingly refined levels of ingenuity, it is still the case that the reasons mediating these demands are of independent interest and that it is dubious to classify institutions simply by the demands that they are said to meet.[64]

'When we read a sign-board, "Trespassers will be prosecuted,"' Bergson writes, 'we begin by perceiving the prohibition; it stands out clearly ... In the same way the prohibitions protecting the social order first stand out, just as they are.'[65] Here, if we can tolerate another (and certainly incongruous) comparison, his argument joins up with the most rigorously nominalist strands of modern political thought. 'To cite a principle,' wrote T.D. Weldon in a celebrated paper, 'is to put a stop to demands for reasons and explanations'; such principles 'have a well-recognized function akin to that performed by "keep-out" notices.'[66] All further requests for reasons are misguided: 'Thus in a Communist state it is pointless to ask why the means of production should not be privately owned. The only answer which can be given is "Because profits involve the robbery (or exploitation) of man by man." It does not require a genius to see that "because" here is misleading. What is offered is not a reason but simply a restatement of the principle in question.'[67] Nor does it require a genius to see that, given this approach to inquiry, much of what was traditionally meant by political theory loses any meaning. We are back to *you must because you must*. Inquiries into 'the grounds of political obligation' or 'the nature of the state' can move only in circles, everything being settled by the starting-point, which is imperatively and recurrently reaffirmed. We can expect political theory to do no more. Of course, what distinguishes Bergson from such a position is that he is not only a political theorist; he sees the polity as open to moral revolutions, and his chief interest is in the manner in which its closure can be (partially) overcome; but as far as his conception of politics goes, we are held in a world of circularity no less firmly than we are by the Anglo-Saxon political philosophy of the next generation. So different are the styles involved that the comparison may seem strained; but what has been suggested above is that the single most important feature of Bergson's political argument is its rejection of any idealist conception of the state in which value is presented as immanent in organization. If Bergson at first seems distant from T.D. Weldon, compare both with, say, T.H. Green.

Views such as Weldon's were to provoke criticisms, many of which, with suitable emendations, apply no less to Bergson. Political concepts are not (or not only) labels persuasively applied with a view to recommending or prohibiting behaviour. It has become a common-place that concepts take their meaning from social practices, which carry with them a web of interdependent meanings and justifications. We thus cannot (simply) attribute the use of words to an intention to praise or blame, for the concepts for which they stand govern the notions of praiseworthiness or blameworthiness themselves. In under-mining a pervasive view of the state as an essential bearer of moral ends Bergson also tends to undermine its essential connection to political language: he implausibly represents it as an institution antecedent to languages of justification – it compels, obliges, binds, and prohibits, and then discovers words with which to do so. But perhaps in political language, or in the concept of politics itself, there is more than that: perhaps it expresses not only the notion of (obligatory) order but also a distinctive conception of an order that is public, that is hence diversely viewable, and that thus requires justification under conditions of reciprocal persuasion. If all that is so, then order conflicts not merely with progress, as Bergson imagines, but also with itself. Political order may contain disparate reflexive pictures of its own character and to that extent does not depend upon intrusive moral revolutions for its life. From such a perspective, we must concede, if anyone insists, that *The Two Sources* was not a work *of* political thought; but it may have made, nevertheless, a uniquely valuable contribution *to* it in stressing so vividly that civic ends are not in any unmediated sense the expressions of moral imperatives.

Conclusion:
Moral Community and
Political Order

These studies have been doubly selective: they have left out theorists for whose inclusion a case could be made if a history were to be written; and they have left out much that is of interest, though less immediately relevant, in those views that are discussed. The point of this selectiveness, however, has not been to imply the existence of a school of thought or anything like that, not even a (single) tradition: it has been, rather, to point to some significant contrasts. These are of interest, as it is perhaps obvious to say, only because the views contrasted have something in common, displaying concerns that are recognizably comparable and drawing sometimes upon the same sources, though viewing them, for the most part, very differently. Along the lines sketched in the Introduction, some contrasts have been drawn out and some shared sources – both political and intellectual – identified. Not much will be offered by way of summary here. What may be worth considering, instead, is the extent to which the views examined here lend themselves to a single substantive theme or to a conclusion. A common problem was identified in Part I, that of discovering an order of relations in which the values of citizenship can be justified and sustained, and it was then suggested that this problem is reflected in several areas of inquiry that are important to the modern state: the relationship between the legitimacy of the state and political processes (Part II), between the state and other associations (Part III), and between political and religious loyalties (Part IV). But to what extent do these studies suggest an answer?

In the Introduction and in many of the studies above, the topic of secularization assumes evident importance. But that notion may be understood in many distinct and rival ways, which themselves reflect different articulations of the relation of citizenship to order. Does it mean, as both Comte and Durkheim believed at times, the transference of religious themes to a secular order? We have seen the internal complexities of even that one view, which dissolves into a cluster of positions often different in their political implications. But the thesis of transference is not the only thesis to have attracted French theorists and others in the nineteenth century. By no means did all believe, in the manner of Comte and Durkheim, that social organization was to take on a religious quality; they believed, rather, in releasing institutions and practices from direct investment by religion. Again, however, further distinctions must be made. Is secularization to be imagined in terms of the *separation* of religious and political objectives and institutions, and the recognition of a realm of life in which religious authority and religious behaviour are inappropriate? In that sense it was sought by Tocqueville, who had so acute a sense of the different contexts of life and whose hope was that the entanglement of religious and political loyalties could be avoided. He put the American example to use in trying to persuade French Catholic opinion that there was no incompatibility between religious and democratic belief, for the world's most democratic society, as he insistently pointed out, is also a very religious one. The influence of religious beliefs and institutions can be detected repeatedly in American civil life. Unfortunately, this has sometimes led to the view that Tocqueville was a theorist of civil religion.[1] He was not, for his object in stressing the impact of religion on civil life was precisely to show that this impact is strengthened, not weakened, by religious disestablishment and that French Catholics would therefore do well to abandon any political claims on behalf of the majority faith. It was as a (politically) 'latent' system that religion could flourish and would be valued for its diffuse impact on attitudes and behaviour, not as a direct symbolization of political order. The desperate circumstances of mid-century France were, it is true, to modify the conclusions he had drawn from America, and he was to regret that the Church's teaching did not sufficiently present citizenship as a virtue;[2] but what he was to call for was expressed in strictly universal terms, and we are still very distant from what theorists of American culture have called a 'civil religion,' in which particular national ends are celebrated.[3] Naturally, Tocqueville's stress upon the essentially transcendent nature of religion also set him sharply against any 'religion of humanity,' and what he thought about the conflation of relgious sentiments and human ends is clearly set out in the *Old Regime* in his comparisons of political movements with religious revolutions. Sympathetic where Maistre had been curtly dismissive, Tocqueville explores the possible alternative expressions of *humanité* as an ethical doctrine, but he is no more a theorist of the religion of humanity than he is of theocracy, rejecting both, in fact, for the same reason: that universals of any kind have only mediated application to circumstances and that the space between general beliefs and political action should be institutionally observed.

Or should we think, rather, in terms of *rejection*, a theme exemplified by the religious and social theories of Proudhon? When Grotius sought to show that there was a 'human right' arising from 'mutual aid and reciprocal service,' he contended that the rules that such practices supply would hold good 'even if we should concede that which cannot be conceded without the utmost wickedness, that there is no God.' Proudhon, however, contends that the *droit humain* of mutual aid and reciprocity can be realized only if there *is* no God, and he provocatively takes delight in voicing what Grotius cautiously described as the utmost wickedness: 'Dieu, c'est le mal.'[4] It is God who stands behind all those malign 'absolutes' that make men obedient rather than free, faithful rather than autonomous. To achieve a human right is not merely to dispense with God but to hunt the *idea* of God out of one's mind, the idea of God containing in its penumbra habits of submission that enslave us. What Proudhon regards as a secularized society is not merely a society in which religious institutions have been relieved of political authority, nor even a society that has dispensed with God for any purpose, but a militantly atheist society that detects oppressive godliness in any institution that contains a hint of necessary submission. His anarchism apart, Proudhon is the unrecognized ancestor of later notions of a secular-libertarian culture, in which liberty is equated with the erosion of religious belief. Needless to say, such an equation differs fundamentally from the separation thesis as Tocqueville developed it, for that thesis does not merely *not* require the erosion of religious belief but may even require its persistence, in order that the political realm may be saved from the spilling over of modes of consciousness that appropriately belong elsewhere.

Of the three views it is the second, Tocqueville's, that is politically the most novel, even if it is theologically the most innocuous. It does not challenge any theological claims at all (except, of course, to the extent that a theology makes political claims). But it proposes a political life that is self-sustaining in the sense that it does not require to be ordained by religious beliefs as traditionally understood, or by religious beliefs as understood by Comte or Durkheim, or by the sort of anti-religion evolved by theorists such as Proudhon.

It is the very possibility of such political life, however, that is emphatically denied by theorists of 'loss,' who can see in politics such as that favoured by Tocqueville nothing but impoverishment. What it is that we have lost is variously described, and various accounts are given of when and why it happened. But loss theories generally focus upon the idea of community, which, it is claimed, is no longer provided by societies termed 'liberal.' Social and political relations have become more abstract, less warmly and intensely symbolized, and less sustained by immediacy of meaning than they once were; the idea of participation in a shared order has given way to rational mutuality of interest. Rather frequently, such themes are connected directly with the loss of a religious dimension to common life. Such a view is stressed particularly by Alasdair MacIntyre in what may be the most sophisticated development of this topic. 'Religion, when it is the religion of a whole society, may have functions other than the expression of the natural and social order, but it is always at least an expression of a society's moral unity, and it lends to that unity a cosmic and universal significance and justification.'[5] What is lost is not merely a sense of belonging or of fellowship, as some theorists stress, but above all the capacity for public moral argument, which is possible only when there are shared criteria of legitimation, in the light of which fundamental questions can be raised and answered. Though he prefers to cite Marx and Engels, what MacIntyre calls or hopes for was anticipated more relevantly by Comte: a new consensus that will put an end to the moral disorder of liberal society and perform the symbolizing functions for which we can no longer look to traditional religion.

The evidence discussed above suggests a different view of the situation of social and political theory. It has been argued that modern social and political theory *took on* the task of representing the polity as a moral community, not just in the sense that moral terms could be applied to it and within it but in the stricter sense that the polity was itself to be viewed as *constituted* by moral relationships – by *generalization*, a moral conception that was called upon not only to regulate the decisions and actions of a polity's members but to define political society itself. The discipline may have failed in this task, but to fail in a self-imposed task is not the same as losing something that one antecedently had. The task was new because, conceived of as a human association, a polity could no longer be identified as a *realm*, subjected to an authority generated elsewhere. It had to be identified in terms of principles that made both its distinct existence and its internal hierarchy intelligible as things that would be rightfully chosen or adopted or willed. These principles were to be universal ones, the polity becoming a local instance of *humanité*; the revolution, Tocqueville wrote, 'did not merely aim at defining the rights of the French citizen but sought also to determine the rights and duties of men in general towards each other in a political context.'[6] It was for this reason above all that Rousseau was so important as an influence or source or symbol, for what he had achieved was a plausible (if unstable) integration of universal principle and particular loyalty, obviously a troublesome duality in this frame of thinking. It was this theme above all that Durkheim was to reassert in supplying the French republic with its civic education. And it was this theme above all that Bergson tried to bring to light, through his sympathetic but quite destructive unpicking of the French civic mind; it is a mind that *cannot* bring itself to see in the particular anything but an instance of the universal, but it is wrong, even if – sometimes – happily so.

Now a theme of instantiation, of discovering universal ends in particular purposes, is one that has been given a much broader application and has been compellingly presented as fundamental to the experience of civic life itself. But it is important to note that what is instanced, in the views of the French theorists considered here, is not a City. Particular states are not instances of the universal city. Why they are not is an interesting and complex question. Montesquieu may supply part of the answer, for later views of citizenship were to draw more upon his image of a participatory monarchy, as it may be called, than upon his sternly drawn picture of republican *civisme*. Beyond Montesquieu's influence there lay the more diffuse influence of a mode of thinking traceable to Montaigne, a mode that stressed the intractable self and thus envisaged social order as multi-centred, as a morally attenuated association of beings who absolutely decline to see themselves as parts of a whole or as bearers of civic roles. They may be obedient but they are not plastic, and society can only be a complex series of adjustments among obdurate individualities. Imagined as, primarily, a matter of horizontal mutual adjustments rather than vertical identifications, society is in principle without boundaries. It thus can lend itself to an essential pacifism, and in some cases the identification of the ancient model of the city with war may have limited its persuasive use; it is certainly noteworthy that among the theorists considered here it is Sorel, a theorist of war though not of the state, who makes the most vigorous use of a civic paradigm. If there is a general reason for the paradigm's absence, however, it is surely that to have pictured the state as a city would not have answered one of the questions set. Theorists who feel obliged to explain why obligations are particular when principles are universal cannot advance their case by appealing to a model that is inherently closed and exclusive. They have to take an inclusive model and justify exclusions. Perhaps that is why, if states were not claimed to instance the city as a universal, they were claimed in a different sense to instance the universal city. They are not imagined as replicas, even differentiated replicas, of a single type, but as portions or fragments of human association.

It was not the thought of the classical city-state that was recalled but, as we have repeatedly seen, that of the end of the classical period: of the Stoics and of Augustine. Both reminiscences may have been evoked by the resemblance, which Tocqueville noted, between a state (first royal, then democratic) that was contemptuous of particularity and an empire that had absorbed diversity under uniformity of right. Also, the two reminiscences have much in common, as Bergson noted, though he stressed rather, given his purposes, the differences between the two. What they have in common is that they lend political citizenship a conditional and limited value: on the one hand meeting one's civic obligations can be included in the requirements of *humanitas*, and on the other civic obligation can be justified only as an imitation – albeit a pale one – of membership in the *civitas Dei*. What sets them apart is that the former was indirectly to license a trend of assimilation that presented civic obligations as effectively primary if ultimately only conditional, the ultimate becoming, however, in Durkheim's case, little more than a distracting whisper; while the latter was to lend itself to radical dissimilations, in which the force of civic attachment was denied or demystified or transferred elsewhere. These two trends of thinking mark the polar boundaries of the ideas discussed above. In one, polity and moral community are identified as completely as the underlying mode of argument allowed; in the other, polity and moral community are so distanced that only traces of analogy relate them, traces that allowed Sorel to approve of *dreyfusisme* and Bergson to approve of French patriotism in the world war, both, it seems, regretting their approval somewhat afterwards.

It has been suggested above that in such an intellectual context legitimations of the state are inherently vulnerable. To claim that states are embodiments or vehicles or expressions of moral commitment is at once to invite the counter-claim that other things are too, or that other things are more so. In the anarchist picture of layered associations in stateless co-operation, or in visions of the displacement of states by corporation or Church, or in theories of class war as something no less legitimate than national war, we may see these inevitable counter-claims being made. In Proudhon's case the images and terms of universal order are simply returned to their original place, 'general society,' the state being dispensable as their bearer; in Comte's, the religious potential of *humanité* is exploited with literal-minded rigour and the state is thus dissolved; in Sorel's, the images and terms of civic life itself are dispersed and redistributed. These approaches are as obviously different in their structure as in their result. But what they have in common is that all are fundamentally the work of moralists, whose objection to states is that they cannot offer the moral experiences on the provision of which (it is assumed) their legitimacy rests. More pointedly still, such moralists deny to the state that very generality that Rousseau claimed for it and that imported direct moral significance into the state so decisively. They discover generality in social, economic, or institutional relations, in historical patterns, in the structure of cognition, anywhere but in political relations, to which even at best only a *sort* of general character can be ascribed. Political citizenship is denied because it is not in politics that the general order required by morality is to be found. At issue, it would seem, is not the loss of moral community but the failure of the state's claim to represent it. Whether or not there is a moral community is an important as well as a difficult question; but politically speaking, a prior question is whether it is possible to imagine that it is states that embody it, if it exists.

That states can and must embody moral community is taken for granted by theorists who believe community to be an indispensable foundation for authority itself. 'For the notion of authority can only find application in a community and in areas of life in which there is an agreed way of doing things ... There being an agreed right way of doing things is logically prior to the acceptance of authority as to how to do things.'[7] However, as noted above in connection, especially, with Rousseau, two rather different kinds of authority must be distinguished from one another. Authority may be conferred by rightness or by propriety; the agreement on which it is founded may be either substantive or procedural, a matter of shared ultimate principles or of methods of decision. Are these exclusive alternatives, the latter assuming prominence when the former fail, liberal notions of compromise and toleration – as it is often claimed – dominating public discourse when a substantive consensus vanishes?

If we consider again for a moment the consensual society described by MacIntyre, it soon becomes evident that it too requires a procedural consensus. For agreement on ultimate principles does not rule out severe disagreement over political purposes. Within the community of discourse 'different and rival answers were given'[8] by the members of consensual society. Plainly, such disagreements cannot be resolved authoritatively if the only authority is that conferred by rightness: for it is *over* the topic of rightness – rightness, that is, in applying the shared principles to the issues of real life – that there is disagreement. The society's unity in the political sense, then, rests upon beliefs in propriety or on the acceptance of procedures establishing the assignment, use, and limitation of power. And if that is so, the conflation of political and moral authority and of political and moral community is surely indefensible. States may be influenced in this or that way by moral consensus or the lack of it, but to the extent that they are systems of power with the capacity to impose solutions in the face of disagreement, they are not the *same* as associations constituted by agreement on what is right. That, perhaps, is the strongest point made by *The Two Sources*, and the reason for taking Bergson seriously as a thinker who had something important to say about politics.

One feature of the principles that the state was required to embody was their moral universality, a universality that was made to coexist with distinctive civic or national identities.[9] Another feature was their immanence; and here the sociological tradition, as one would scarcely guess from Comte's or Durkheim's critiques of eighteenth-century rationalism, continued a project originated by theorists of *droit humain*. Legitimation was required to be drawn from principles of association that were displayed in social relations themselves or were to arise from society's 'own nature and condition.' The original model was of course the device of contract, and it was largely in making central use of this device that early modern political theory was distinctive. But the idea of contract could point to two different conceptions of association, which also were capable of being formulated and developed without any reference to contract at all. A contract implies mutual recognition –

parties to it are equal in the formal sense that neither has a prior claim on the other's obligation; it is in this sense that contract and status can be said to oppose one another. The notion of contract thus lends itself, as in Rousseau's argument, to conceptions of political equality in which resemblance is stressed, differences of role or power being justifiable only as the product of agreement on the basis of prior equality. What is general is what is typical or shared, and the analogies between the symbol of contract and a moral theory of generalization are apparent. But contracts of exchange also can be taken to imply initial differentiation: they express a complementarity of interest, and that naturally depends upon their being some difference in the parties' situation – as Proudhon stressed. His mutualism is fundamentally linked to that division of social labour that Rousseau had so disliked, as something incompatible with political equality and hence with freedom. Proudhon, like Durkheim, stresses the diverse and organic nature of a society for which exchange has become the principle of association; it is not homogeneity but differentiation that is the condition of freedom. The institution of credit, for example, to which Proudhon gave such close and constructive attention, makes his point well: it is only because individual lives are diverse and unsynchronized that mutual credit is possible, and it is only because mutual credit is possible that society can free itself from the new feudalism of capital.

Either Stoic or Christian themes or an indistinct compound of both could sustain the first conception: human association springs from a resemblance that may be overlaid or distorted or ignored but that is fundamental. It requires us, as Rousseau argued, to set aside the particular or privileged, not to see things 'from this or that point of view,' in Seneca's words, and thus merges political order with an ancient universal vision. The second conception, however, is sustained by a different root image, one of *plenitude*, an image developed in medieval and Renaissance thinking – as by Bodin – but traceable ultimately to Plato. Here unity is imagined in terms of mutual indispensability, differentiation being necessary to the completion of order; as a social doctrine it stresses interdependence, diversity, divided labour, and contiguity rather than similarity.

Now to describe the two themes in this way may well seem to exaggerate their distinctness, for similarity and diversity can be taken to be different features of a situation rather than rival situations, different features that Tocqueville's God could grasp instantaneously and without conceptual differentiation. But a recurrent trait is the identification of social and political types in terms of one associative principle or the other. Durkheim's organic and mechanical solidarities would be the classic instance if it were not that the distinction is complicated, after *The Division of Labour*, by the insertion of a principle of resemblance into the organic society. But Bergson too gives the distinction an equally primary if less obvious importance: the closed society of nature has imposed 'variety,' intending that individuals should fulfil specialized roles unreflectively, while the open society is identified with a desire to 'resemble' – he follows the later rather than the earlier Durkheim in identifying freedom with resemblance, constraint with variety. Before Durkheim, the two models figured in Tocqueville's contrast between aristocratic and democratic societies, the former united structurally by interdependence, the latter united morally by a sense of resemblance or human fellowship. They figured, too, in Proudhon's contrast between political monism and economic diversity. And in turn Proudhon (overtly) and Tocqueville (diffusely) derived their views of democratic politics from Rousseau, who had seen unity as something self-imposed, through laws, by essentially independent individuals and had contrasted this with the false unity of social interdependence. Repeatedly, then, French political thought has attached importance to the distinction between two ways of thinking of association: between *le pays légal* of equal official status and *le pays réel* of intractable diversity.

The case of Comte is also of interest here, but not because he identified resemblance and difference as the associative principles of different societies. He made the distinction emphatically (if only, as we have seen, after some initial confusion) and developed from it his intriguing further distinction between *representatives* and *agents* of humanity. Some men, and all women (excepting such as Mme Comte), are humanity's representatives, in bearing the capacity to love, in which what is generically human is at once displayed and valued. Some men (no women) are humanity's agents, in bearing some distinctive and special capacity that advances man's technical and spiritual command over his condition. To celebrate *humanité* is to celebrate at once what is generic and what is specialized; there are, consequently, two kinds of celebrations, 'les fêtes statiques' and 'les fêtes dynamiques,' the former celebrating the morality of generic love, the latter celebrating history rather than morality and thus recognizing the special contributions made by men to the achievement of the positive age. [10] There is, then, a conceptual harmony claimed, even if political tensions between secular priests and their grumbling bankers are admitted; the ideas of generic value and specialized function are no more than two facets of a single mode of organization. They become contradictory only when generic value is expressed in the false language of *rights*, when indeed it takes a form that is subversive of all organization whatsoever.

In somewhat abstract terms, then, two kinds of response can be distinguished. One is to privilege one associative principle over the other and to define order and citizenship within it in terms of the logic of resemblance or of diversity, taking one or other to be constitutive of what society is. A second is to suppose conflict between the two principles to be merely contingent, the product of faulty organization, the two expressing complementary rather than competing features of social life. In either case consistency is achieved, and a polity can be viewed as the expression of a moral order grounded in the essential logic of human association itself. But a third response, too, must be noted, one that is implicit in *Democracy in America* and in *The Two Sources* (two texts whose dissimilarity in almost every other respect is very marked): that neither principle is exhaustive, though both tend to exclusiveness. Both Tocqueville and Bergson see democratic beliefs as resting upon a principle of resemblance ultimately deriving, as they both insist, from Christian notions of equality and fraternity. They both insist, however – though for different purposes – that this principle must be compromised if it is to enter political life. Democratic society, Tocqueville argues, is led by its principle to stress analogy and to ignore structure; though drawn together morally, its citizens do not easily grasp their interdependence with one another, or the fact that collective action has features that make it more than a repetition of individual actions. Associations, which bring this fact to light, are the source of their political liberty, only equality and fraternity being supplied by their unmediated beliefs. Bergson's argument runs in the opposite direction; it is the open principle of resemblance that is the corrective, moderating the closed compulsions by which hierarchies are sustained and individuals attached uncomplainingly and ant-like to their roles. While the two arguments run contrary courses, they are formally parallel in detecting in civil life an unstable amalgam of associative principles rather than a single principle of an overarching unity of principles. There is, then, no self-consistent order.

Now Bergson is content to draw a veil over the inconsistency that he had brought to light, for it could undermine not only social obligation but also that degree of openness with which obligation had been tempered; he agrees in this as in other things with 'the greatest of our moralists,' who had insisted that some deceptions were fortunate ones. For Tocqueville, however, this collision of principles was an indispensable condition of political life. It was not a collision between belief systems, such as the Revolution had displayed, that he had in mind – the Revolution was more like a religious than a political event, he says, a sort of violent and temporary category mistake. What he had in mind was, rather, a collision between belief and reality. Some things are settled by belief; others are not; when a society is convinced of the fact and value of equality, we know a great deal about what its moral life will be like, but we know nothing about its political life. What that is like – or whether it exists at all – depends upon how the society comes to terms with what its beliefs do not settle: the facts of interdependence and the structures of responsibility through which those facts are recognized.

Interdependence will not, of course, take the form that it had taken in pre-revolutionary society. It has no necessary connection with social hierarchy or even with inequality, and Tocqueville's description of associations as aristocratic, while intelligible in terms of historical imagery, seems distracting rather than illuminating. But he describes them in this way because, historically, aristocracies offered the most vivid examples of the active co-operation that he valued; conceptually, because what he calls 'equality' is often something much more like resemblance, and he wishes to make a contrast between a society in which differentiation is weakly perceived and a society in which differentiation is manifest. He takes it for granted that there will be differentiation, manifest or not; it need not be vertical, though he has little doubt that it will be in part, and rather little concern about the fact, it must be said; there are differences of interest and (as, like Proudhon, he stresses) of locality; there may not be very large differences of fundamental viewpoint, he predicts, but more important, there are differences of personal capacity and attitude that are brought to light only in situations in which active co-operation is demanded. They are not brought to light when, to borrow Proudhon's revealing phrase, 'the citizen has nothing to do.' It is when there *is* something to do that citizenship is present; it is, in other words, in the mediation *between* believing and doing that citizenship or its absence is displayed. The point is symbolized institutionally in the role that both Tocqueville and the later Proudhon assign to administration, with which we may usefully compare Rousseau's view: for Rousseau it is the generalizing conscience that underpins legitimacy, the rightness of law hinging upon the rightness of the legislators' belief, the process of executing or doing belonging to a realm that is of interest to political sociology but not to *droit*.

The implications of this for questions of legitimation are considerable. It is not, in the trend of thinking that Tocqueville best represents, the beliefs of a political society that establish its legitimate or tyrannical character, but its processes. It is not order of a certain kind that gives legitimacy to citizenship; it is citizenship that gives legitimacy to an order.[11] The point is not to be confused with the democratic one (though it is not incompatible with it either); what creates legitimacy is not the assertion of a popular will – which in turn requires normative and perhaps moral justification – but the presence of a certain kind of life that the term 'citizenship' conveys well enough but that Tocqueville, sometimes, simply called 'political.' It is a life characterized by a sense that things can be done as opposed to suffered or enjoyed, that one can oneself do them or contribute to them, that there are others who will wish to do them too, and that what eventually is done will reflect the distribution of both shared and contrasting interests and goals. It requires equality in the sense that one must recognize in others at least the status of being agents like oneself, and it requires recognition of interdependence at least in the minimal sense that what each agent does will be constrained, or reinforced, by the decisions of other agents. That something is shared does not obliterate the things that are not shared: locality, interest, or unevenly dispersed opportunities. That some things are not shared does not instantly override the common status that *is* shared or imply that others are something other than agents who may help or resist but in any event are distinct will-bearing creatures. The shared and the exclusive collide. This essential duality is not captured by either of the models of order on which revolutionary or post-revolutionary thought had drawn. What may be the most central question to pose, therefore, is whether human association, taken as a source of legitimating principles, yields a single consistent normative model or whether, rather, it yields a problem. In the one case the space of citizenship is morally defined, while in the other it is constituted by political questions, human association having discontinuous features.

Tocqueville describes the circumstances of citizenship as circumstances of 'concours,' or of the coming together of wills, each of which is capable of distinct expression. He contrasts the appreciation of *concours* with the understanding of what we may term 'discours,' or the construction of orders over which one mind alone is sovereign. Specialists in *discours*, the writers who directed reform and revolution in eighteenth-century France, figured poorly in the role of statesmen, a role to which the understanding of *concours* is quite essential. Tocqueville's implied contrast becomes still sharper if we take discourse in a later sense, as entailing discussion that cannot but end in unanimity. In such discussion *will* has no standing and dissolves, for it is not a matter (as in Tocqueville's *concours*) of finding common ground among distinct personal intentions and perspectives but, rather, of resolving differences into matters of fact or logic to which the holding of any personal intention or perspective is quite irrelevant. Such resolution may occur through the collaboration of distinct minds, but it need not do so at all; it could as well occur within one mind, and the fact that it is collaborative, if it is, adds nothing whatsoever to the legitimacy of the outcome. It is clear that such an approach is far removed from what Tocqueville proposes, an approach that identifies the legitimacy of an order with the extent to which it rests on civic collaboration or the extent to which it permits points of convergence between wills to be discovered. In this respect legitimacy in its political sense necessarily does assume the distinctness of minds and is thus different from whatever legitimacy might mean in a purely cognitive context. Just why politics might not be amenable to a model of purely cognitive process is, of course, a very large question; but Tocqueville seems to be implying that if politics is a field of contending criteria, requiring that we recognize both the demands of equality and the demands of interdependence, then there is no reason to suppose in advance that political discussion will necessarily end in unanimity or that what is to be done politically can be known in the manner by which matters of fact or logic may be known.

When the theme of citizenship was first introduced above, Aristotle's importance was noted; his importance may be noted again here but – interestingly – for a different and perhaps contrary reason. Bodin's Aristotle is a monist who places politics in a context of cosmic imperatives and finds for citizenship a justification in the order of nature itself. That Aristotle can be thought of in this way can scarcely be denied. But we may detect in some political thinking an echo of another Aristotle who, *within* the field of politics, uncovers a fundamental discontinuity in the idea of order as a political goal. If we ask what politics is, doubtless we invite cosmological answers that identify political life as an essential part of some natural sequence. But if we consider the kind of association that makes politics possible, we are led to a conceptual dualism rather than a monism.

In *The Politics* Aristotle contrasts political association with two other kinds of association. One is the household, in which we may easily recognize a principle of emphatic differentiation; it forms a unity because its components are diverse. Rational man, indecisively rational woman, not-yet-rational child, and irrational slave are complementary to one another by nature. The second is friendship, which in its perfect form can exist only between those who 'resemble one another in their goodness'; in its extended or debased form of economic exchange it depends upon submitting desires to the 'common measure' of money and thus upon determining equivalence. Both household and friendship are essential to politics, but politics is reducible to neither, for it shares in the associative logic of both. 'The state consists not merely of men, but of different kinds of men; you cannot make a state out of men who are all alike.'[12] At the same time it is also an association 'as far as possible of those who are alike and equal,'[13] and with an absolutely superior man – as superior to other citizens as master is to slave – one cannot have a political relationship. These two conditions are both essential to politics. They are adopted as rival and exclusive principles by the oligarchs and democrats whose competition, according to Aristotle, provides the characteristic basis of politics; but each of these has grasped only one of the two features of political existence.

In *On the Jewish Question*, published three years after the final volume of *Democracy in America* (and drawing slightly upon it to make its point), Marx likewise commented upon the theme of duality of status. 'Where the political state has attained to its full development, man leads, not only in thought, in consciousness, but in *reality*, in *life*, a double existence.'[14] In the political community man enjoys formal equality of status; in civil society he is embedded in networks of inequality. But his abstract political status offers only illusory relief from real inequality; political emancipation does not achieve social emancipation any more than political secularization brings emancipation from religion, as the case of America shows. The duality is, therefore, a contradiction and must be overcome. 'Human emancipation will only be complete when the real, individual man has absorbed into himself the abstract citizen; when, as an individual man, in his everyday life, in his work, and in his relationships, he has become a *species-being*; and when he has recognized and organized his own powers as *social* powers so that he no longer separates this social power from himself as *political* power.'[15] In Marx's 'species-being' we may of course see something strongly parallel to the *humanité* of French thought. Properly understood, it supplies an identification that (conceptually) overcomes duality; and when duality is overcome, the political is overcome too (at least as a separate realm).

Marx's projected overcoming of duality is presented as the outcome of qualitative social and economic change. Aristotle's thesis of permanent duality is accompanied by a notorious social conservatism. Tocqueville, whose own thesis of duality interestingly though silently recalls Aristotle's, was scarcely progressive in his social and economic views; he does not get far beyond Aristotle's blunt opinion that political society 'is bound to be divided into classes,' though he believes that there are politically important differences in the forms that classes take. But to assume that what is at stake here is at bottom a social and economic issue is simply to beg the question by assuming the truth of Marx's answer (or of some other nineteenth-century answer). Whether or not social and economic change can confer 'self-identity'[16] or a unique status is just the question that has to be raised – that has been raised, in ways that intriguingly recall the later Proudhon, by those who question the reducibility of political questions to questions of economic change and stress the shared occupancy of space as the continuing source of political life.[17] If change cannot produce what Marx supposed, then the apparatus and values of a distinct political realm cannot be assumed to be dispensable. If what is generated by social relations is not a self-consistent model of association but a problem, then an institutional context for its solution is required. Such a context must be detached from social and economic institutions if it is to exert leverage upon them, and it is only if it can exert leverage upon them that it can function, with any effect, as a medium through which discontinuities, or failures of consistency, can be given expression.

It may be quite true that the distinction between private and public is archaic in the form in which Aristotle formulated it, again a Comtean as much as a Marxian point. It may be quite true that the state envisaged by theories of representative democracy falls short of the demands that its theorists and its critics may impose upon it. But it does not follow that citizenship should therefore be transposed or 'absorbed' elsewhere, for other sites may be incapable of expressing its meaning. It requires a space that is, as it were, indefinite in content, as opposed to the defined spaces supplied by institutions whose purposes are given by prior commitments or whose functions are socially established. It is self-definition, not moral identification, that must be achieved: or, if a kind of identification is involved, it is of a kind that leaves the objects of identification open, the nature of public objects being exactly what political action has to establish and not something settled immediately by conviction.

It would be dogmatic and unnecessary to claim that a space thus understood can only be provided by states. The point at issue here is simply that states can be legitimate only if they *do* provide it. The self-imposed problem of much social and political thought in France, from Rousseau to Durkheim, was that of finding an order that citizenship could express or in which a substitute for citizenship could be achieved; but this may be to turn things upside-down and to imitate the logic of older forms of order that have vanished. What can give political circumstances the features of order is not that they express a principle or vision that is independently and antecedently right but that they express the actions of citizens under conditions that give scope to their capacity to *do*. To regard the civic process as simply a vehicle for discovering antecedently right answers is obviously to render it dispensable in principle at least – an implication that Comte was to derive from the Rousseauan conception of legitimacy when he reduced consent to the authorization of administrative rule.

Well-justified constraints may be placed upon the scope of civic processes, and the conditions under which they are to operate *require* good justifications; citizens, moreover, may be ideally represented as acting with good justifications and are frequently held to learn to do so through civic experience itself. All this is merely to say that politics, while distinct as a category, cannot be thought of as a separate process but is linked in innumerable ways with convictions of various kinds, including moral ones. However, it is hard to see what secure status can attach to citizenship if everything is settled by the application of moral convictions or if a single model or pattern of relationships is held to exhaust the features of association, so that what is shared or what is exclusive assumes decisive primacy. And it is hard to see what legitimacy can attach to states unless the civic processes that they contain have a distinct rather than a derivative value. 'Qui cherche dans la liberté autre chose qu'elle-même est fait pour servir,'[18] Tocqueville wrote. This is a suitably rhetorical point at which to end, but I hope to have shown that it is not *merely* rhetorical and that it expresses the most plausible conclusion that can be drawn from the positions examined here.

Notes

INTRODUCTION

1 For views such as these, see, for example, Gabriel Almond's introduction to *Politics of the Developing Areas*, repr. in his *Political Development*, 79–151, and David Apter, *The Politics of Modernization*.
2 See W.H. Greenleaf, *Order, Empiricism and Politics*.
3 Henri Bergson, *Oeuvres*, 692
4 Pierre-Joseph Proudhon, *Philosophie du progrès*, 124
5 Alexis de Rocqueville, *Oeuvres complètes*, I. 2. 89–90
6 John H. Schaar, 'Legitimacy in the Modern State'
7 Ibid., 107–10
8 Tocqueville, *Oeuvres complètes*, I. 1. 246
9 Proudhon, *Du principe fédératif*, 114
10 Auguste Comte, *Cours de philosophie positive*, II. 50
11 See F.M. Barnard, 'Will and Political Rationality in Rousseau.'
12 See J.H. Hexter, *The Vision of Politics on the Eve of the Reformation*, 171–2.
13 See Jurgen Habermas, *Legitimation Crisis*.
14 Parallels to the remarks on Rousseau above are to be found in Philip Pettit, 'Habermas on Truth and Justice,' 212–16.
15 Jean-Jacques Rousseau, *Political Writings*, I. 139
16 Comte, *Cours de philosophie positive*, II. 664
17 Proudhon, *Idée générale de la révolution au XIXᵉ siècle*, 141
18 Tocqueville, *Oeuvres complètes*, I. 1. 56
19 Schaar, 'Legitimacy,' 111

CHAPTER 1: FROM BODIN TO ROUSSEAU

1 Nannerl O. Keohane, *Philosophy and the State in France*, 81. Keohane's

book contains indispensable discussions of all the theorists considered in this chapter. It should be mentioned here that Keohane stresses the continuities between Bodin and Rousseau and should be read as a corrective to the position developed below.

2 This and subsequent references in the text in this section are to the book and chapter numbers of Bodin's *Six livres de la république*.

3 W.H.Greenleaf, *Order, Empiricism and Politics*, 128

4 Stanley Hoffmann, 'The Areal Division of Power in the Writings of French Political Thinkers,' 116

5 For a balanced discussion, see M.J. Tooley's introduction to his translation of *Six Books of the Commonwealth*.

6 J.U. Lewis, 'Jean Bodin's "Logic of Sovereignty"'; see also David Parker, 'Law, Society and the State in the Thought of Jean Bodin.'

7 *Political Writings*, ed. C.E. Vaughan, II. 34. Subsequent references are to the volume and page numbers of this edition, cited as PW.

8 This and subsequent references in the text in this section are to the book and essay numbers of Montaigne's *Essais*.

9 Quoted in E. Zeller, *Stoics, Epicureans and Sceptics*, 307n

10 This and subsequent references in the text in this section are to the Lafuma numbering of Pascal's *Pensées*.

11 See Alban Krailsheimer, *Pascal*, espec. 21–6.

12 Montaigne, *Essais*, III. 8

13 Nigel Abercrombie, *Saint Augustine and French Classical Thought*, 91

14 Zeller, *Stoics*, 306n

15 *The City of God*, 1073

16 Blaise Pascal, *Oeuvres*, II. 139

17 Montaigne, *Essais*, I. 26

18 *Lettres persanes*, letter 80

19 See Albert O. Hirschman, *The Passions and the Interests*, pt 1.

20 This and subsequent references in the text in this section are to the book and chapter numbers of *L'Esprit des lois*.

21 Louis Althusser, for example, declares roundly that for Montesquieu the age of republics is past (*Politics and History*, 61); but see Keohane, *Philosophy and the State*, 417–18.

22 On *la thèse nobiliaire*, see Keohane, *Philosophy and the State*, 346–50.

23 This view is taken by Tzvetan Todorov, 'Droit naturel et formes de gouvernement dans *L'Esprit des lois*,' 38–40. Durkheim, however, regards the laws of nature as an irrelevance: see *Montesquieu and Rousseau*, 19. Friedrich Meinecke sees, rather, a fundamental ambivalence; see *Historism*, 90–143.

24 *Montesquieu and Rousseau*, 83
25 *PW* I. 140–1
26 *PW* I, 451
27 J.G.A. Pocock, *The Machiavellian Moment*, 533
28 *PW* I. 448–9
29 John Plamenatz discusses some analogies in 'Pascal and Rousseau.'
30 *PW* II. 36
31 *PW* I. 452
32 *PW* I. 139
33 See Robert Derathé, *Jean-Jacques Rousseau et la science politique de son temps*.
34 Bossuet, *De la politique tirée des propres paroles de l'Ecriture Sainte*, 177
35 Hugo Grotius, *The Law of War and Peace*, 12–13
36 *PW* I. 196
37 Derathé, *Jean-Jacques Rousseau*, 49
38 Included in *PW* (I. 429–33)
39 See W.G. Runciman and A.K. Sen, 'Games, Justice and the General Will.'
40 *PW* I. 452 (emphasis added)
41 *PW* I. 454
42 John B. Noone, 'Rousseau's Theory of Natural Law as Conditional'
43 See F.M. Barnard, 'National Culture and Political Legitimacy: Herder and Rousseau.'
44 Alasdair MacIntyre, *After Virtue*, 44
45 As is stressed by Peter Gay, in *The Enlightenment: An Interpretation*
46 See especially Kennedy F. Roche, *Rousseau: Stoic and Romantic*.
47 *PW* I. 453
48 *PW* I. 453
49 *PW* I. 250–1
50 Friedrich Meinecke, *Cosmopolitanism and the National State*, 30
51 Quoted in Zeller, *Stoics*, 306n. It is sometimes maintained, however, that Rousseau's general will is to be understood as something emerging from a diversity of particular standpoints: see, for example, Keohane, *Philosophy and the State*, espec. 447–8. In support of such a view, the passage in *Social Contract*, II. 3, should be noted: 'Mais ôtez de ces mêmes volontés les plus et les moins qui s'entre-détruisent, reste pour somme des différences la volonté générale' (*PW* II. 42). No summary explanation of this notoriously difficult sentence is likely to be convincing: my own view, however, is that the 'pluses' and 'minuses' refer to the positive and negative attitudes of the citizens in terms of their varied particular wills. These cancel out in the sense that, in a homoge-

234 Notes to pages 41–5

neous society, we may expect the numbers of positive and negative views to be approximately equal. When these are 'taken away,' the 'sum of the differences' (taking 'differences' in the arithmetic sense) amounts to the sum of the views that citizens have as citizens, in abstraction from their particular viewpoints.

52 Cf Roche, *Rousseau*, 2. This is one of the few points on which I would dissent from this lively and illuminating discussion.

53 *PW* II. 104. This could also perhaps be regarded as an instance of 'Laconism' or Spartanism, *short* speeches belonging eponymously to the Laconic tradition. See Elizabeth Rawson, *The Spartan Tradition in European Thought*, 19–20. To stress Rousseau's Stoicism is not at all to dispute Rawson's evidence (see espec. 231–41) for stressing the importance of Sparta for him; see also Judith N. Shklar, *Men and Citizens: A Study of Rousseau's Social Theory*. But Spartanism, or idealization of other city-states, is remote from the question of obligation. For a suggestion that the Stoic and Spartan images may have something in common, see Rawson, 88–90.

54 See Zeller, *Stoics*, 312n; Seneca, *Letters from a Stoic*; F.H. Sandbach, *The Stoics*, 34.

55 *PW* I. 251

56 *PW* I. 162

57 *Emile*, 326

58 *PW* I. 243

59 *PW* I. 449. If innocence had been maintained, Rousseau writes, 'il n'y aurait ni bonté dans nos coeurs ni moralité dans nos actions.'

60 See Alexis de Tocqueville, *L'Ancien Régime et la révolution francaise*, part I, chap. 3. See also Elie Kedourie, *Nationalism*, 9–19.

61 Plutarch, *Moralia*, 393. On Plutarch's importance, see Roche, *Rousseau*, 19–21.

62 *PW* I. 242–3

63 G.D.H. Cole's view of Rousseau tended in this direction. For some critical remarks, see Richard Vernon, introduction to G.D.H. Cole, *Guild Socialism Re-Stated*.

64 *PW* II. 63

65 *PW* I. 495

66 *PW* I. 252

67 *Emile*, 7

68 Compare, for example, H.D. Rempel, 'On Forcing People to be Free,' and Ernst Cassirer, *Rousseau, Kant, Goethe*.

69 *PW* II. 23

70 This seems to stand in the way of the interesting solution offered by Andrew Levine, *The Politics of Autonomy*, 40.
71 The necessity of making this distinction is also urged by Hanna Fenichel Pitkin, 'Justice: On Relating Private to Public,' 345.
72 *PW* II. 95
73 *Emile, PW* II. 52
74 *PW* I. 251
75 *PW* I. 495
76 See Stephen G. Salkever, 'Virtue, Obligation and Politics.' Salkever rightly notes (92n) Rousseau's debts to 'the language of legitimacy and obligation on the one hand and the language of virtue on the other.'
77 See Patrick Riley, 'A Possible Explanation of Rousseau's General Will.'
78 *PW* II. 53 (emphasis added)
79 Hannah Arendt, *On Revolution*, 186
80 *PW* I. 503 (emphasis added)
81 *PW* I. 365
82 Auguste Comte, *Système de politique positive*, III. 596–7

CHAPTER 2: MAISTRE AND PROUDHON

1 P.-J. Proudhon, *Idée générale de la révolution au XIXᵉ siècle*, 141
2 Rousseau, *Political Writings*, II. 31
3 See also ibid., II. 38.
4 See Hanna Pitkin, 'Obligation and Consent,' 81, for the importance of this.
5 Joseph de Maistre, *Oeuvres complètes*, I. 344. Subsequent references are to the volume and page number of this edition, cited as *OC*.
6 *OC* I. 407
7 As is noted by Richard A. Lebrun, 'Joseph de Maistre and Rousseau,' 892
8 *OC* I. 312
9 *OC* I. 465
10 *Idée générale*, 258
11 *OC* I. 353
12 *OC* I, 236
13 *OC* I. 237–8
14 *OC* I. 354
15 *OC* I. 117
16 *OC* I. 473
17 *OC* I. 91

18 *OC* I. 53
19 *OC* I. 406
20 *OC* I. 435
21 *OC* I. 329
22 *OC* I. 351
23 *OC* I. 2
24 *OC* I. 280–1
25 *OC* I. 284; see also *OC* I. 3.
26 *OC* I. 88
27 *OC* I. 287–8
28 *OC* I. 147–8
29 *OC* I. 246
30 *OC* I. 147
31 *OC* I. 35–7
32 *OC* I. 16–20
33 *OC* I. 125
34 *OC* I. 357–62
35 *OC* I. 389
36 *OC* I. 26–7. See the translator's explanatory notes in *Considerations on France*, Richard A. Lebrun, ed. and trans., 49.
37 *OC* I. 408
38 *OC* I. 125
39 *OC* I. 56
40 *OC* I. 409
41 See Richard A. Lebrun, *Throne and Altar*, 70–3.
42 *OC* I. 3
43 *OC* I. 80 (emphasis added)
44 See the editor's introduction to *Considerations on France*, 15–16.
45 *OC* I. 312–13
46 *OC* I. 111
47 *OC* I. 467
48 *OC* I. 131
49 *OC* I. 467
50 See Aaron Noland, 'Proudhon and Rousseau,' and Silvia Rota Ghibaudi, *Proudhon e Rousseau*, for accounts of Proudhon's view of Rousseau.
51 *OC* I. 28–40
52 *La Guerre et la Paix*, 481
53 *Idée générale*, 298
54 *OC* I. 376

55 *Idée générale*, 142
56 Ibid., 254
57 Ibid., 141
58 *Système des contradictions économiques*, 41
59 Ibid., 38
60 *Philosophie du progrès*, 108
61 *Idée générale*, 141
62 *De la justice dans la révolution et dans l'eglise*, I. 494
63 *Philosophie du progrès*, 66
64 *Idée générale*, 113
65 Ibid., 74
66 *Philosophie du progrès*, 83
67 See Alan Ritter, *The Political Thought of Pierre-Joseph Proudhon*. 136–7.
68 *Idée générale*, 245
69 *De la justice*, I. 486
70 *Idée générale*, 43
71 Ibid., 237–8
72 Ibid., 142
73 Ibid., 89
74 Ibid., 314 (emphasis added)
75 Ibid., 89
76 *Système des contradictions économiques*, 34
77 *Philosophie du progrès*, 67
78 *OC* I. 244
79 *OC* I. 4
80 *Idée générale*, 8–9
81 Ibid., 318
82 *Système des contradictions économiques*, 392
83 *De la capacité politique des classes ouvrières*, 148
84 Cf *De la justice*, II. 67, 75.
85 *Philosophie du progrès*, 29
86 Ibid., 41
87 Ibid., 124
88 Georges Sorel, *Les Illusions du progrès*, 7–8
89 *Idée générale*, 11
90 *Philosophie du progrès*, 65
91 Ibid., 124
92 *Idée générale*, 158
93 *De la justice*, I. 480
94 Ibid., 482

95 *Idée générale*, 299
96 *OC* I. 76
97 *Idée générale*, 139
98 Ibid., 137; cf Maistre, in *OC* I. 76–7.
99 *OC* I. 242
100 *Idée générale*, 260
101 *Philosophie du progrès*, 80
102 *OC* I. 545
103 *OC* I. 74
104 *OC* I. 90
105 *OC* VII. 54
106 Rousseau, *Political Writings*, 63, 103
107 Rousseau, *Confessions*, 377

CHAPTER 3: PROUDHON'S FEDERALISM

1 *Du principe fédératif*, 42
2 Ibid., 97
3 For some accounts of this transition, see Nicolas Bourgeois, *Les Théories du droit international chez Proudhon*; Bernard Voyenne, *Le Fédéralisme de P.-J. Proudhon*; Richard Vernon, introduction to *The Principle of Federation by P.-J. Proudhon*.
4 Franz Neumann, *The Democratic and the Authoritarian State*, 161
5 *Principe fédératif*, 80
6 Ibid., 82
7 Ibid., 94–5
8 Ibid., 101
9 Ibid., 100–1
10 Ibid., 107–16
11 Ibid., 20
12 Ibid., 21
13 *Critique of Hegel's Philosophy of Right*, 29–30
14 See S.-R. Taillandier, 'L'Athéisme allemand et le socialisme français.'
15 *The German Ideology*, 86
16 *L'Esprit des lois*, VIII. 16
17 Ibid., IX. 1
18 *Principe fédératif*, 83–5
19 Ibid., 57
20 Ibid., 58
21 Ibid., 79–80, 108

22 Ibid., 36
23 Ibid., 55–6
24 Ibid., 109
25 Ibid., 119
26 Ibid., 106
27 Ibid., 84
28 Ibid., 36
29 Ibid., 60
30 Ibid., 117–24
31 *On Revolution*, 217–85
32 V.I. Lenin, *State and Revolution*, 60–4
33 *Principe fédératif*, 44
34 Ibid., 99
35 Ibid., 53
36 Ibid., 313
37 But see Hoffmann, 'The Areal Division of Powers,' 133, for a contrary view.
38 See J.G.A. Pocock, 'The Mobility of Property and the Rise of Eighteenth-Century Sociology.'
39 *Principe fédératif*, 97
40 Ibid., 83
41 See, for example, Neumann, *Democratic and Authoritarian State*, 216–32; William H. Riker, *Federalism*, 139–45; Preston King, 'Against Federalism' and, more recently, *Federalism and Federation*.
42 *Principe fédératif*, 80
43 Ibid., 61
44 See Isaiah Berlin, *Four Essays on Liberty*; Gerald C. MacCallum, 'Negative and Positive Freedom'; John N. Gray, 'On Negative and Positive Liberty.'
45 MacCallum, 'Negative and Positive Freedom,' 176
46 Raymond Aron, *An Essay on Freedom*, pt 2
47 Ibid., pt 4
48 Ibid., 157
49 *Capacité politique*, 207
50 *Principe fédératif*, 114

CHAPTER 4: TOCQUEVILLE AND THE HUMAN POINT OF VIEW

1 Alexis de Tocqueville, *Oeuvres complètes*, II. 1. 246. Subsequent references are to the volume, part, and page numbers of this edition, cited as *OC*.
2 *OC* II. 1. 92

3 *OC* II. 1. 87–90
4 *OC* I. 1. 304–6
5 *OC* I. 1. 310; *OC* I. 2. 29
6 See Doris Goldstein, *Trial of Faith*, espec. 15–27.
7 See Guy H. Dodge, *Benjamin Constant's Philosophy of Liberalism*, 126.
8 Robert A. Nisbet, 'Many Tocquevilles'
9 *OC* I. 91. 268–70
10 *OC* I. 2. 20
11 *OC* I. 1. 430
12 *OC* I. 2. 172
13 *OC* I. 1. 46–50
14 *OC* I. 2. 93
15 *OC* I. 2. 106
16 *OC* I. 2. 173–4
17 See Melvin Richter, 'Tocqueville's Contributions to the Theory of Revolution,' 80.
18 *OC* I. 2. 30–1
19 *OC* I. 2. 338
20 Cf Marvin Zetterbaum, *Tocqueville and the Problem of Democracy*, 24.
21 *OC* I. 1. 239, 259
22 *OC* I. 1. 296
23 *OC* I. 1, 335–6, 378
24 *OC* I. 2. 174
25 *OC* I. 2. 106
26 *OC* I. 2. 109
27 *OC* I. 2. 166–7
28 *OC* I. 2. 247
29 *OC* I. 2. 89–90
30 *OC* I. 2. 163
31 *OC* I. 2. 144
32 See Jon Elster, *Logic and Society*, 99.
33 *OC* I. 2. 301n
34 *OC* I. 1. 268–70
35 As is rightly stressed by Melvin Richter, in 'The Uses of Theory,' 81–82
36 *OC* I. 2. 305 (emphasis added)
37 *OC* II. 1. 147
38 *OC* II. 1. 94
39 As J.S. Mill grasped: 'Now, as ever, the great problem in government is to prevent the strongest from becoming the only power' (introduction to *Democracy in America*, 2. li).
40 *OC* I. 2. 107

41 *Leviathan*, 240, 255
42 *OC* I. 1. 94
43 See Gunnar Myrdal, *Value in Social Theory*, 206–30.
44 *OC* I. 2. 327
45 *Du principe fédératif*, 105
46 Georges Sorel, *Matériaux d'une théorie du prolétariat*, 112
47 'Les Dissensions de la socialdémocratie en Allemagne,' 63
48 Henri de Saint-Simon, *Oeuvres*, II. 195–200
49 *Système de politique positive*, IV (app.). 1–3
50 See Raymond Aron, ed., *World Technology and Human Destiny*, 3–26, 55–66.
51 *OC* I. 1. 94
52 *OC* II. 1. 232
53 *OC* I. 1. 14
54 *OC* II. 1. 200. This theme is explored in a different context in F.M. Barnard and Richard Vernon, 'Recovering Politics for Socialism.'
55 As Roger Boesche argues in 'The Strange Liberalism of Alexis de Tocqueville.' His case seems to me to depend in part on attributing altogether too much tranquillity of mind to Mill's liberalism (523). Tocqueville and Mill are indeed different (see below, this section), but not in the way that Boesche suggests.
56 See, for example, W.B. Gallie, 'Essentially Contested Concepts.'
57 See, for example, Isaiah Berlin, *Four Essays on Liberty*, 190–1.
58 See, for example, John N. Gray, 'On the Contestability of Social and Political Concepts'.
59 *OC* I. 2. 16. The independence valued here is independence from government rather than the independence from other citizens that (see n 40 above) Tocqueville did not welcome.
60 *OC* I. 1. 42.
61 Mill, *On Liberty*, 133
62 Ibid., 106–7
63 *OC* XII. 102–5

CHAPTER 5: COMTE AND THE WITHERING AWAY OF THE STATE

1 In 'The Areal Division of Powers in the Writings of French Political Thinkers,' 113
2 *Cours de philosophie positive*, II. 37–8. Subsequent references are to volume and page numbers of this edition, cited as *C*.
3 'Considérations sur le pouvoir spirituel,' reprinted in the appendix to the fourth volume of *Système de politique positive*, 198. The *Système* is cited below as *S*, with volume and page numbers.

4 *Ecrits de jeunesse*, 93–4
5 Ibid., 46
6 *s* IV (app.) 63–70; *s* II. 270
7 *s* IV. 71
8 *s* IV. 76
9 See Henri de Saint-Simon, 'L'Organisateur,' in *Oeuvres*, II. 17–26.
10 See Frank E. Manuel, *The Prophets of Paris*, 251–60.
11 *c* II. 35
12 *s* IV (app.) 177
13 *s* IV (app.) 188
14 *s* IV (app.) 201
15 *c* II. 33, 418
16 *c* II. 783
17 *c* II. 37–8
18 *c* II. 49
19 *c* II. 85
20 *c* II. 366
21 *c* II. 511–12, 518
22 *c* II. 176
23 *s* II. 290
24 *s* II. 291
25 *s* II. 305
26 *s* II. 308
27 *Catéchisme positiviste*, 131
28 *s* II. 306
29 *s* II. 320
30 *Catéchisme*, 241
31 *s* IV. 421–2
32 There is a partial listing of provinces in *Du principe fédératif* (100), which coincides with Comte's as far as it goes. But Proudhon was uncertain about the right number; see Bernard Voyenne, *Le Fédéralisme de P.-J. Proudhon*, 181n.
33 *Du principe fédératif*, 80
34 *s* II. 316
35 *s* II. 315
36 *Catéchisme*, 252
37 F.A. Hayek, *The Counter-Revolution of Science*, 168
38 J.S. Mill, *Auguste Comte and Positivism*, 125
39 *s* I. 4
40 *c* II. 663

41 *c* II. 186
42 *c* II. 200
43 *s* IV. 67–8
44 Cf *s* IV. 31 and 108–09.
45 *s* III. 100
46 *c* I. 24
47 *s* II. 283–6
48 *s* I, 335
49 *s* II. 97
50 *s* II. 290
51 *s* IV. 441–2
52 *Catéchisme*, 35, 43
53 *s* IV. 394
54 *s* I. 363; cf *c* II. 670.
55 *c* II. 671
56 *Catéchisme*, 79
57 *c* II. 150
58 *s* I. 342
59 *s* II. 315
60 *s* II. 312
61 *s* II. 301, 319; see also *Catéchisme*, 204–5.
62 *s* II. 297; see also *Catéchisme*, 247.
63 *Catéchisme*, 217
64 *c* II. 667; cf 674, 681–2.
65 *Catéchisme*, 217
66 Ibid., 47
67 *s* IV. 82, 84
68 *Catéchisme*, 35, 45
69 J.G.A. Pocock, *Machiavellian Moment*, 550
70 See Michael James, 'Pierre Louis Roederer, Jean-Baptiste Say, and the Concept of *industrie*.'
71 *s* II. 312–13
72 *Catéchisme*, 247
73 Ibid., 677
74 *s* II. 263–4
75 *Catéchisme*, 233
76 Ibid., 218, 234
77 Ibid., 217
78 *Ecrits de jeunesse*, 58
79 *c* II, 583

80 *s* II, 333–4. Comte evidently feels – correctly – that the partial explanation offered in the *Cours* (II. 677) is inadequate.
81 *c* II. 32
82 *s* IV. 108–9
83 *s* IV. 62
84 *Catéchisme*, 99
85 *c* I. 882
86 *Catéchisme*, 97, fig. A
87 Ibid., 100–1
88 See *c* I. 47, where this task is assigned to an intermediary class of engineers.
89 *Catéchisme*, 205
90 Ibid., 51–5, 265–71
91 *Passages from the Letters of Auguste Comte*, 12
92 *City of God*, 154
93 *s* IV (app.) 198
94 *s* II. 97
95 *Catéchisme*, 80
96 *s* II. 296
97 *Catéchisme*, 247
98 See Manuel, *Prophets of Paris*, 260–3.
99 See above, n 43.

CHAPTER 6: GEORGES SOREL

1 Sheldon S. Wolin, *Politics and Vision*, 352–434
2 Ibid., 433
3 Ibid., 423
4 G.D.H. Cole, *Guild Socialism Restated*, 12
5 Carole Pateman, 'Sublimation and Reification'
6 *D'Aristote à Marx*, 67
7 In, for example, 'Virtue and Commerce in the Eighteenth Century,' J.G.A. Pocock stresses that it was the *rentier* rather than the merchant who attracted the fears of theorists of virtue; 'independent proprietorship' of land *or* capital was accepted, he shows, as a qualification for citizenship. However, it evidently was Sorel's view (see n 9 below) that the merchant lacked the crucial quality of 'independence,' in France at least.
8 See Melvin Richter, 'The Uses of Theory.'
9 *Le Procès de Socrate*, 172
10 *La Ruine du monde antique*, 311

11 *Réflexions sur la violence*, 434–8
12 *Le Procès de Socrate*, 176
13 Ibid., 6–7
14 *Matériaux d'une théorie du prolétariat*, 189
15 *Réflexions*, 173
16 *Le Procès de Socrate*, 378–9
17 Ibid., 167
18 *La Ruine du monde antique*, 317–18
19 Preface to F. Pelloutier, *Histoire des bourses du travail*, 6–7
20 *La Ruine du monde antique*, 314
21 *Réflexions*, 376
22 There is, of course, Machiavelli's discussion of the benign effects of class conflict in the *Discourses* (I. 4). But Sorel's 'classes' are not Machiavelli's – see *Réflexions*, 73–6 – and conflict between them is meant to be terminal, not the social basis for a mixed constitution.
23 *La Révolution dreyfusienne*, 21
24 *Politics and Vision*, 223
25 J.G.A. Pocock, *Politics, Language and Time*, 94–5
26 *La Ruine du monde antique*, 138
27 *Matériaux*, 73n
28 St Augustine, *City of God*, 74
29 *Réflexions*, 221
30 Preface to Pelloutier, *Histoire*, 12
31 J.G.A. Pocock, *Machiavellian Moment*, 550
32 Michael James, 'Pierre-Louis Roederer, Jean-Baptiste Say, and the Concept of *industrie*'
33 See *The Politics*, I. 7.
34 Felix Markham, introduction to *Henri de Saint-Simon*, xxvi
35 *Système de politique positive*, IV (app.) 64
36 Preface to Pelloutier, *Histoire*
37 *Réflexions sur la violence*, 12–24
38 *D'Aristote à Marx*, 227
39 *Cours de philosophie positive*, II. 73
40 *La Décomposition du marxisme*, 60
41 *La Ruine du monde antique*, 320
42 But not wholly unique; see Peter F. Drucker, *Concept of the Corporation*, for similar views.
43 *Les Illusions du progrès*, 282–3
44 I mean that Sorel found Comte's distinction unpalatable, not that he believed in the unity of theory and practice in its Marxist sense. His

distinction between prospective and retrospective knowledge would appear to rule out unity in that sense. See Richard Vernon, 'The Disunity of Theory and Practice.'

45 *Le Procès de Socrate*, 179
46 *Réflexions sur la violence*, 96. Here Sorel abandons his earlier objection to the use of the term *conquest*, in *D'Aristote à Marx*, 202.
47 See Richard Vernon, *Commitment and Change*, 23–37, for a fuller account.
48 Preface to S. Merlino, *Formes et essence du socialisme*, xv (emphasis added)
49 *Les Illusions du progrès*, 38–44
50 Giambattista Vico, *The New Science*, 916–46
51 *La Ruine du monde antique*, 245
52 *Matériaux*, 17
53 *Réflexions*, 189
54 Ibid., 407
55 See 'L'Avenir socialiste des syndicats,' in *Matériaux*, 77–167.
56 Preface to Merlino, *Formes*, xvi
57 Preface to Pelloutier, *Histoire*, 28
58 *Matériaux*, 69
59 See Henry Tudor, *Political Myth*.
60 J.G.A. Pocock, *Politics, Language and Time*, 242–3
61 *Réflexions*, 436
62 Preface to Pelloutier, *Histoire*, 27–8
63 *Matériaux*, 60–1
64 Ibid., 69
65 Preface to Pelloutier, *Histoire*, 28
66 *La Ruine du monde antique*, 272
67 *Les Illusions du progrès*, 354–5
68 *D'Aristote à Marx*, 179
69 *De l'utilité du pragmatisme*, 432
70 See, for example, G.D.H. Cole, *Guild Socialism Restated*; Peter M. Bachrach, *Theory of Democratic Elitism*; Carole Pateman, *Participation and Democratic Theory*.
71 Pateman, *Participation*, 110
72 Bachrach, *Democratic Elitism*, 80–1
73 See F.M. Barnard and Richard Vernon, 'Pluralism, Participation and Politics,' for a fuller discussion of this point.

CHAPTER 7: DURKHEIM AND THE SECULAR POLITY

1 *L'Education morale*, 131
2 Ibid., 4–5

3 'Individualism and the Intellectuals,' 28. See Steven Lukes's commentary on this translation and his account of Durkheim's *dreyfusisme* in *Emile Durkheim*, 332–49.

4 Gurvitch, quoted in Melvin Richter, 'Durkheim's Politics and Political Theory,' 170–1

5 'Individualism,' 25

6 Cf Fred H. Willhoite, 'Rousseau's Political Religion.'

7 *Cours*, II. 83: *Système*, IV. 30

8 *Cours*, I. 21–2

9 *Système*, III. 63. But see Warren Schmaus, 'A Reappraisal of Comte's Three-State Law' (a critique, in part, of the position developed here).

10 *Cours*, II. 68

11 *Cours*, II. 331, 389

12 *Cours*, II. 340; *Système*, IV. 23

13 *Cours*, II. 377, 379

14 *Cours*, II. 24, 124, 222–3, 381

15 *Système*, II. 290; IV. 29

16 *Cours*, II. 363

17 *Montesquieu and Rousseau*, 111–12

18 Ibid., 127

19 *De la division du travail social*, 26

20 Ibid., 158

21 Ibid., 392

22 Ibid., 178

23 'Individualism,' 26

24 *Leçons de sociologie*, 134

25 On Durkheim's Stoicism see Georges Davy, introduction to *Leçons*, xxviii.

26 *Leçons*, 87–90

27 Ibid., 134

28 *Division du travail*, 119

29 'Individualism,' 23

30 *Division du travail*, 143

31 Anthony Giddens, *Emile Durkheim*, 54

32 *Education morale*, 8–12 (emphasis added)

33 See Robert A. Nisbet, *The Sociology of Emile Durkheim*, 31–2; Melvin Richter, 'Durkheim's Politics,' 192–3.

34 *Leçons*, 68

35 Ibid., 31

36 Ibid., 78; see Nisbet, *Sociology of Durkheim*, 148.

37 *Leçons*, 78

38 Ibid., 96–108
39 *Division du travail*, 253
40 *Leçons*, 10
41 Ibid., 87–8
42 See Davy, introduction to *Leçons*, xxi–xxii.
43 *Education morale*, 64
44 Ibid., 65; *Leçons*, 88–91
45 *Leçons*, 201
46 Ibid., 85
47 *Education morale*, 66–7
48 *Leçons*, 85
49 *Division du travail*, 274
50 *Education morale*, 7–8
51 Giddens, *Durkheim*, 34
52 'Individualism,' 25
53 Ibid., 24
54 See Richard K. Fenn, 'The Process of Secularization'; and Roland Robertson, *The Sociological Interpretation of Religion*, 40–1.
55 See David Apter, *The Politics of Modernization*; and Robert Bellah, 'Civic Religion in America,' in Richey and Jones, *American Civil Religion*, 21–44.
56 See David Martin, 'Towards Eliminating the Concept of Secularization'.
57 Numa Denis Fustel de Coulanges, *The Ancient City*, 520
58 *Education morale*, 5
59 See Richter, 'Durkheim's Politics,' 181, 196.
60 Lukes, *Durkheim*, 44
61 *Education morale*, 6
62 Henri Bergson, *Oeuvres*, 1025–6
63 See Richter, 'Durkheim's Politics,' 175, 203.
64 David Martin, *The Religious and the Secular*, 35

CHAPTER 8: HENRI BERGSON'S TWO CITIES

1 A.P. d'Entrèves, 'Political Obligation and the Open Society,' in Dante Germino and Klaus von Beyme, eds., *The Open Society in Theory and Practice*, 26–31
2 Melvin Richter, 'Some Views of the Closed Society,' in Germino and von Beyme, *Open Society*, 99–100
3 I owe this point to Ph. Merlan, 'Le Problème de l'irrationalisme dans les

Deux Sources de Bergson,' 314, where Ernest Renan's notions of open and closed religions are noted.

4 Henri Bergson, *Oeuvres*, 1046
5 Ibid., 993–4
6 Ibid., 1006
7 Ibid., 1003
8 Cf Rousseau: 'Considered in relation to society, religions can be divided into two types ... ' (*Political Writings*, I. 500).
9 *Oeuvres*, 1001, 1007, 1174, 1202
10 Ibid., 1002; cf Rousseau, *Political Writings*, I. 252.
11 *Oeuvres*, 1033–41. Bergson's account recalls in some ways the discussion by Giorgio del Vecchio in *La Giustizia* (first published 1922); the English translation is entitled *Justice*.
12 *Oeuvres*, 1017–18. For a parallel, see the classic paper by H.A. Prichard, 'Does Moral Philosophy Rest on a Mistake?'
13 *Rules of Sociological Method*, liv (n), emphasis added
14 *Oeuvres*, 1043
15 Ibid., 1209
16 Ibid., 1218–19
17 Ibid., 1000
18 Ibid., 1000–1
19 *Education morale*, 63
20 *La Signification de la guerre*, 40
21 Ibid., 13–14. For a discussion of this theme, see Anthony Parel, 'Political Society and the Open Society,' in Germino and von Beyme, *Open Society*, 32–52.
22 See Steven Lukes, *Emile Durkheim*, 505.
23 *Oeuvres*, 1052
24 *Leçons de sociologie*, 119
25 Ibid., 126–7
26 *Political Writings*, I. 251
27 Ibid., 365
28 *Oeuvres*, 1208. On 'conjectural history,' see Richter, 'Some Views of the Closed Society,' 101.
29 *Oeuvres*, 1078
30 *Political Writings*, I. 182
31 *Oeuvres*, 1143–4
32 Ibid., 983
33 Ibid., 1051
34 Ibid., 986

35 Ibid., 1203
36 Ibid., 1052
37 Ibid., 1047–50
38 Ibid., 1051–2; see also 1204.
39 Ibid., 1051
40 Ibid., 1131
41 *Leçons de sociologie*, 90
42 *Oeuvres*, 1007
43 Ibid., 1029
44 Ibid., 1025
45 Ibid., 1007–8
46 Ibid., 1146
47 Ibid., 1078, 1086
48 Ibid., 1202; cf Pascal, *Pensées*, 418.
49 *Pensées*, 44
50 *Oeuvres*, 1076
51 Ibid., 983
52 Jacques Maritain, *Bergsonian Philosophy and Thomism*, 285–8
53 Ibid., 324–45
54 Jacques Maritain, *Man and the State*, 82
55 Ibid., 62–3
56 Ibid., 82–100
57 Jacques Maritain, *The Person and the Common Good*, 55
58 *Man and the State*, 10
59 *Oeuvres*, 985
60 Ibid., 1022
61 See Merlan, 'Problème de l'irrationalisme,' 319.
62 See Emmanuel Mounier, *Personalism* 70.
63 Ibid., 94
64 See, for example, Peter Winch's critique of Pareto in *The Idea of a Social Science*, 95–120.
65 *Oeuvres*, 1081
66 'Political Principles,' 27
67 Ibid., 30

CONCLUSION: MORAL COMMUNITY AND POLITICAL ORDER

1 Cf Cushing Strout, 'Tocqueville and Republican Religion,' and the reply by Peter Dennis Bathory, 'Tocqueville on Citizenship and Faith.'
2 See Doris Goldstein, *Trial of Faith*, 91.

3 See Russell E. Richey and Donald G. Jones, eds., *American Civil Religion*.

4 *Système des contradictions économiques*, 384

5 Alasdair MacIntyre, *Secularization and Moral Change*, 12

6 *Oeuvres complètes*, II. 1. 89

7 MacIntyre, *Secularization*, 53

8 Ibid., 29–30

9 See Friedrich Meinecke, *Cosmopolitanism and the National State*, 30.

10 *Système de politique positive*, I. 342

11 See F.M. Barnard and Richard Vernon, 'Recovering Politics.'

12 *The Politics*, II. 2

13 Ibid., IV. 11

14 *Early Writings*, 13

15 Ibid., 31

16 Leszek Kolakowski and Stuart Hampshire, eds., *The Socialist Idea*, 18–44

17 See William E. Connolly, 'A Note on Freedom under Socialism.'

18 *Oeuvres complètes*, II. 1. 217

Select Bibliography

Abercrombie, Nigel. *St Augustine and French Classical Thought*. New York: Russel and Russel 1972

Almond, Gabriel A. *Political Development*. Boston: Little, Brown 1970

Althusser, Louis. *Politics and History: Montesquieu, Rousseau, Hegel and Marx*. London: New Left Books 1972

Apter, David E. *The Politics of Modernization*. Chicago: Chicago University Press 1966

Arendt, Hannah. *On Revolution*. New York: Viking Press 1965

Aristotle. *The Politics*. Harmondsworth: Penguin 1962

Aron, Raymond. *An Essay on Freedom*. New York: New American Library 1970

Aron, Raymond, ed. *World Technology and Human Destiny*. Ann Arbor: University of Michigan Press 1963

Augustine, St. *Concerning the City of God against the Pagans*. Harmondsworth: Penguin 1972

Bachrach, Peter. *The Theory of Democratic Elitism*. Boston: Little, Brown 1967

Barnard, F.M. 'National Culture and Political Legitimacy: Herder and Rousseau.' *Journal of the History of Ideas* 44 (1983): 231–53

– 'Will and Political Rationality in Rousseau.' *Political Studies* 32 (1984): 369–84

Barnard, F.M., and Richard Vernon. 'Pluralism, Participation and Politics: Reflections on the Intermediate Group.' *Political Theory* 3 (1975): 180–97

– 'Recovering Politics for Socialism: Two Responses to the Language of Community.' *Canadian Journal of Political Science* 16 (1983): 717–37

Bathory, Peter Dennis. 'Tocqueville on Citizenship and Faith: A Response to Cushing Strout.' *Political Theory* 8 (1980): 27–38

Bergson, Henri. *Oeuvres*. Paris: Presses Universitaires de France 1963

Berlin, Isaiah. *Four Essays on Liberty*. London: Oxford University Press 1969

Bodin, Jean. *Six livres de la république*. 1583. Facsimile edn, Darmstadt: Scientia Aalen 1961

– *Six Books on the Commonwealth*. 1606. New York: Macmillan 1955

Boesche, Roger C. 'The Strange Liberalism of Alexis de Tocqueville.' *History of Political Thought* 2 (1981): 495–524

Bossuet, Jacques Bénigne. *De la politique tirée des propres paroles de l'Ecriture Sainte*. 1709. Geneva: Droz 1967

Cassirer, Ernst. *Rousseau, Kant, Goethe*. Princeton: Princeton University Press 1970

Cole, G.D.H. *Guild Socialism Re-stated*. New Brunswick, NJ: Transaction 1980

Comte, Auguste. *Ecrits de jeunesse*. 1816–28. Paris: Mouton 1973

– *Cours de philosophie positive* 1830–42. Paris: Hermann 1975

– *Système de politique positive*. 1851–54. Paris: Société Positiviste 1929

– *Catéchisme positiviste*. 1852. Paris: Garnier-Flammarion 1966

– *Passages from the Letters of Auguste Comte*. London: Adam and Charles Black 1901

Connolly, William E. 'A Note on Freedom under Socialism.' *Political Theory* 5 (1977): 461–77

Derathé, Robert. *Jean-Jacques Rousseau et la science politique de son temps*. Paris: Presses Universitaires de France 1950

Dodge, Guy H. *Benjamin Constant's Philosophy of Liberalism: A Study in Politics and Religion*. Chapel Hill: University of North Carolina Press 1980

Drucker, Peter F. *Concept of the Corporation*. New York: Mentor 1975

Durkheim, Emile. *Montesquieu and Rousseau*. 1892, 1918. Ann Arbor: University of Michigan Press 1965

– *De la division du travail social: étude sur l'organisation des sociétés supérieures*. 1893. Paris: Alcan 1902

– *The Rules of Sociological Method*. 1895. Glencoe: Free Press 1964

– 'Individualism and the Intellectuals.' 1898. Trans. with commentary by Steven Lukes, *Political Studies* 17 (1969): 14–30

– *L'Education morale*. 1925. Paris: Presses Universitaires de France 1963

– *Leçons de sociologie: physique des moeurs et du droit*. Paris: Presses Universitaires de France 1950

Elster, Jon. *Logic and Society*. Chichester: Wiley 1978

Fenn, Richard K. 'The Process of Secularization: A Post-Parsonian View.' *Journal for the Scientific Study of Religion* (1970): 117–30

Fustel de Coulanges, Numa Denis. *The Ancient City*. Boston: Lothrop, Lee Shepard 1873

Gallie, W.B. 'Essentially Contested Concepts.' *Proceedings of the Aristotelian Society* 56 (1956): 167–98

Gay, Peter. *The Enlightenment: An Interpretation.* London: Weidenfeld and Nicholson 1967

Germino, Dante, and Klaus von Beyme, eds. *The Open Society in Theory and Practice.* The Hague: Nijhoff 1974

Giddens, Anthony. *Emile Durkheim.* New York: Viking 1979

Goldstein, Doris S. *Trial of Faith: Religion and Politics in Tocqueville's Thought.* New York: Elsevier 1975

Gray, John N. 'On the Contestability of Social and Political Concepts.' *Political Theory* 5 (1977): 331–48

– 'On Negative and Positive Liberty.' *Political Studies* 28 (1980): 507–26

Greenleaf, W.H. *Order, Empiricism and Politics: Two Traditions of English Political Thought 1500–1700.* London: Oxford University Press 1964

Grotius, Hugo. *The Law of War and Peace.* Indianapolis: Bobbs-Merrill 1925

Habermas, Jürgen. *Legitimation Crisis.* Boston: Beacon 1975

Hayek, F.A. *The Counter-Revolution of Science.* Glencoe: Free Press 1955

– *Studies in Philosophy, Politics and Economics.* London: Routledge 1967

Hexter, J.H. *The Vision of Politics on the Eve of the Reformation.* New York: Basic Books 1973

Hirschman, Albert O. *The Passions and the Interests.* Princeton: Princeton University Press 1977

Hobbes, Thomas. *Leviathan.* Harmondsworth: Penguin 1968

Hoffmann, Stanley. 'The Areal Division of Powers in the Writings of French Political Thinkers.' In *Area and Power*, ed. Arthur Maas, 113–59. Glencoe: Free Press 1959

Holmes, Stephen. 'Two Concepts of Legitimacy: France after the Revolution.' *Political Theory* 10 (1982): 165–83

James, Michael. 'Pierre-Louis Roederer, Jean-Baptiste Say, and the Concept of *industrie.*' *History of Political Economy* 9 (1977): 455–75

Kedourie, Elie. *Nationalism.* London: Hutchinson 1961

Keohane, Nannerl O. *Philosophy and the State in France: The Renaissance to the Enlightenment.* Princeton: Princeton University Press 1980

King, Preston. 'Against Federalism.' In *Knowledge and Belief in Politics*, ed. Robert Benewick et al., 151–76. London: Allen and Unwin 1973

– *Federalism and Federation.* Baltimore: Johns Hopkins University Press 1982

Kolakowski, Leszek, and Stuart Hampshire, eds. *The Socialist Idea.* London: Weidenfeld and Nicholson 1974

Krailsheimer, A.J. *Pascal.* Oxford: Oxford University Press 1980

Lebrun, Richard A. *Throne and Altar: The Political and Religious Thought of Joseph de Maistre*. Ottawa: University of Ottawa Press 1965
– 'Joseph de Maistre and Rousseau.' *Studies on Voltaire and the Eighteenth Century* 88 (1972): 881–98
Lenin, V.I. *State and Revolution*. Peking: Foreign Languages Press 1965
Levine, Andrew. *The Politics of Autonomy: A Kantian Reading of Rousseau's Social Contract*. Amherst: University of Massachusetts Press 1976
Lewis, J.U. 'Jean Bodin's "Logic of Sovereignty."' *Political Studies* 16 (1968): 206–22
Lukes, Steven. *Emile Durkheim: His Life and Work*. New York: Harper and Row 1972
MacCallum, Gerald C. 'Negative and Positive Freedom.' In *Philosophy, Politics and Society*, ed. Peter Laslett et al., 174–93. 4th ser. Oxford: Blackwell 1972
MacIntyre, Alasdair. *Secularization and Moral Change*. London: Oxford University Press 1967
– *After Virtue*. Notre Dame: University of Notre Dame Press 1981
Maistre, Joseph de. *Considerations on France* 1797. Montreal: McGill-Queen's 1974
– *Oeuvres complètes*. Lyon: Vitte 1891
Manuel, Frank E. *The Prophets of Paris*. Cambridge: Harvard University Press 1962
Maritain, Jacques. *Man and the State*. Chicago: Chicago University Press 1951
– *The Person and the Common Good*. Notre Dame: University of Notre Dame Press 1966
– *Bergsonian Philosophy and Thomism*. New York: Greenwood 1968
Martin, David. 'Towards Eliminating the Concept of Secularization.' In *Penguin Survey of the Social Sciences 1965*, ed. Julius Gould, 169–82. Harmondsworth: Penguin 1965
– *The Religious and the Secular*. London: Routledge 1969
Marx, Karl. *Early Writings*. New York: McGraw Hill 1963
– *Critique of Hegel's Philosophy of Right*. Cambridge: Cambridge University Press 1963
Marx, Karl, and Friedrich Engels. *The German Ideology*. New York: International 1970
Meinecke, Friedrich. *Cosmopolitanism and the National State*. Princeton: Princeton University Press 1970
– *Historism: The Rise of a New Historical Outlook*. London: Routledge 1972
Merlan, Ph. 'Le Problème de l'irrationalisme dans les *Deux Sources* de Bergson.' *Revue Philosophique* (1959): 305–19

Mill, John Stuart. Introduction to Alexis de Tocqueville, *Democracy in America*. 1835, 1840. New York: Schocken 1961
– *On Liberty*. 1855. Harmondsworth: Penguin 1974
– *Auguste Comte and Positivism*. 1865. Ann Arbor: University of Michigan Press 1961
Montaigne, Michel de. *Essais*. 1580, 1588. Paris: Presses Universitaires de France 1965
Montesquieu, Baron de. *Lettres persanes*. 1721. Paris: Garnier-Flammarion 1964
– *L'Esprit des lois*. 1748. Paris: Garnier 1961
Mounier, Emmanuel. *Personalism*. 1950. London: Routledge 1952
Myrdal, Gunnar. *Value in Social Theory*. London: Routledge 1958
Neumann, Franz. *The Democratic and the Authoritarian State*. New York: Free Press 1957
Nisbet, Robert A. *The Sociology of Emile Durkheim*. London: Heinemann 1975
– 'Many Tocquevilles.' *American Scholar* 46 (1976): 59–78
Noland, Aaron. 'Proudhon and Rousseau.' *Journal of the History of Ideas* 28 (1967): 33–54
Noone, John B. 'Rousseau's Theory of Natural Law as Conditional.' *Journal of the History of Ideas* 33 (1972): 23–42
Parker, David. 'Law, Society and the State in the Thought of Jean Bodin.' *History of Political Thought* 2 (1981): 253–85
Pascal, Blaise. *Pensées*. Harmondsworth: Penguin 1966
– *Ouevres*. Paris: Hachette 1908
Pateman, Carole. *Participation and Democratic Theory*. Cambridge: Cambridge University Press 1970
– 'Sublimation and Reification: Locke, Wolin and the Liberal-Democratic Conception of the Political.' *Politics and Society* 5 (1975): 441–67
Pettit, Philip. 'Habermas on Truth and Justice.' In *Marx and Marxisms*, ed. G.H.R. Parkinson, 207–28. Cambridge: Cambridge University Press 1982
Pitkin, Hanna. 'Obligation and Consent.' In *Philosophy, Politics and Society*, ed. Peter Laslett et al., 45–85. 4th ser. Oxford: Blackwell 1972
– 'Justice: On Relating Private and Public.' *Political Theory* 9 (1981): 337–52
Plamenatz, John. 'Pascal and Rousseau.' *Political Studies* 10 (1962): 248–63
Plutarch. *Moralia*. London: Dent, n.d.
Pocock, J.G.A. *Politics, Language and Time*. London: Methuen 1972
– 'Virtue and Commerce in the Eighteenth Century.' *Journal of Interdisciplinary History* 3 (1972): 119–34
– *The Machiavellian Moment*. Princeton University Press 1975

- 'The Mobility of Property and the Rise of Eighteenth-Century Sociology.' In *Theories of Property*, ed. Anthony Parel and Thomas Flanagan, 141–66. Waterloo: Wilfrid Laurier University Press 1979
Prichard, H.A. 'Does Moral Philosophy Rest on a Mistake?' *Mind* 21 (1912): 21–37
Proudhon, Pierre-Joseph. *Système des contradictions économiques ou philosophie de la misère*. 1846. Paris: Rivière 1923
- *Idée générale de la révolution au XIXᵉ siècle*. 1851. Paris: Internationale 1868
- *Philosophie du progrès*. 1853. Paris: Rivière 1946
- *De la justice dans la révolution et dans l'église*. Paris: Garnier 1858
- *La Guerre et la Paix*. 1861. Paris: Rivière 1927
- *Du principe fédératif*. 1863. Paris: Dentu 1863
- *The Principle of Federation by P.-J. Proudhon*. Toronto: University of Toronto Press 1979
- *De la capacité politique des classes ouvrières*. 1865. Paris: Rivière 1924
Rawson, Elizabeth. *The Spartan Tradition in European Thought*. Oxford: Clarendon 1969
Rempel, Henry David. 'On Forcing People to be Free.' *Ethics* 87 (1976): 18–34
Richter, Melvin. 'Durkheim's Politics and Political Theory.' In *Emile Durkheim*, ed. Kurt H. Wolff, 170–210. Columbus: Ohio State University Press 1960
- 'Tocqueville's Contributions to the Theory of Revolution.' In *Revolution*, ed. Carl J. Friedrich, 75–121. New York: Atherton 1966
- 'The Uses of Theory: Tocqueville's Adaptation of Montesquieu.' In *Essays in Theory and History*, ed. Melvin Richter, 74–102. Cambridge: Harvard University Press 1970
- 'Towards a Concept of Political Illegitimacy: Bonapartist Dictatorship and Democratic Legitimacy.' *Political Theory* 10 (1982): 185–214
Riker, William H. *Federalism: Origin, Operation, Significance*. Boston: Little, Brown 1964
Riley, Patrick. 'A Possible Explanation of Rousseau's General Will.' *American Political Science Review* 64 (1970): 86–97
Ritter, Alan. *The Political Thought of Pierre-Joseph Proudhon*. Princeton: Princeton University Press 1969
Robertson, Roland. *The Sociological Interpretation of Religion*. New York: Schocken 1970
Roche, Kennedy F. *Rousseau: Stoic and Romantic*. London: Methuen 1974
Rota Ghibaudi, Silvia. *Proudhon e Rousseau*. Milan: Giuffrè 1965
Rousseau, Jean-Jacques. *Political Writings*. Ed. C.E. Vaughan. 2 vols. Oxford: Blackwell 1962

- *Emile*. 1762. London: Dent 1911
- *The Confessions*. 1781. Harmondsworth: Penguin 1953
Runciman, W.G., and A.K. Sen. 'Games, Justice and the General Will.' *Mind* 74 (1965): 554–62
Saint-Simon, Henri de. *Social Organization, The Science of Man, and Other Writings*. New York: Harper 1964
- *Oeuvres*. Paris: Anthropos 1966
Salkever, Stephen G. 'Virtue, Obligation and Politics.' *American Political Science Review* 68 (1974): 78–92
Sandbach, F.H. *The Stoics*. London: Chatto and Windus 1975
Schaar, John H. 'Legitimacy in the Modern State.' In *Legitimacy and the State*, ed. William Connolly, 104–33. Oxford: Blackwell 1984
Schmaus, Warren. 'A Reappraisal of Comte's Three-State Law.' *History and Theory* 21 (1982): 248–66
Seneca. *Letters from a Stoic*. Harmondsworth: Penguin 1969
Shklar, Judith N. *Men and Citizens: A Study of Rousseau's Social Theory*. Cambridge: Cambridge University Press 1969
Sorel, Georges. *Le Procès de Socrate*. 1889. Paris: Alcan 1889
- *D'Aristote à Marx*. 1894. Paris: Rivière 1935
- Preface to Saverio Merlino, *Formes et essences du socialisme*. Paris: Giard et Brière 1898
- 'Les Dissensions de la socialdémocratie en Allemagne,' *Revue Politique et Parlementaire* 6 (1900): 33–66
- *La Ruine du monde antique*. 1901. Paris: Rivière 1933
- Preface to Fernand Pelloutier, *Histoire des bourses du travail*. Paris: Schleicher 1902
- *La Décomposition du marxisme*. 1908. Paris: Rivière, nd
- *Les Illusions du progrès*. 1908. Paris: Rivière 1947
- *Réflexions sur la violence*. 1908. Paris: Rivière 1930
- *La Révolution dreyfusienne*. 1909. Paris: Rivière 1911
- *Matériaux d'une théorie du prolétariat*. Paris: Rivière 1919
- *De l'utilité du pragmatisme*. Paris: Rivière 1921
Strout, Cushing. 'Tocqueville and Republican Religion: Revisiting the Visitor.' *Political Theory* 9 (1980): 9–26
Taillandier, Saint-René. 'L'Athéisme allemand et le socialisme français.' *Revue des Deux Mondes* (1848): 280–322
Tocqueville, Alexis de. *Oeuvres complètes*. Paris: Gallimard 1951
Todorov, Tzvetan. 'Droit naturel et formes de gouvernement dans *L'Esprit des lois*. *Esprit* 3 (1983): 35–48
Tudor, Henry. *Political Myth*. New York: Praeger 1972
Vecchio, Giorgio del. *Justice*. Edinburgh: Edinburgh University Press 1952

Vernon, Richard. *Commitment and Change: Georges Sorel and the Idea of Revolution*. Toronto: University of Toronto Press 1978
- 'The Disunity of Theory and Practice.' *Canadian Journal of Political and Social Theory* 4 (1980): 199–205
Vico, Giambattista. *The New Science*. Ithaca: Cornell University Press 1970
Voyenne, Bernard. *Le Fédéralisme de P.-J. Proudhon*. Paris: Presses de l'Europe 1973
Weldon, T.D. 'Political Principles.' In *Philosophy, Politics and Society*, ed. Peter Laslett. 1st ser. Oxford: Blackwell 1956
Willhoite, Fred H. 'Rousseau's Political Religion,' *Review of Politics* 27 (1965): 501–14
Winch, Peter. *The Idea of a Social Science*. London: Routledge 1958
Zeller, E. *The Stoics, Epicureans and Sceptics*. London: Longman's 1870
Zetterbaum, Marvin. *Tocqueville and the Problem of Democracy*. Stanford: Stanford University Press 1967

Index